"Never put off till tomorrow what you can do, day after tomorrow just as well."
— Mark Twain

MAKO Publishing Co.

The Pirate's Guide to Lake St. Clair (1st Edition). *The Pirate's Guide to Lake St. Clair & Surrounding Waters* (2nd Edition). Copyright© and Trade Mark® registered with the Library of Congress and the U. S. Patent Office. All rights reserved. Printed in the United States of America. ISBN 0-9616963-0-3. No part of these books may be reproduced, or similar infringement of work or idea duplicated or copied in any manner, including electronic, mechanical, photocopying or infringement without written permission, except for the purpose of reviews.

Library of Congress Cataloging in Publication Data

1. Boating/Travel

The unauthorized reproduction or distribution or similar facsimiles of this trademarked and copyrighted work is illegal. Criminal copyright or Trademark infringement, including without monetary gain is investigated by the FBI and is punishable by up to 5 years in Federal Prison and a fine of $250,000.

"People and boats have one main thing in common, the only ones that make waves are the ones moving."
-Bradley

Amazon.com

Welcome to the second edition of the *Pirate's Guide to Lake St. Clair & Surrounding Waters*, a voyage of intrigue, adventure and discovery. This new edition has been revised, redesigned and expanded to delight the thousands of recreational and commercial boaters in the legends and hidden treasures of the heart of the Great Lakes system. The graphics, illustrations and design have been selected to create an atmosphere of maritime lore, both past and present. As stated in the first edition "In today's complex society, guide books are published on thousands of subjects, Lake St. Clair, until this date has not been graced with any complete information regarding its being and surroundings. This is a book of that information." The second voyage of the *Pirate's Guide* is comprised of ten chapters and numerous special features that flow thru the dockside bistro's to the Cajun and Creole kitchen's of Jean Lafitte's Pirate's Pantry. The chapter on *Navigation and Seamanship* covers the technical and educational marine information; for novice or professional. A new chapter on *Fishing*, has been included to help lure that trophy Wallege aboard. *Cities, Towns and Harbors* discussed historical and current characteristics of the varied communities that surround Lake St. Clair. *Aerial harbor photographs* is the most complete photostudy of this region with a seagulls' view of the ports of call. The aerial photos are displayed to assist with entry to foreign harbors, especially night entry. *Weather Information* explains the how's and why's of Mother Nature's various personalities. *Fairs, Festivals, Races and Regattas*, a summer events calendar is the first directory ever assembled to inform the reader of the hundreds of events ranging from the Curious George's Kite Flying Contest to the Sandcastle Competition, with $2,500 in prizes. Special thanks to the Chambers of Commerce that forwarded this special and unique information to showcase the many celebrations, that until now, have only been known to the local communities. It is a *Pirate's Guide* original and jewel for this new edition. *Charters, Rides and Instruction* informs beginner and experienced of the many alternative courses to follow, prior to a major yacht investment. *Surrounding Waters* expands the first edition with data regarding the connecting liquid arteries and small lake charts of Cass and Elizabeth. *Nautical publications* briefly reviews the many recreational and commercial boating publications to expand your special maritime interest, power or sail, canoe or crusier. Special features include original sea stories and The *Golden Doubloon Awards* presented to special people and places during the creation and completion of this edition.

Our contributors have varied from travel bureaus, Ministry of Tourism, librarians, researchers and watermen. The *Pirate's Guide* is a result of their information and direction. Treasure is defined as a thing of great worth; something rare and precious. Hopefully, you will find this second edition of the *Pirate's Guide* capable of that definition. It is for dock boys and dreamers, young people and old people, it is a gift. Created in the spirit of Jean Lafitte, Long John Silver, Young Jim Hawkins and Anne Bonnet, it is with great pleasure I give you this second publication. A wholehearted Welcome Aboard. We tightened our lines.

Bill Bradley

Table of Contents

Chapter 1 — 5
FOOD & GROG
RESTAURANTS & SALOONS

Chapter 2 — 44
NAVIGATION & SEAMANSHIP

Chapter 3 — 60
FISHING

Chapter 4 — 69
CITIES, TOWNS & HARBORS

Chapter 5 — 86
AERIAL HARBOR PHOTOGRAPHS

Chapter 6 — 134
WEATHER INFORMATION

Chapter 7 — 148
FAIRS, FESTIVALS, RACES & REGATTAS,
SUMMER EVENTS CALENDAR

Chapter 8 — 165
CHARTERS, RIDES & INSTRUCTION

Chapter 9 — 179
SURROUNDING WATERS

Chapter 10 — 190
NAUTICAL PUBLICATIONS

SPECIAL SECTIONS

GULF STREAM NORTHERN	161
FIRST TIME OUT	162
SAILING SINGLES	178
GOLDEN DABLOON AWARDS	164
PIRATE'S PANTRY	34

The Crew

Mark Rutowski (cover) a true artist, Mark is presently living and painting in his Boston studio overlooking the Mystic River and communting to one man shows in New York City. A local artist that also created the cover for the first edition and graduate of the Center for Creative Studies. Sketch pad and camera, seagulls and thought exploded this original oil and acrylic on canvas for our new cover.

Gloria Goeddeke (fine line drawings) graced the text with her own personal style. A Michigan artist with her work in both public and private collections, described as romantic impressionism. Gloria's pen and palette are the nucleus of lectures, demonstrations and teaching. Paper, canvus, pin or brush, Gloria illustrated the first edition and expanded her collection to flow thru number two.

Susan McDonald (copy editor) has been a newspaper and manuscript editor for over a decade. Her ability to refine, embellish and channel raw copy into polished text is a seasoned art. Editorial and graphic direction was a constant inspiration. The quality of this publication would not have been possible without her support, guidence and imagination.

Seth Lampe, APR (publication consultant) a public relations consul with decades of media experience accepted this project while still on the drawing board. His guidence, persistence and life lines refined and directed the technical and logistical aspects from conception.

Minstrals, poets and singers of songs have entertained and informed Kings and Captains throughout history. Our present musicians struggle with the same creative process in their bars, boats and recording studios as the minstrals of yore. Theirs are the stories of love and passion, death and dying, the simplest of things, the most complex of things. The lyrics and quotes used in this book have been placed to spark the veins of intrigue and to enhance the stimulation of the reader.

The great present day poets, singers and writers blend with their predecessors with electricity. As Thomas Edison left Port Huron to ignite the world, the balladers, rock n' roll bands and singers have ignited our senses.

The moon, stars, sun, streams, sea and storms — have been the Pirate's Guide's inspiration. The guide was created to help, to entertain and inform.

The title of this publication has been created not in a negative sense that sometimes accompanies the term Pirate. It is devoted to the romance of conquest and maritime ethics that accompanied the famous pirates like Lafette, Sam Lord, Ann Bonnet, Mary Reed. Many of the pirates who captured slave ships from the Carribean waters gave the slaves an option, they could leave as free men or stay with the pirates and liberate other slave ships as men of the sea. Jean Lafette was pardoned by the U.S. government in return for his aid in the battle of New Orleans in 1814. At the side of General Andrew (Old Hickory) Jackson, Lafette defended a large invasion force of British, which some say saved the city of New Orleans and won the war.

Questions about the ethics of the pirates ring true, including the quote by Lafette: "To steal on land you are a thief, to steal from the sea, you're a Buccaneer." At times in our society we quickly place a label on events, without searching for the proper description. The head lines and video statements made during the Achille Lauro crisis stated that pirates siezed an ocean liner. Terrorists are not pirates. The only skill they might have is killing innocent women and children, and never doing battle man to man, ship to ship, cannon to cannon. I find it hard to believe that a man who nobly assisted one of our great patriots, General Jackson, should be placed in the same category with terrorists who kill old men in wheel chairs. The journalists and video jockey's who used such terms should call the event what it was and not blurr it in society with what it's not, for the purpose of selling papers or intriguing viewers. The same applies to the coined term that accompanies to the killers who presently hijack yachts. Killers of a wife and husband unarmed after responding to a theatrical may day are greed-driven criminals, not pirates. Auto theft, yacht thief, what's the difference? In his eloquent observation "A Pirate Looks at Forty," Jimmy Buffet states "Occupational hazard is, occupation, just not around." The only true pirates today are etched in the paintings like Marooned, or in the imaginations of Walt Disney and the dreams of Mel Fisher, and you and me. As we speed through the twentieth century, let's not make the mistake of artificially ascribing legends and romance of the past to events and people of the present.

The title, The Pirate's Guide, was created in the romantic, entertaining, and mystic spirit that accompanied the swashbucklers of days gone by. Long John Silver, Young Jim Hackins and Captain Hook are pleasure dreams, exciting dreams. The only difference between Long John's silvers, treasure maps, never, never land and our charts, is ours are real. The title and publication were created to be a positive, exciting and intriguing experience, not a negative one. Let's try and keep our legends in perspective and enjoy our present dreams.

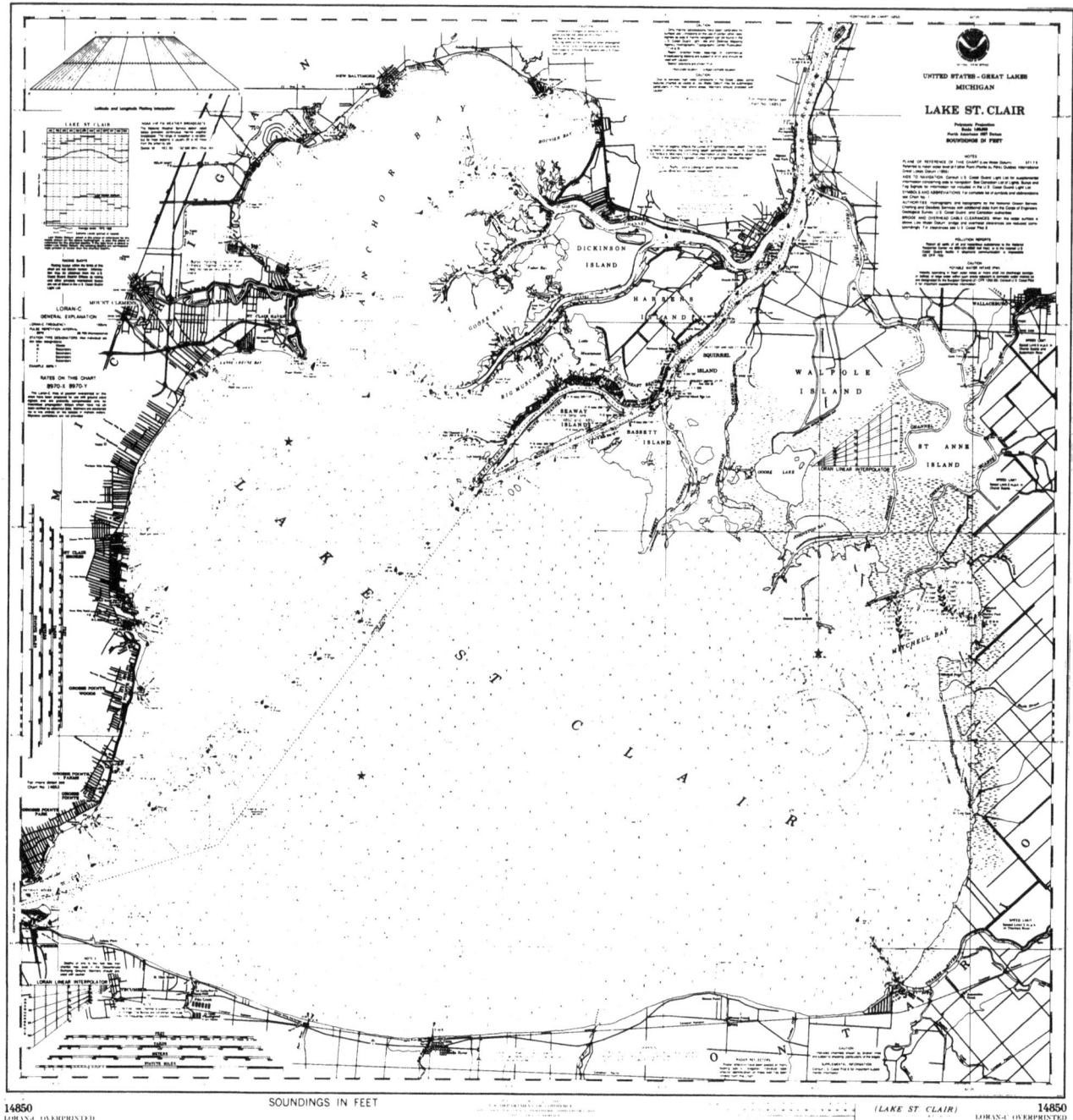

Lake St. Clair is an expansive shallow basin, having low and marshy shores and flatly sloping bottom formation, with a natural depth of approximately 24 feet. Irregular depths of from 2 to 18 feet extend out from the shore around the lake at distances varying from one to 7 miles, and local knowledge improves approach to local shores. The ship channel for large vessels, trending northeast and southwest through the lake, has been provided by the construction of St. Clair Flats Canal and by dredging across the lake and in the Grosse Pointe Section leading to the head of the Detroit River, affording a through depth of 27½ feet. The minimum width is 700 feet at the upper end and a width of 800 feet across the lake. An earth dike, about 7,200 feet long, lies along the easterly side of the channel at the South Channel outlet. The channel, dredged through the shoal at the foot of Lake St. Clair and leading from the deep water at the head of the Detroit River to the turn abreast Lake St. Clair Light, is an almost straight cut 11¼ miles long, 800 feet wide and 27½ feet deep. The channel is subject to shoaling along the sides. Depths adjacent to the channel vary from 10 to 15 feet. The depths vary with seasonal change, with the highest stages in the summer months and the lowest stages in the winter months. During a 73 year period (1898-1970), **the range of fluctuation between the highest and lowest monthly mean stages was 5.84 and the greatest annual fluctuation was 3.32 feet and the least annual fluctuation was 0.88 foot.**

Chapter 1

FOOD & GROG
RESTAURANTS & SALOONS

"Where is the trader of London town?
His gold's on the capston
His blood's on his gown
And it's up and away for St. Mary's Bay
Where the liquor is good and the lasses are gay."

Pirate's Chantey 1697

The following reviews have been researched and included for the purpose of enhancing your boating trip and making you aware of the many fascinating, unique and mandatory portions of your liquid adventure. The Food & Grog Restaurant and Saloon Section is directed specifically to one of the major responsibilities of all Captains and crew who seek to receive Golden Dabloon Awards and not keel hauling. The ability to eat, drink, cook and make the perfect "Pirate's Gold" separates the Jean Lafitte's from the sea dogs. By land or by sea, cooking, eating, and drinking can be the blessing of the perfect cruise. The recipes originated in the bayous of Louisiana, the drinks from assorted travels. The restaurants and saloons reviewed here border or are within a cheap cab fare of dock side. The research during the first Pirate's Guide and this second edition ignited a curiosity about the Pirates. Their lifestyle, mystery, legends and tales of buried treasure. New Orleans was the only natural place to start digging out the legends and romance, of that elite group. The parallels that were discovered between this region (Detroit/Windsor) and New Orleans and Lake Charles direct a recommendation to our city planners and leaders to look closely at developing this area as the New Orleans of the Midwest. The French came from the New Orleans areas and French Canadians, to establish many of the traditions, names, and lifestyles traditional in Louisiana. There are still dialects of Creole spoken in Windsor. The Junior League of Lake Charles, La. allowed the reprinting of some of their great Cajun and Creole recipes from their excellent cookbook, "Pirate's Pantry." As stated "For more than a hundred years, Lake Charles area residents have dreamed of finding Napolean's jewels, riches purportedly buried along the shores of Calcasieu River or on the bottom of Contraband Bayou by the pirate-captain Jean Lafitte, a frequent guest at the dinner tables of Lake Charles's wealthy Creole planters." Rich shrimp creoles, crab gumbos, the list goes on and on. From the tables of the wealthy Creole planters to the brass rails of the Woodbridge Tavern, here are Food & Grog Restaurants and Saloons.

tugboat restaurant
"OUELLETTE ON THE RIVER"

When boats change hands the name accompanies the new owner, to maintain tradition. The Queen City was the official Tug Boat chartered annually by Pinkey's Blvd. Club, Tugboat Society. The blue prints were in the first issue of the Pirate's Guide before the exchange took place. Capt. Hank Van Aspert refurbished the Queen City from stem to stern creating a masterpiece of brass finely varnished wood to the envy of Queen Mary. Photos of the major overhaul grace the entrance walls. Floating at the heart of the Detroit River, the view of the Ren-Cen and river traffic is great. Railroad barges transporting cargo to the tracks off its starboard stern come close enough to anticipate fending off. Chefs from the British Royal Navy prepare the catch of the day, grilled swordfish, veal Oscar, and delights like posieon platter, i.e. "The Greek God of tempest storms releases to you a variety of seafood including halibut, salmon, mussels, shrimp, scallops and frog legs baked with mushrooms, green onions, butter and spices." A superior array of lobster dinners includes lobster Dieppe, lobster tail sauteed with shallots and tomatoes, flambeed with brandy and finished with cream. Um, Um. Batten down the hatches and hoist the main, with appetizers such as shrimp on a pear, sauteed with garlic, onions, mushrooms, and crab nuggets dijonaise.

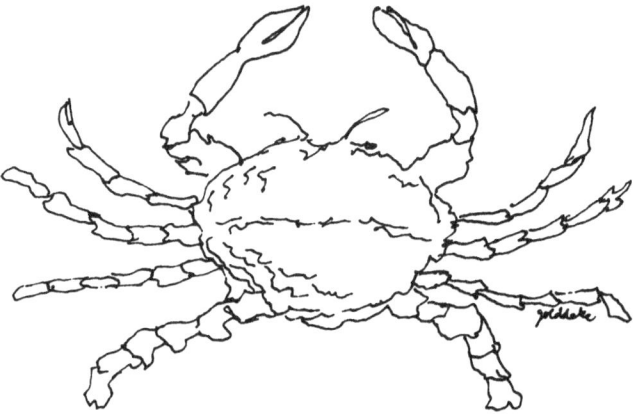

If you haven't tried the Tugboat you'll never receive your Culinary Captain license. Invite the crew for the boatman's stew, a hearty combination of clam chowder, scallops, shrimp, crab, mussels, tender chunks of "Catch of the day," mushrooms and green onions, and you'll never have a mutiny. The Captain's wine locker offers a new wine of the month stowed with 25 other fine wines, by glass, ½ litre, litre or bottle. Dom Perignon, on board, Pommard, on board, Pelle Island Vin Villa, on board.

A full line of liquors and liqueurs includes only premium brands. Jean Lefette would turn over his treasure map after a few Centaure Napoleon Cognac's. Burgers and snacks offer those wishing to test the waters, an excellent diversion from the landlocked routine. Now for the ship's tour. A lake tug 114 feet long, 23 feet wide, 216 ton, built in Kingston, Ontario, and commissioned in 1911. Once powered by steam and later in 1942 fitted with a 37 ton 4 cylinder 1250 H.P. diesel. Retired in the early 70's from ice breaking she became the private vessel of Mr. Bob Adams, a member of the International Tugboat Society. With the start of the International Tugboat Races on the Detroit River, the "Queen City" became the official escort tug and was used as a base by the officials of Detroit and Windsor. Today the top deck offers bar and tables high above the docks with entertainment in the summer that could include moonlight raggee. For Long John Silver's private parties, the Pilot's quarters are available. Call (519) 258-9607 or on your ship to shore radio and the chef will have your order ready for ship to ship delivery. Extending a long pole with fish-net your dinners will be passing with the accuracy the Westcott delivers mail. Hail to the "Queen". MC, AE, V. Open seven days. The Best.

THE OLD FISH MARKET

156 Chatham St. W.
Windsor

Walking in to the high ceilings with international flags draped and a display case of oysters, lobsters and king crabs starts the experience with regatta surroundings. A daily menu of specials at reasonable prices offers the unique traveler a casual lively atmosphere for fun and fish. A long wood bar serves oysters, chowders, including Conch for the southern Captains. Fresh and smoked fish chowder, East Coast cream clam and the oyster bar are great. The main course offers one of the most complete selection of seafood this side of the intercoastal. The Maritime Mixed Grill includes a platter of Snow Crab claws, half a stuffed lobster, baked oysters, fresh fish, smoked black cod, smelts, mushrooms, rice, onion rings and half tomato. If rain and wind has rerouted your cruise, The Market Kettle includes half of lobster, Snow Crab claws, mussels, fresh fish, shrimp, and vegetables in a spicy broth with brandy. The list is so long, you have to see it to believe it. This large open bistro can also handle groups from 25 to 150, sailors delight.

The Louisiana Purchase

3236 Sandwich
Windsor
AE, V

Finally we have a small part of New Orleans a few blocks up from the Detroit River. Owner Camernon Lyon has captured the ambience of my favorite city with taste and good food. Decorated in the quality of part French bistro and New Orleans restaurant the Louisiana Purchase would satisfy Jean Lafitte. Appetizers range from Oysters Roffinac to Shrimp Remoulade to Shrimp Roffinac. Entrees include blackened fish, Cajun prime rib and hot boiled crawfish. Deserts of sweet potato pecan pie, New Orleans bread pudding and praline parfaits. Ethnic eating trends take time to arrive to the Mid-West. The Cajun and Creole dishes have finally arrived. A complete review of these delights is included in the section on the Pirate's Pantry, with background on the creation. With the many French that arrived from the New Orleans area to settle in Windsor and Detroit, it surprises me, more Cajun and Creole restaurants didn't accompany them. The Louisiana Purchase will be the start of this delightful trend. Good wines with small bar accent this lunch or dinner bistro. Menu prices in U.S. and Canadian.

M.V. "QUEEN CITY"

GENERAL ARRANGEMENT

SCALE 1/8" = 1 FOOT.

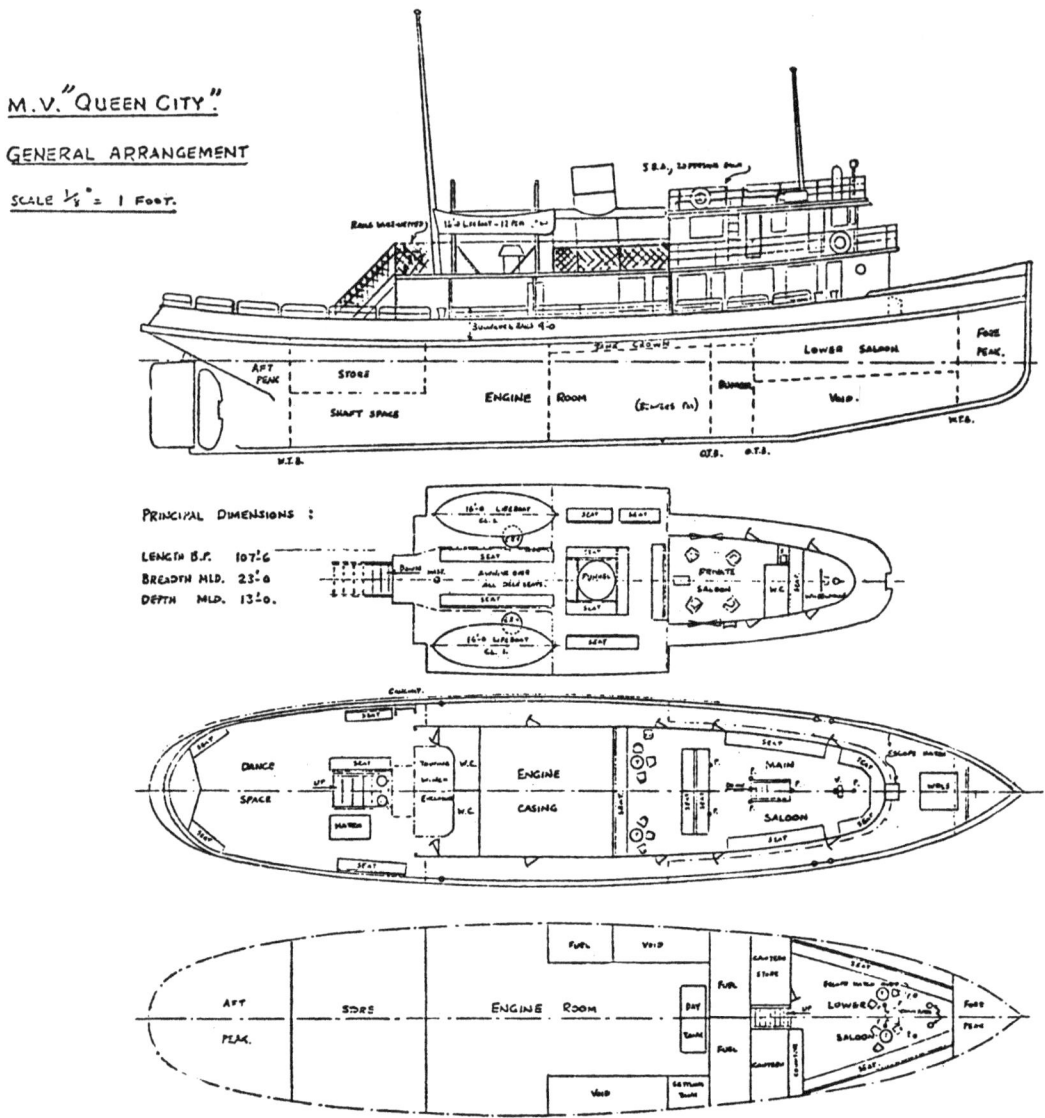

PRINCIPAL DIMENSIONS:

LENGTH B.P. 107'6
BREADTH MLD. 23'0
DEPTH MLD. 13'0

The "QUEEN CITY" was built in 1911 by The Kingston Shipbuilding Co., Ltd. of Kingston, Ontario, as a steam tug, named the "JALOBERT." Later renamed the "MACASSA." She was repowered in 1942 with an Alco-Sulzer Diesel engine, and 1955 was converted by the Hamilton, Ontario Harbour Commission and refurbished as a passenger carrying Harbour vessel. In 1965, she was purchased by Waterman's Services (Scott) Ltd. of Toronto, Ontario, and given her present name QUEEN CITY." She has been used as a sightseeing vessel and quarters boat by Waterman's Services. In April, 1971, the "QUEEN CITY" was sold to Robert M. Adams of Detroit, Michigan.

Principal dimensions and brief detail information are as follows:

    Official Number: 126930, British Registry
    Name: "QUEEN CITY" - Port of Registry: Toronto, Ontario, Canada
    Built: 1911 by Kingston Shipbuilding Co., Ltd. Kingston, Ont.

    Propelling Machinery: 4-cylinder, "ALCO-SULZER" (American Locomotive Co., Type 4-TM, 720 Brake horsepower, Straight drive, direct reversible, diesel engine, turning an 8" shaft, and driving a 5 bladed (72" x 48") propeller.)
    Auxiliary Machinery: 2 - 20 KW diesel generators, 5 HP air compressor motor, 7.5 HP fire pump, 3 HP general service pump, etc.

There are quarters for 10 men in 3 staterooms below forward, in addition to the Captains stateroom abaft the Pilot House.

LIFE SAVING EQUIPMENT consists of individual life jackets for 120 persons, located in the main Deck Saloon. Various life rings with water lights about vessel, 2-20 man floats on the pilot house roof. (Note that the Life Boats you see are 2 16' - 12 person boats, but are currently not approved, but kept in the Davits position for appearance only)

There is a galley in the main deckhouse, amidships, and forward of that is the main saloon. The engine room is enclosed by the after portion of the main deckhouse. The pilot house and master's cabin are on the upper deck, and the sightseeing observation deck is just between the lifeboats davits, and around the stack, abaft the pilot house. A stairway to the upper deck is located aft on the main deck. Heads (toilets) are located on the main deck port and starboard, in the after end of the deckhouse.

MORO'S

9550 Riverside Drive East
Windsor

Across from Peche Island

Moro's is the former site of the Thomas Inn, a speakeasy in the rum-running days that began many of the restaurants and taverns on the Canadian shore. Photos and Hiram Walker memorabilia are displayed on the walls of this new California style full service restaurant. Contemporary brass, wood and brick establish a pleasurable, casual yachting atmosphere. The dining room seats 180-190, lounge 60 and a beautiful patio, 140. The view is lucious. Twenty cleats are available along the boardwalk for docking, no bumpers provided. The Windsor City marina, with 300 docks, is next door and contact to the harbormaster can provide overnight docking. Diesel and regular gas are available with power and water. There's no minimum charge at the restaurant with light jazz entertainment on the patio, periodically. Full course meals are offered with dinner specials, such as Lake Superior whitefish, lake perch, lobster and

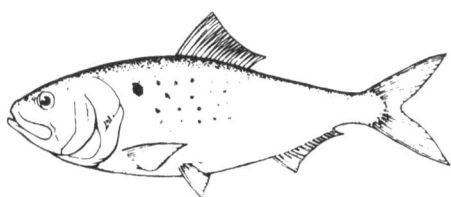

the full additional range of fish and seafood. Veal, chicken and beef entrees from chicken cacciatore, veal Moro (slowly cooked in a mushroom sauce), New York sirloins and filets are just a sampling of this complete menu. Reservations are suggested for parties of six or more. Approximately 50 wines, champagnes and apertif's would go nicely with fruits of the sea appetizers (a combination of shrimp and escargots, sauteed in butter and garlic, and served with steamed mussels). Open seven days a week. AE, V, MC, DC. The hostess Vanessa displays warmth and friendliness to make your late night snack, dinner or overnight stay a pleasant one. A stroll around the boardwalk watching the river activity go by, is the perfect dessert.

An Invitation To Join Mystic Seaport

An opportunity to join with like-minded individuals dedicated to the restoration and preservation of our national maritime heritage. Annual dues materially strengthen Mystic Seaport. And a member receives tangible benefits and privileges.

Mystic Seaport is a unique 40 acre museum open daily year-round, dedicated to positive action in saving artifacts related to the Age of Sail. A nonprofit educational and research center, the museum offers a broad spectrum of interest, including:

- The whaleship *Charles W. Morgan* and other major vessels
- Historic buildings
- Formal exhibits—scrimshaw, paintings, ship models, figureheads
- More than 130 historic small craft
- Shops in which skilled artisans demonstrate crafts vital to whaling and shipbuilding
- Lectures, demonstrations and planetarium shows
- A wide variety of educational programs for all ages
- An extensive research library
- Special programs, seminars, workshops and other events year-round

Members of this nonprofit educational and research organization are entitled to:
Unlimited admission to Mystic Seaport grounds without charge.
The LOG of Mystic Seaport, the museum's quarterly magazine
The *Wind Rose*, a monthly newsletter.
A discount at Mystic Seaport Stores, Inc.
Twenty-four-hour free boat dockage extended to members in the membership classifications higher than individual.
The Annual Report and other special reports.
Eligibility for subscriptions to the Mystic Seaport Adventure Series.
The privilege of purchasing guest ticket books.

The following classifications of membership are renewable annually:

Individual $15.00   Participating $ 50.00
Family   25.00   Sustaining   100.00
                       Associate   250.00

To: Mrs. Flora Fairchild
Mystic Seaport, Inc.
Mystic, Connecticut 06355

I would like to help preserve our priceless maritime heritage by enrolling as a _____ member.
I enclose my check for $_____
Name_____
Street_____
City or Town_____
State_____ Zip Code_____

Mystic Seaport is a publicly funded organization. Gifts are tax deductible to the full extent allowed by law.

MYSTIC SEAPORT
MUSEUM OF MARITIME AMERICA

Island View TAVERN

7880 Riverside Drive East
Windsor, Ont.

A true Canadian tavern, with view of Belle Isle, thus named Island View. It's divided into three sections, dining room with band and dance floor, dining room and bar, and stand-up bar for those great Canadian ales and goldens. The perogys with fried onions and sour cream are home made and delicious. The full menu offers pickerel, lake perch, frog legs, t-bone steaks and sandwiches in this friendly all-ages River nugget. Dockage is available. A pool table and juke box add to the friendly atmosphere. The U.S. has a tendency of trying to put people and things into categories, over 20, under 40, singles, families, etc. Canadians welcome everyone. The young don't bother the old and the old enjoy the young. Very informal. Wednesday through Saturday night there's rock bands and dancing. It's always hard to write reviews about places like the Island View. You just want to get up and go there, spend the day or night and really enjoy what taverns were meant to be. As Bob Dylan stated "Don't put on any airs when you're down on Rou Morgue Avenue." Don't put on any airs at the Island View, have a perogy and an ice cold Canadian Golden. Cash only.

MENARD'S TAVERN
494 Riverdale
Windsor
MC, V

Up a few blocks from the Detroit River, Menard's is open seven days. Perch and pickerel are the specials. Haddock, salmon, rainbow trout and smelt accompany the full menu and bar service. Live band (country/soft rock) and dancing. Friendly neighborhood tavern with special every two weeks.

HOLIDAY INN
480 Riverside Drive West
Windsor

One of the best views of the city of Detroit and River activity is here. The large glass windows in both the riverside room and dining room provide a comfortable view and good food. The Sunday brunch and buffets in the dining room are excellent. The bar has sofas and cocktail tables for the best view right on the Detroit River. Then some of the rooms open up right at the river with walkway and water underneath. The tasteful nautical decore in the river room provide the tranquility that enhances the flow of the river. There are very reasonable weekend price packages and excellent views and service.

12010 Riverside Dr. E.
Windsor, Ontario
(519) 735-6021

On chart # 14850 the breakwall entrance is about two miles east of the Peche Island light. There is a huge lakeside tavern and restaurant with plenty of docks and tie up facilities, a quick sail across the lake from the Detroit river waters. Acres of green lawn roll down to lake side for wandering around. Canadians know how to maintain the lake and riverfront.Cut the lawn and plant flowers. The lake, freighters, sailboats, pleasure craft, river, moon, sun and stars will do the rest. Too bad you have to go up six floors in the Ren-Cen to see that. In Canada the water comes first. Catering to yachtsmen/women for years, the Rendevous is divided into a tavern, from the days when women weren't allowed in, and vast dinner room, dance floor and private banquet rooms for all occasions. A 6 meter buffet course for Sunday brunch and dinner would satisfy the crew of the Courageous II. The Vuicic family prepares dinners of Roadhouse style Louisiana shrimp, Nova Scotia scallops, one pound snow crab, steaks, chicken, and burgers, highlighting the other 20 or so entrees. A new light menu offers pickerel, 8 oz. New York strips and other delights for the weight watchers on board. Windows expose the entire restaurant to the lake. Oil paintings of the Great lakes freighters and classic events like "Rounding the Horn" develop part art museum for gazing pleasure. The full liquor roadhouse is a welcome haven close to Detroit but miles from the hussle   Live entertainment on the weekends with large dance floor. New expansion will seat 700. Open seven days. AE, DC, MC, V.

BELL BUOY
930 Old Tecumseh Rd.
Puce, Ontario

Tom and Susan Bell operate restaurant, saloon and boat yard on the Puce River. The Puce River inlet is between Windsor and Belle River. About 20 wells and breakwalls are there for tie up. Washrooms, showers, fuel and pump out facilities create a great sailing destination from the U.S. The interior is wall papered with charts of the Bahamas and a huge flag over the fireplace stating the famous "Don't give up the Ship" slogan. My curiosity had been ignited. Why do you have charts on the Bahamian waters in a rustic wind swept restaurant on Lake St. Clair? Says Tom Bell, "For all the sailors that are headed for the Bahamas. They can chart their course from here." Sounds good to me! You can also enjoy an array of fresh, home cooked and prepared meals and snacks including fresh perch, pickerel and seafood. The outdoor patio enhances the fresh Canadian lake air with entertainment on the weekends. Marine radio supplies the background music for an afternoon cocktail at the bar. The view allows observance of the boats tying up and a review of craft and crew. Having a Dock Boy heritage, it's always one of my favorite activities. Both Tom and

Susan are sailors and from the party photos on the wall, they are maintaining the Pirate's Guide tradition. Leaving one day, Tom stopped me in the yard, pulled me back into the bar until I was convinced I'd found Margaritaville. Open seven days. Summer. MC, V.

New Sails

Repairs

North/Harken Furling Gear

Zip-Stop Mains

Covers

NORTH SAILS DETROIT

22960 Industrial Drive, West
St. Clair Shores, MI 48080
(313) 776-1330

The Lighthouse Inn
"ON LAKE ST. CLAIR"

Mouth of the Thames River, Lighthouse Cove
Tilbury, Ontario

Tradition has a way of returning rightful possessions to rightful owners. The Cookes maintained the Lighthouse at the mouth of the Thames in the days when you rowed out and changed the filament and poured fuel in the system to keep the lights burning, long before computerized data based switch panels. They are one of the nicest families on the Lake and their family inn is one of the finest points on Lake St. Clair. The restaurant changed hands about three years ago, but the Cooke sparkle was absent. Back in the hands of the traditional owners, the sparkle is back. Overnight dockage is available at the moorings. A very large dining room, porch, and red wood patio sweep out to weeping willows on a full lawn. Daily specials, buffets, steaks, seafood, lake food and combination dinners include the "Admiral's dinner of lobster tail, perch and shrimp". Children's menu and light dinner menu complete this Canadian tradition for generations. Full color lithographs of many prize yachts gracefully accent the spotless tight ship that Captain Cooke would be proud to be a part of. Open seven days. Docks for 25 boats. AE, MC, V.

MARINER'S

Lighthouse Cove, Mouth of the Thames,
Tilbury, Onatario
(519) 682-1836

Located next to the lighthouse, Mariner's is another very large full service restaurant, with 100 docks with overnight available. The Lighthouse Cove community also has marinas close by if repairs are in order. It's open seven days with an all-you-can-eat special of frog legs and perch that draws people from far and near. The activities at the Mariner and Lighthouse Cove don't stop when the ice comes. There's standing room only during the ice fishing season. MC, V.

WHEELS RIVER INN

On the Thames River
Chatham
(519) 354-5030

"The Oasis of the Thames" takes about two hours from Light House Cove, (motoring, with spots to sail). Formerly a Holiday Inn, the standards have been maintained if not improved. The Wonderful World of Wheels Inn operates a seven acre recreational facility that includes, 19 indoor tennis, squash and racquetball courts, three swimming pools, a bowling alley, miniature golf, day care for children, spa and sports medicine facility right down the road from the Wheels River Inn. Overnight dockage is available for up to 80 boats. The Granary offers full menu and liquor, with comfortable rooms and swimming pool, a complete package for the berth weary Captain and crew. The purpose of the Pirate's Guide is to dig out the information that doesn't get into the brochures or headlines. Arriving at the summer Sunday concert at the Oasis on the Thames is a hidden treasure. The lawn sweeps down the river bank with three outdoor bars and roaring grills, cooking up hot dogs, burgers and chicken at a price that's minimal. A pavilion in the open air surrounds the rock 'n roll to a pirate's delight. It usually runs from 5 to 9 p.m., so don't miss a minute. There's great food, lovers hand in hand, cool breezes and uncrowded green grass that flows to the river. Small, clean, healthy and civilized. Chatham is a great little city and the concerts on the banks of the Thames offer all the pleasures, and none of the problems. AE, MC, V.

GREAT LAKES LIGHTHOUSE KEEPERS ASSOCIATION

P.O. Box 2907
Southfield, MI 48037

Dedicated to the preservation of the history of Great Lakes Lighthouses and the people who kept them.

The Great Lakes Lighthouse Keepers Association was incorporated in November 1983. The formal organization was a culmination of over two years of effort on the part of a growing number of persons interested in the history and preservation of lighthouses on the Great Lakes.

It was founded to facilitate the accumulation and exchange of information about the histories of the lighthouse stations and their keepers, so that life at these stations, as it was, may be accurately interpreted and its history preserved.

The Association is currently working to establish and support a network of Great Lakes Chapters whereby efforts at preservation and restoration may be coordinated.

Chapters...
The Lake Michigan Chapter of the Association was the first to be formed. Chapters have since been organized on Lakes Huron and Superior, with an ongoing effort to establish chapters on Lakes Erie and Ontario.

Each chapter is headed by a coordinator who serves to accumulate information and to keep the membership informed of the history of and changes to lighthouses in his/her area. This information is published in THE BEACON and is shared at annual conferences.

Conferences...
Each chapter coordinator organizes at least one conference yearly. At these conferences, usually held near a different lighthouse, the participants share information about the lighthouses and their keepers, discuss and illustrate restoration projects in their area, and seek ways to address issues of common concern.

The BEACON
THE BEACON, published quarterly, contains information from the coordinators and articles submitted by the members, which are edited for content and historical accuracy by THE BEACON staff. The newsletter also announces conference dates and occasionally includes special features such as tour charts, lists of lighthouse museums, and other material of interest to the membership.

Membership...
We invite you to join the Great Lakes Lighthouse Keepers Association, a means for historians, keepers' descendants, artists, teachers, photographers, and others interested in the history and continuing concerns of Great Lakes lighthouses and life, to further explore and preserve this unique heritage.

Individual	$ 10
Family	$ 15
Sustaining	$ 50
Patron	$100
Life	$150

Membership includes receipt of THE BEACON and special mailings that provide preservation and historical information for your enjoyment of our Great Lakes lighthouses.

THAMES RIVER LIGHTHOUSE
Mount of the Thames River at Lake St. Clair

Construction of the lighthouse by the Cartier family in 1818 and its predecessor. A frame structure destroyed by fire in the latter years of the War of 1812. Established an enduring land mark at the mount and a dynasty by the Cartier family as lighthouse keepers that lasted 150 years.

The lighthouse became the property of the Federal government in 1837 and had continued in use until 1966 when it was replaced by automatic light. The structure was obtained by the lower Thames Valley Conservation Authority through a grant from her Majesty the Queen Elizabeth II on November 6, 1972 and has since been restored.

RETURN TO THE RIVER

WOODBRIDGE TAVERN
287 St. Aubin
Detroit

It has been a family tradition since 1905 when Euphrasie and Henry Brunelle arrived from Belgium in 1905 and opened a grocery store bordering on the Detroit River. The sailors came in for provisions and the sale of spirits started to exceed the sale of provisions. Dick's Bar continued through the war years and the saloon was operated by daughters and son-in-law Marce. The saloon was sold to their daughter Marcia in 1975. Having the same instincts that Euphrasie had in 1905, Marcia re-named the restaurant the Woodbridge Tavern. She started building, cooking and adding entertainment that will guarantee any sailor from Maine to Martinique a variety of delights. The Woodbridge Special includes ham, pastrami, bacon and tomato, topped with melted Swiss cheese on an English muffin and horseradish sauce and cole slaw on the side. Lake perch, pan fried, quiche, steaks, and prime rib just accents a few of the treats of this full-service menu. Carry outs are available on all items including delicious square deep dish pizza and Award winning burgers, for that hungry crew.

Now for the fun part. Weekend entertainment includes sing-a-long Dixieland, and at times the band that was found by Marcia up north and imported to be the recipient of the Golden Dabloon Award for best party band, the infamous "Keel Haulers". Florida has Jimmy Buffin & the Coral Reefer Band, New Jersey has Bruce Springstine and Michigan the Keel Haulers. You have to see it to believe it. They're great. The roof-top

---

WOODBRIDGE TAVERN

259-0578   289 St. Aubin

Boaters welcome - join the enjoyment of fine food, fun and frolic in historic setting of a Rivertown tavern.

- full menu - lunch and dinner
- imported beer from around the world
- carry outs or catering for your boating party - "picnic fare" with your favorite bottle of wine...

- "toe-tappin" music Monday thru Saturday evenings
- Alfresco Dining - patio or rooftop
- large parties welcome
- open Sunday thru Saturday
- all major credit cards accepted

Custom Catering   Casual or Chic

deck, one of the first in the city, is the perfect setting, day or night, to enjoy the open air and summer breezes. Ester, the day bartender, is one of the best from port to starboard. Marcia Cron is a boat owner and will cater to any needs you or your party may have. Liquor, imported beer and wines are on hand from all over the world, Woodbridge is a treasure by day or night. Open seven days.
AE V, DC, MC, CB

Pontchartrain Wine Cellars

234 W. Larned
Detroit

Bistro: (nParisian argot) a small or unpretentious wineshop or eating place. Webster has just described the Wine Cellars, it's both. Not to be confused with the Ponchartrain Hotel, but right across the street for coastal nagivators. Continental cuisine is served in a wood, brick and French Impresionist cafe setting. Step into a Detroit tradition that originated Cold Duck in the States. It's a special place for clients or commodores/Commordoreses. The French ambience and culinary awards (Holiday Magazine) define both menu and environment. Noisettes of lamb, tournedos of beef tenderloin/pommes Delphine just mention a few. A small standup bar serves beer, wine and aperitifs. A few couples' tables allow drinks before or after the Grand Prix. When in France do as the French do. When in Detroit head leeward to the Wine Cellars.

Benno's

1436 Brush
Downtown Detroit

My first encounter with Benno occured during the travels of the first Pirate's Guide. Not wanting to disturb the closed street entrance in the old Indian Village location, it was down the back alley to the rear kitchen and inquiring to some gentlemen cooking and delicately pouring wine on what was cooking. "I'm writing a book on Lake St. Clair and would like to talk to someone about Benno's restaurant. Come in off the alley, you can talk to me, I'm Benno." Wow, what a place to hold an interview, in the kitchen with the infamous recipient of all awards possible, including Holiday Magazine, Travel and Leisure, gold this and silver this. What a great guy. At that time the Pirate's Guide was about two clicks off a bar napkin blueprint and light years from publication. We talked as he quickly attended his award winning creations. I never felt or wanted my blue jeans to get past the alley or past the kitchen. We're talking amature author here. Benno apologized for being so busy and then requested the other person in the kitchen keep a crow's nest watch on the ovens. Entering then to one of the most magnificent dinner rooms this side of the new Caribbean Room in the Pontchartrain Hotel in New Orleans. Not the same Ponchartrain as Detroit, by a nautical mile. The movement to the new location maintains the same elegance and superior food the old did, if not more so. Benno and I talked as he served beers, wines and samples of his treasures. Many local restaurant critics reference his temperamental attitude. I can't understand it. I've seen him at his restaurant and at other local spots, and he's always been bright and accommodating. When told some of the boaters may not have suits or ties when arriving, he said he would wave the dress requirements, only to the traveling yachtsman. Reservations are, however, required. Salmon, beef Wellington, oysters and wild rice, delicious. The people who have complained about the service or the temperament are obviously in waters over their head. Dining at Benno's is an experience, not a junk food slot machine. One of the few restaurants that could compete with five star New Orleans rooms and win. Highly recommended. Wine and beer only. MC, V.

624 3rd
Downtown Detroit

The Galleon was created by Katy Stock and sailor, Brady, who rumor has it, is now spinning his compass and sailing in that direction. The Golden Galleon's helm has been turned over to Katy. It is one of the only true nautical restaurants/saloons in the city. Large wood beams support numerous

maritime artifacts that intrigue and excite even the novice, from pirate parrots to life size oil paintings of the sea, its ships, and their sailors. Homemade soups, burgers, specialty sandwiches and dinners are offered. The Seafarer Sandwich (open faced with crabmeat and melted Swiss, warmed on an English muffin) is an example of the sailor's treats on board in the galley. The cruising yachtsman can enjoy the fabulous Mount Gay rum, not familiar to these waters, while swapping sea stories with bankers and bosun's mates. It's a tight ship without the artificial atmosphere some restaurants attempt at the nautical decore. You can almost hear the timbers creak and the sea flow around you. After a few Mount Gays you will think you're sailing!

With restauranteurs using sophisticated marketing research, food unit specialists, and subliminal interior designers, it's a relief to see a true nautical saloon sail past them all. Very reasonable and highly recommended.

STAR OF DETROIT
Detroit River behind Cobo Hall

A beautiful dinner cruise ship is worth its weight in gold. Finally we have a real ship to cruise the river and lake on those warm romantic nights. Enjoy a full course dinner with full liquor and walk the decks from stem to stern while viewing the diamonds created by the glow of the silvery moon.

There are many variations of dinner cruises, lunch or just cocktails and jazz. If working is not part of your yachting agenda, the Star will hoist the lines, serve the cocktails, sautee the mushrooms and steer a true course of elegance. Beautifully decorated and spotless in true Yachting tradition, Detroit should be proud of this treasure that's finally arrived.

1
289 ST. AUBIN
DETROIT, MICHIGAN 48207
259-0578

2
673 FRANKLIN
DETROIT, MICHIGAN 48226
259-8202

3
1977 WOODBRIDGE
DETROIT, MICHIGAN 48207
567-6020

4 **RICHARD'S**
225 JOS. CAMPAU
DETROIT, MICHIGAN 48207
259-3675

5 **ANDREWS**
201 JOS. CAMPAU
DETROIT, MICHIGAN 48207
259-8325

6 *Taboo*
1940 WOODBRIDGE
DETROIT, MICHIGAN
567-6140

7 **The Rhinoceros**
265 RIOPELLE
DETROIT, MICHIGAN 48207
259-2208

8 **Soup Kitchen Saloon**
1585 FRANKLIN
DETROIT, MICHIGAN 48207
259-1374

9 **It's Only ROCK-n-ROLL**
1538 FRANKLIN
DETROIT, MICHIGAN 48207
259-9447

10 **Pekin Pavilion** 北京亭
3177 EAST JEFFERSON AVE.
DETROIT, MICHIGAN 48207
259-1510

Discover RiverTown

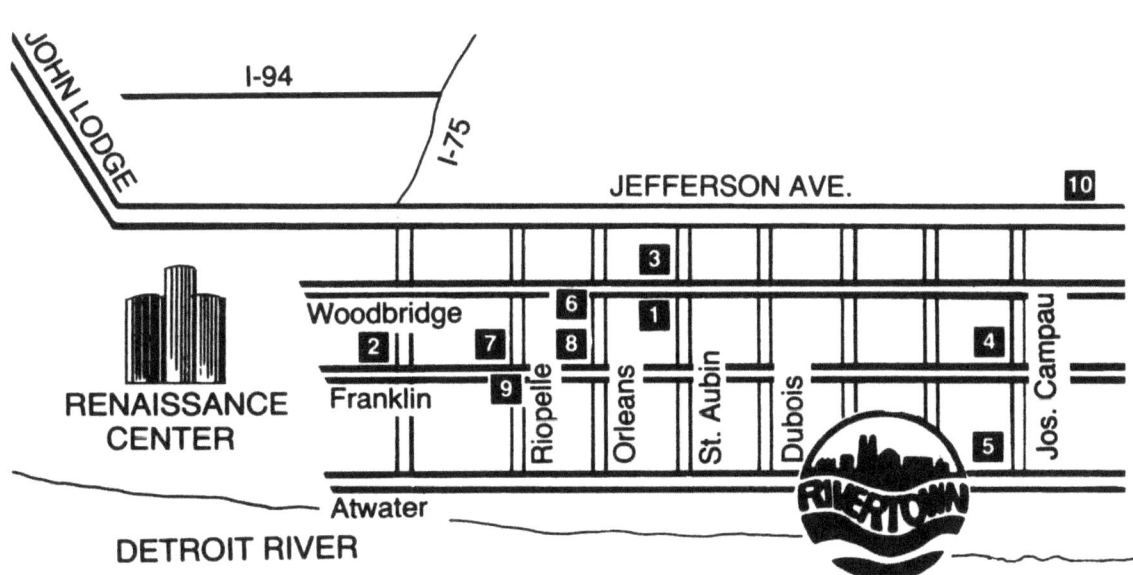

LANDSDOWNE
201 At Water
Detroit River
AE, CB, DC, MC, V

This classic barge built in 1884 to ferry railroad cars from Detroit to Windsor is anchored at the foot of Hart Plaza, a floating lunch and dinner restaurant, but no rides. There are two main floors with upstairs for entertainment, drinks and dancing. Steaks, seafood and veal are served with views of Windsor and river traffic. Very unique seating arrangements make every room a bit different.

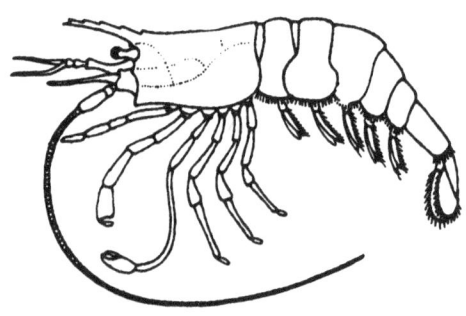

JACOBY'S SINCE 1904
624 Brush
Detroit
AE, CB, DC, MC, V

A German restaurant and saloon with sailors and legal pirates spliced together. Across from the City-County building, Jacoby's has been feeding and servicing the legal and political community of Detroit for decades. Jacoby's love for the lake and its yachts decorates the walls from stem to stern. Here is a hearty German fare with imported beers and full liquor service. Lunches and dinners provide fast service on the main dining room or aloft on the second floor. Many a private party has echoed the halls of the second floor, from regatta winners to retirement bashes. Jacoby's caters to the racing elite, whether Canadian Cup or Mackinac mark, yacht racing is spoken here. Saturday and Sunday brunch is served for captain and crew.

Pinkey's Boulevard Club

110 E. Grand Boulevard
Detroit
All Major Credit Cards

A tradition for years, Fran Rogers operates one of the best restaurants in the city. Across from the Belle Isle bridge Pinkey's will please Captains Crew and Commodores. It's a small bar where Roy Nickols created legends. The most important ingredients to a successful restaurant are the owner, the bartender, the chef, the waitresses/waiters and valet. Pinkeys has them all. With wrought iron rails, fresh flowers, cloth covered tables, Fran runs the tightest ship on the River. For the yachtsmen who's tired of the DYC or Boat Club atmosphere, jump across the bridge for superior food and drink. Dover sole, tenderloin tips, burgers, and omelettes, just to name a few of the Golden Dubloon award ratings. Once home port of the Tugboat Society, Fran is both Pilot and Yachtswoman. The next time Webster defines Hostess, Fran Rogers should be included. At night the piano bar ignites with sing-alongs from Vaudeville to the Marine Corps Hymn. All ages sing and meet and mingle, till the wee hours, in this 105 year old converted home. Open six days, Monday through Saturday. Private parties available. Highly recommended.

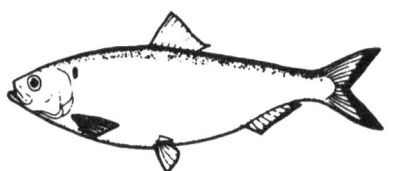

2000 Gratiot
Detroit
AE, MC, V

A Detroit tradition for decades, Joe's is not to be confused with the Chuck Muer chain. Joe Muer's is Joe Muer's. Joe Muer is a legend in his own time and the restaurant is why. Seafood specialties are famous, the place is famous and Joe Muer is famous. Line up on the weekends, but it's worth the wait. Service is fast and the line moves quickly. Deep red leather chairs and booths create an intimate atmosphere with service for hundreds. Sport coats and ties are needed, but it's worth it. If you've just bought that 60 footer or just sold it, this is the place to celebrate. Dignitaries and diplomats rub elbows with local celebs and upward mobiles.

Pinkey's Boulevard Club

...and old & quaint

"Pinkey's is only 7 minutes from Downtown,
serving excellent food and cocktails
11 a.m. to Midnight Monday through Friday, Saturday 5:00 to 12:00
Cocktails 'til 2:00 a.m.   Entertainment every evening.

BOATERS WELCOME

110 EAST GRAND BOULEVARD   DETROIT, MICHIGAN
Attendant Parking
Corner of E. Jefferson at the Foot of the Belle Isle Bridge
824-2820

Clementine's Kitchen

CLEMENTINE'S KITCHEN
271 Jos Campau
Detroit/Warehouse District

Lou and Millie have maintained this saloon for years. At night the dim bar lights can't help but invite you in. By day, it's a local spot for Ross Roy yuppies, Stoph's employees and other folks that want something a little different. By night the clientele varies from Hill Street Blues to searchers from the other warehouse district taverns. Expect anything and anyone, including Greektown belly dancers. Many of the local bartenders and waitresses meet here after work for attitude adjustment. Food is served by day, roast beef, homemade soups, salads, burgers and a daily special. Detroit memorabilia enhance this old time saloon with wood floors, booths, pool table and juke box. Imported beers and good drinks top off this warehouse district institution.

8900 E. Jefferson
Detroit
In the River House, at the City Marina

Hoy Tin or translated "View of the River" is precisely what this Oriental treasure offers. Chinese, Cantonese, Japanese and American foods at very reasonable prices, escort the dragons and exotic cocktails with views of freighters, sea gulls, and marina activity. A side room offers Japanese dining with official tatami floors for the adventurers. Carry out is available for the unique Captain who wishes to serve the Pu Pu platter of Chinese ribs, rumaki, bali miki, egg roll and puffed shrimp appetizers, prior to complete dinners, with the Far East delicacies. Warren Fong overseas his fast, efficient staff seven days a week. For the crew that seeks something different from the burgers, steaks, seafood normal bill of fare, the Hoy Tin offers that diversion. Dockage at the city marina is reserved for season holders but usually some are open long enough to place a to go order or get permission for dinner. Variety is the spice and the view of the River offers that spice. Open seven days.

100 St. Clair
Detroit River

AE, DC, MC, V

As stated in the first edition, Sindbad's is "one of the greatest boating galleys from the Azores to Mitchell's Bay". Under the direction of Buster's sons Mark and Brian Blancke run the same tight ship that was created by Buster and H. Van Hollebeke. It has 92 boat wells, is open seven days a week with a full liquor cabinet and full service

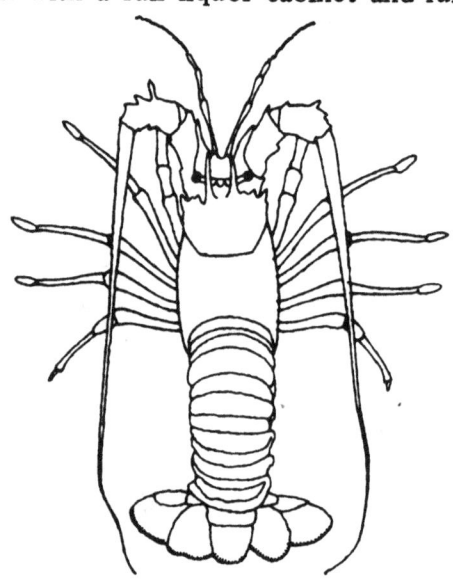

menu. A tradition of the boating community from its days as a one room saloon to its present five expansions later. Steaks, seafood, burgers and breakfast are served anytime for the night watch. Founded February 23, 1949 by two brothers through marriage, a saloon with a boat yard for a parking lot, grew into a 280-seat capacity restaurant. Sea stories and the best drink on the river accompany homemade chili, homemade clam chowder, frog legs, fresh pickerel and superior surf and turf. For the Captain who wants to get away from his or her crew to the crew of Calipyso, Sindbad's can handle it. Bartenders and waitresses rapidly serve at an America's Cup pace, never missing a mark. The only word of caution is not to tell too big of a sea story. You may find out the story started there. As the menu states, for empty Bilges, names like Dinghy Special, Gang Plank, Deck Hand's Delight, Gulf Stream, Mermaid and Neptune's Delight reflect the true Sindbad's spirit from drink to dinner.

The Post Bar
408 W. Congress,
Detroit

Yachting and the Post Bar have a great deal in common. When you head out to the open seas, just about anything can happen. Welcome to the Post with the Most. For the Captain and crew that are seeking the ultimate party, place 408 W. Congress on the weekend log. A long narrow saloon, with pool table in the back forty, decorated by patrons giving American folk art a new meaning. A Detroit original that has created some of the most unique and cerebral activities to hit the front pages of the Dailies. Remember the elephant foot prints during the rebublican convention that sauntered from the back doors of Cobo Hall to the third bar stool of the Post Bar? While the battalions of other saloon keepers were staying up nights pulling their hair for that perfect slogan, triple deck bus or dancing girl to reel in the anticipated delegates, the foot prints where dry for the international media crews, that arrived weeks in advance, resulting in weeks of flowing elephantiasis. The best juke box and sound system from Martique to Mitchell's Bay occational live entertainment depending on who wants to compete with the saloon that had to move the tables out due to the many patrons going aloft without their Bosun's chair. If after a few rums, you think you're seeing double, you are? But you're not? The Proprietors, Pat and Michael Wheeler are identical twins, Phyllis, Jane and Andrea assist in the excitement, friendliness and flow of this Detroit tradition. Cash. Pirate's Paradise.

Art's Tavern
15316 E. Jefferson
Grosse Pointe Park

A family restaurant and tavern Art and Fran Kreft operate a full service, Mon-Sat legend. Burgers, fish, chicken dinners or munchies, ice cold drafts or ice cream hummers. Art's will fill the order. The homemade soups are probably the best on the Great Lakes. When the Gales of November come early head to Art's for his famous soups. Spotless would be an underestimation of ship and rigging. A very warm atmosphere for lunches, dinners or cocktails and good conversation. This hidden jewel on East Jefferson glows under the helm of Art and Fran, all their children have bartended, cooked, waitressed while pursuing colleges, careers, and marriages. The Kreft's have always offered a helping hand to Pirate's and Princesses. In a world that sometimes seems to be based only on the "all mighty buck" steer a course to 15316 E. Jefferson and see what a wonderful world we could have, if we followed the outstanding and unique example set by the Kreft's for decades. Highly recommended.

SURF NORTH
10069 Dixie Hwy. (M-29)
Anchorville

Robert and Sharon Bracci operate one of the finest restaurants on Lake St. Clair. A wonderful view of Anchor Bay with boat docking right out side the door. Specialties include fish, steaks and excellent ribs. Friday and Saturday nights provide a complete evening of dinner, drinks and dancing to the Big Band sound. Lunch and dinner served seven days a week. Tie up for the day or the night, the Braccis have been catering to boaters for years. Recommended.

The Old Place
15301 W. Jefferson
Grosse Pointe Park

For the cruising yachtsman that is laying over at one of the Grosse Pointe Yacht Clubs or harbors a few of the many restaurants in this area will be listed. The Old Place is one of Diamond Phillips' fleet. The Golden Lion and Little Harry's also offer valet parking as a start into the world of Diamond's. All are designed to satisfy diners and drinkers. The bars are all briefly separated from the formal dining areas. All provide piano bars with contemporary tunes and request lines open. If the yacht clubs start to get boring any one of these three will spice up the night. Grosse Pointe debs and occasional Mrs. Robinsons can be found for cocktails and conversation. The weekends start to unwind on a small dance floor with a fantastic glittering mirrored ball shooting laser streaks of light through the Gimlet glasses. Preppys come and go on weekends depending on whose party or date received the deep six award. Dinners are very good and like some of the finer restaurants in the area, the Yachting term prevails. If you have to ask the price, you can't afford it. The host, Hiller has been there for years and always has a pleasant welcome. Why does he always seem to project the knowledge that he's seen it all.
Oyster bar opens at four. Closed Sunday. AE, DC, MC, V.

XOCHIMILCO

3409 Bagley, Detroit, North of Vernor and the Ambassador Bridge

Open Sunday through Saturday 11 a.m. – 4 a.m.

A bit of the sea lanes the Xochimilco is well worth travelling across land to reach. Unlike many ethnic restaurants the Xochimilco, is about as authentically ethnic as any dining spot north of the border. The prices are almost unbelievably low and the food excellent. For sea food lovers the Xochimilco offers fish soup on Fridays and Shrimp Ranchero style. For the true lover of Mexican cuisine the Xochimilco provides a full range of traditional Mexican meals cooked with a suburbly original touch.

1585 Franklin, Detroit at Orleans just south of Jefferson

Open Monday-Thursday, 11 a.m. – 1 p.m.; Friday 11 a.m. – 2 a.m.; Saturday Noon – 2 a.m. Reservations are not necessary.

Located just off the Detroit River the Soup Kitchen was in days past known as the Ship Inn a place which attracted sailors in interested quenching a variety of thirsts whether downstairs at the bar or upstairs at "the hotel." Today a tamer variety of sea goer can stock up on the hearty soups and sandwiches the Soup Kitchen offers and order from a wide variety of domestic and foreign beers, while surrounded by the relics of the bar's more colorful past.

18431 Mack
Detroit
MC, V

Farina's Granary

One of the treasures of the Grosse Pointe area. It's a family tradition, with Leonard Farina, his wife and children all crewing in this intriguing bistro. The stained glass on the walls embellish this family tradition back to Europe and the initial granary. The atmosphere is intimate and warm. Tables and high back booths offer private dinners and memorable lunches. The homemade daily specials are outstanding. A complete menu with many of the family's diverse European favorite regatta flags. Sandwiches or four course dinners are the bill of fare. The price is also a treat. The quality is high, but not the price. Mr. Farina also operates a full catering service, so if the galley slaves on the Christian Nordich want to surprise the crew, call the Granary and pick up your full course dinners for twenty. Highly recommended. Monday thru Saturday. Private parties Sunday.

17131 E. Warren
Detroit
DC, MC, V

Here is a separate dining room and bar with excellent food, and seafood flown in from all over the world. Very large portions and very reasonable prices put this full service restaurant on the chart even though it's a little past dock-side.

For the Captain and crew who are looking for the hidden treasures tucked away from the standard rum lines, this is the place. The seafood is not on a formula system, each dinner is prepared perfectly for you, including home made pasta. The owners and staff project the feeling of a family restaurant with friendly service. For those seeking an excellent meal without mortgaging the yacht, try the Blue Pointe.

PHONE 881-3086

18431 MACK   DET. MICH 48224

DYLAN'S
Raw Bar & Grille

15402 Mack Avenue
Grosse Pointe, Michigan
(313) 884-6030

Hours of Operation
Monday-Thursday

Kitchen: 4:00-11:00 p.m.
Bar: 4:00 p.m.-Close

Friday-Saturday
Kitchen: 4:00 p.m. – Midnight
Bar: 4:00 p.m. – 2:00 a.m.

Sunday
Kitchen: 5:00 p.m.-10:00 p.m.
Bar: 5:00 p.m. –Close

John Montgomery and Rocco Ciqueranelli took over partnership of Tom's Oyster Bar and re-named it in tribute to singer songwriter Bob Dylan.
A great local spot with a Great Lakes flavor. Music, Live Music, Music in part of the soul of this wonderful place.

Little Tony's
Lounge in the Woods
20513 Mack Ave.
Grosse Pointe Woods, MI

In 1970, Carol and Tony Alfonsi opened Little Tony's Lounge in the Woods on Mack Ave. in Grosse Pointe Woods. Carol Alfonsi remains the owner and hostess to this day.
This cozy neighborhood landmark offers a full bar and beautiful patio for outdoor dining. Little Tony was an avid boater and had a sharp yacht, Lounge in the Woods! Boater's welcome!

15117 Kercheval
Grosse Pointe Park
822-0266

A contemporary bistro navigated by Darrell and Liz Finken. The blend of Darrell's excellent wine and culinary knowledge and Liz's art and artist design create one of the most unique restaurants to enter the 20th century. From the sky lights and art treasures to the black tie bartenders individuality explodes. Fine wines, duckling terrine, angle hair pasta and mesquite start to define one of the most creative menus state side. A large bar rafts an assortment of corporate heirs and corporate crews. When asked by a local gossip columnist why not offer entertainment, Darrell replied, "it's already here". It's listed in the Official Preppy Handbook as one of the Preppy foundations. Bartenders and waitresses supply excellent service to a very demanding group. A Sunday brunch fit for Ted Turner accompanies lunch, dinner and "after the regatta's over" late night treats. Miles Davis, Billie Holliday or Ravel's Bollero float through the sound system, symbolic of the uncharted waters Liz and Darrell have successfully created. AE, DC, MC, V.
My favorite part is the wall of wine corks, but that's a secret.

Julio's ZANTE

FRESH SEAFOOD
STEAKS & CHOPS
GREEK DISHES

DAILY SPECIAL
LUNCHES & DINNER

FULL LIQUOR
CARRY OUT & CATERING

 OPA!

SQUARE GREEK PIZZA

THURS. - SAT.
PIANO ENTERTAINMENT

OPEN 7 DAYS
11:00 - 2:00
12-12 SUN.

20930 Mack Ave.
885-7979 Grosse Pointe Woods, MI 48236

24420 E. Jefferson
St. Clair Shores
All Major Credit Cards

24935 Jefferson
St. Clair Shores
AE, MC, V

Owner Al Wagner is the recipient of the Golden Dabloon Award for the Best Lake St. Clair Waterman. He's a yacht owner, marine operator, nice person and operator of Brownie's on the Lake. Located in the Jefferson Beach Marine complex, Brownie's has been a boating tradition for years. Don't look twice but the gentleman handing out the menu and seating the diner's just might be Al.

Located near the heart of the nautical mile, Moore's is a full service restaurant with full menu from burgers to Prime rib. The deep dark woods and brass trim comfort Captain or Commodore. The seating design offers your choice. Booths are set off from the main stream for private and intimate dining and drinks. For review of the sunken treasure maps the booths are the way to go.

Commander of one of the fastest paced restaurants on the lake, Mr. Wagner oversees his fleet of waitresses, bartenders, chefs and busboys, like Reichover commanded the U.S. Navy. Entering through the transom of a 40 footer should be your first clue to what's in the galley. It's one of the largest circular bars on the lake, if not the largest, bartenders work at regatta pace serving the thirsty sailors and powerboaters that sometimes are three deep. The large dining room has a full service menu with Captain size steaks, chops, burgers and fresh seafood. The patio is a dockboys delight. What could be better than sitting back and watching amateur and pros jockeying to dock their 28 or 40 footer. Why watch Divorce Court on TV, when you can see it live! Open seven days. At night the live band warms up for dancing more lines than dockside. There's a full service marina, with hardware and provisions, probably the most complete marine complex on Lake St. Clair. And they can handle the big boys, 110 feet, no problem.

Once the pirate share has been agreed, move into the other rooms for celebration. A beautiful wood bar with stained glass serves a full line of liquor, beer and wine. Tables for eating and/or drinking are available in the bar section. The clam chowder is terrific. A piano bar with very good entertainment and dance floor offers a welcome break from the pitches and rolls at sea. Singles move into the saloon area at night, with many a boat ride invitation offered. Valet parking.

LIDO'S
24028 E. Jefferson
St. Clair Shores
Major Credit Cards

A casual, relaxed atmosphere reigns here, with boating built from entrance to deck. Located at the nautical mile (9½ & Jefferson), Lido's decor has created a feeling of not knowing whether you are in a restaurant or on the back deck of a sixty footer. The patrons have placed their life rings behind the bar with those sacred boat names, like Black Gold, J B & Water, The Other Women, etc., for a unique backdrop. Daily specials range from seafood to steaks. They are famous for the French onion zoupa covered with melted cheese. The deck offers a great view of the many marine activities by day or night. Live band entertainment lights up the evening activities. It's next to the Great Lakes Yacht Club for those going from club to club. Viewing this expansive nautical mile easily shows why Michigan is the Water Wonderland.

BOAT TOWN, U.S.A.
Clinton River, Mt. Clemens

Canada has the beautiful lawns and flowers, the U.S. shore proudly has Boat Town, U.S.A. The business and community pulled together to create this. The public and private community joined forces to secure a historic preservation sea anchor to hold back the development of this community. Located on the North and South shores of the Clinton River, marinas, restaurants, shops, party stores, and associated marine supplier and manufacturers stopped the wreaking balls and bulldozers destined for this prime region of Lake St. Clair. Floating down the Clinton River is a combination of the intercoastal waterway, Newport, Annapolis and Nantucket, all spliced togehter. But don't expect the Intercoastal high-risers, the sea anchor stopped most of that. Sun bleached slopes, wind burned cradles, sleek 40 footers and 16 foot ski boats with tank tops as far as the eye can see. For a break from the high seas of Lake St. Clair, Boat Town is a welcome port. Hundreds of docks to tie up, with showers, provisions, pump-outs, fuel and an array of boating bars and restaurants espose the tradition "boaters have more fun".

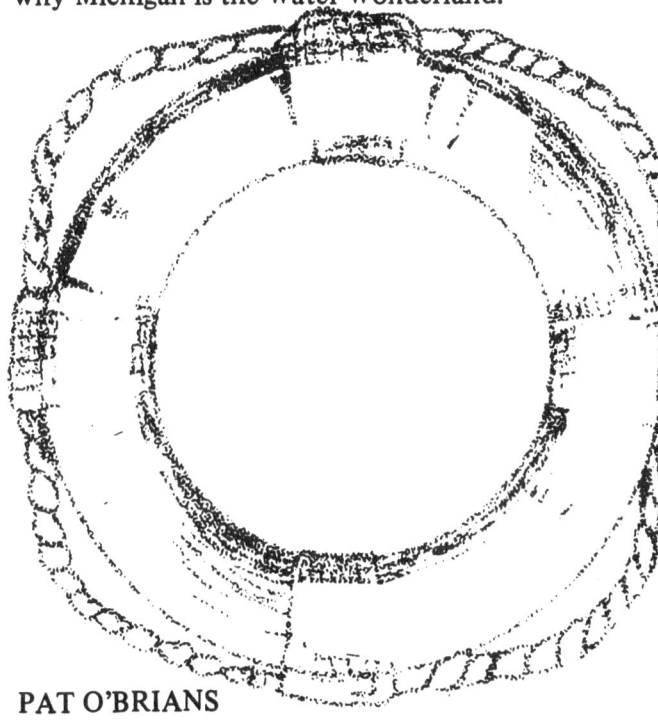

PAT O'BRIANS

Located at Ten Mile and Jefferson, O'Brian's is a pirate's paradise. Very good food, with ribs, fish special, (famous perch), burgers, etc. The restaurant is divided into two sections, one for dining, so bring the family, and one for the bar, so leave the family. A good juke box in the bar area allows bar patrons to listen to the tunes, but not bother the diners. When the crew is sick of the Captain or owner after too many nautical miles, jump ship and head for Pat O'Brian's. Singles come and go by day and night. Full liquor service. Who knows you might meet — a Commodoress! More believe it or not fish and sea stories have been told in this saloon than any other on the lake. Highly recommended.

Wet your whistle but don't drown it.
Don't drink too much of a good thing.
The Distilled Spirits Council of the United States.

CANDLES ON THE LAKE

32760 S. River Road

If Jimmy Buffett ever needed inspiration for his "changes in latitudes, changes in altitudes album," he could find it here. It's divided into bar and dining room, with eight wells right on Lake St. Clair, and the street entrance on South River Road. Jukebox, video games and pool table will take your mind off the compass rose. All age groups blend for burgers, beers, nachos. The view is great. Sailboats, windsurfers, water skiiers, all cruise by the windows in a partly shelter bay past Huron Point. Rolling wood floors, piling tables and open grill separate the bar section from the step up dining area with tables and fireplace. Sea stories, fish stories and the latest in singles stories, change hands like the ticker tapes on Wall Street. Continuing the history of the Blue Boat, don't miss Candles on the Lake. Fried chicken and shrimp. Open seven days. MC, V.

JAC'S BAY LOUNGE
Conger Bay Drive
Mt. Clemens
Cash

Located on Belvedere Bay by the Clinton River, Jac's has fifty boat wells, six with water and electricity. Jac's could easily be a California Laugua Beach bar. There's live music, video games, and a good juke box. Tee shirts, tank tops - surf's up at Jac's. Go for the drinks and the good time. Placed on the second floor of a beach house, sea stories and good tunes top off this unique hideaway.

CREWS INN
31988 N. River Road
(313) 463-8144

An attractive, newly decorated full service restaurant for lunch, dinner or late supper. The premiere chef prepares breast of chicken Isabella, frog legs Provencle, and veal Scallopine, to perfection. Appetizers include wing dings and crabmeat maison. There are hot sandwiches, barbecue spare ribs, pork chops and many other fish and seafood specialties. Desserts of fried ice cream Kaluha, and fresh strawberry Chantilly compliment entrees. From May. 1 to Labor Day, a Sunday buffet breakfast is served from 9:30 a.m. to 1:30 p.m. Full liquor with attractive bar for cocktails and conversation. Eight boat wells. AE, DC, MC, V.

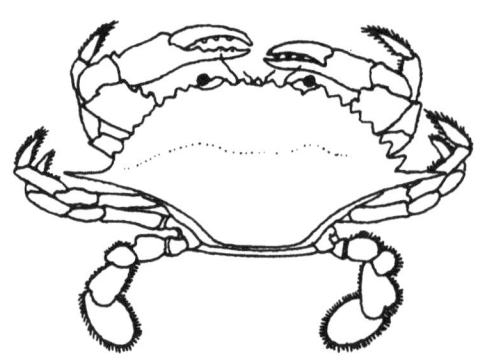

MERMAID BAR
S. River Road

Down the road and river from all the activity, the Mermaid offers liquor and beer for the crew on a budget. Locals swap fish stories and friendly directions for gear or provisions. It's a good place to plan a treasure hunt. The Mermaid bar has to be in the Pirate's Guide, it's a natural.

SHANNON'S STEAK HOUSE
29370 S. River Road
Mt. Clemens
MC, V, AE

A quick cab fare from the many marinas on the Clinton River, Shannon's offers prime aged steaks. A thirty-two-ounce T-bone claims the largest on the lake. The interior is kelly green with a piano bar and full service liquor. It's a very good steak house in an area of boaters that's got lots of wells, but not a whole lot of cattle. If a rare, aged, delicious steak is on the chart, Shannon is the port 'o call. Good after dinner entertainment for sing-along and swapping sea stories or no-wives tales. Eight boat wells, open seven days.

JOHNSON'S
32003 North River Road
Mt. Clemens
Cash

One of the first treasures to be logged in the first Pirate's Guide, Johnson's is a must for all. The Johnson family has been operating this full service restaurant for thirty-seven years with no end in sight. If a T.V. crew would need a hurricane house for a back drop, Johnson's would fill the bill. No glitter and a small sign expose the rolling wood floors and dining room. They measure the amount of fish they serve not by the stringer or bucket, but by the ton. A variety of American fare is offered, with pickerel one of the specialties. Part circus act, part restaurant and all restaurant. Informal. Highly recommended.

BEACHCOMBER
31960 N. River Road

Small and efficient, Beachcomber is next to the Mariner's Yacht Club. Three boat wells move boaters in and out for feasting on the 12 omelets, bacon and eggs, delicious homemade soups and sandwiches. Two small patios open for fresh air, picnic tables and umbrellas to watch the world sail by. Open at 6 a.m. to 9 p.m. daily, the Beachcomber cuts past bar tabs and right to the food. Very casual, comfortable restaurant for singles, families or groups. Carry-out available. No alcohol. MC, V. For the crew that has work to do, this is the place to start.

Corner of Washington & Green streets

725-1717

**Food and Spirits
Sandwiches and Pizza**

Open 10 a.m. to 2 a.m.

Friday and Saturday...Party Night, Dance to your favorite Top 40 Tunes

Drink Special Every Hour!

— COME JOIN THE FUN AT RJ'S —

ST. CLAIR INN
500 N. Riverside
St. Clair
St. Clair River
(313) 329-2222

1337 N. River Road
St. Clair, MI
All Major Cards

"On the river where the world goes by" is a complete restaurant and inn, with meeting rooms and banquet facilities for groups from 25 to 200, audio-visual equipment for the board meeting or video viewing party. The English Tudor projects elegance right down to the brick circular entrance. Rich with leather and wood beams, the view is hypnotic. International shipping lanes seem close enough to touch. Freighters from all over the world forge to many destinations from White Fish Bay to Norway. Nearby marinas offer dockage and shuttle service to the inn is available. Full liquor with seafood trays, prime rib, pan fried chicken, lamb chops, and many Great Lakes fish specials. Don't expect video games or pool tables, but beautifully decorated rooms with small cottages for the perfect get-away or lay over on your way to Georgian Bay or Harbor Springs. Golf, tennis, and swimming facilities top off this jewel of the River. AE, V, MC, DC.

A Chuck Muer nugget. Located on the St. Clair river for another excellent location to watch the freighters and river activity by day or night. Shuttle service is provided from the local marinas. The River Crab motel is attached to the restaurant complex if the berths get too small. Fresh seafood is the Muer tradition with daily specials from shark to swordfish. It's a full service bar and restaurant, open seven days, with Sunday brunch. Mackerel, King Salmon, Whole Black Sea Bass, the famous frog legs, and steaks are also available. This is one of Muer's finest restaurants. Seafood just tastes better when you're two feet from the water. A piano bar offers entertainment in a casual atmosphere. The combinations and specialties live up to the famous Chuck Muer tradition.

On the River, where the world goes by.

"A marvelous place for a meeting"

If you're planning a meeting for any time of the year, think about St. Clair Inn. You'll find the international ambience of a shipping lane, just an hour or so from your office. Freighters from everywhere glide silently by just outside the windows, reminders of the great world of trade.

Meeting rooms for groups from 25 to 200 are ready with the latest and best in audiovisual equipment.

Dining rooms offer fresh-caught lake fish, plus a tempting variety of other entrees. Our wine list is vigorous and varied.

If you've thought about Boyne Mountain, Las Vegas and Atlantic City, think hard about St. Clair Inn. You can get there sooner, enjoy yourself longer.

Call us for details.

St. Clair, Mich. 313-329-2222
Detroit, Mich. 313-963-5735

DECKER'S LANDING

9081 Anchor Bay Drive, Fair Haven at M-29

Hours 11 a.m. — 2:30 p.m. Sunday through Saturday. No reservations. VISA and Master Charge accepted.

Decker's provides the lusty salt with good food and plentiful grog. Open a little later than many of its neighbors Decker's offers safe harbor for the midnight sailor.

HENRY'S

408 M-29, Algonac, near St. Clair Drive

Hours: Monday through Friday, 11 a.m. until Midnight; Saturday and Sunday, 11 a.m. — 2 a.m. Reservations are suggested especially in season.

VISA and Master Charge accepted.

Henry's provides a good view of the lake and an outstanding perch dinner. One word of warning — be sure to call ahead during the boating season to insure your crew seats.

BROSNAN'S BAR & GRILL

15019 E. JEFFERSON
GROSSE POINTE PARK, MICHIGAN 48230
(313) 331-9653

Proprietor: John Brosnan

STROH'S ICE CREAM
Now Available in Florida

(813) 623-6299

5806-B North 53rd St.
Tampa, FL 33610

We handle...
The Larson Company • Henry Colt Enterprises, Inc. • Viking Seafoods, Inc.
Pierre Frozen Foods, Inc. • New York Bread (Tampa, Orlando)
Texas Custom Bakers • Celestial Farms • New England Shrimp Co., Inc.

THE FOGCUTTER
511 Fort Street, Port Huron, On top of the People's Bank Building

Reservations required Friday and Saturday. All major credit cards accepted. Open Monday-Thursday 11 a.m. – 10 p.m.; Friday and Saturday 11 a.m. – 1:30 a.m.; Sundays 2 p.m. – 7:30 p.m.

From his perch in the crow's nest your host Jerry O'Conner serves up such taste treats as Petitte Frog Legs Belle Provence, Almond-Fried Jumbo Gulf Shrimp, and Duckling a l'Orange. For the more adventurous dinner there is broiled filet of young white shark. The Swiss Onion Soup is unsurpassed. If all of this is not enough enjoy the entertainment offered seven nights a week or visit the adjoining Vagabond Gift Center.

THE LITTLE BAR
321 Chartier, Marine City just east of M-29

Hours Monday through Saturday 11:30 a.m. – Midnight. Reservations during the week, but not on weekends. VISA and American Express accepted.

The Little Bar, located between two marinas, offers a fine selection of steaks and seafood and provides the thirsty salt with one of the best stocked galley of spirits to be found anywhere. The Little Bar is small but cozy as your ship's cabin. For variety try the daily luncheon and desert specials.

THE PIERS
7479 Dyke Road, Fair Haven on Anchor Bay

Hours Wednesday-Friday 3 p.m. – 2 a.m.; Saturdays and Sundays, Noon – 2 a.m.; Open holidays that fall on Monday. Reservations are required for parties of six or more. VISA, Master Charge, and MOBIL cards accepted.

Something is always going on Tom Santo's Marina complex. There are a variety of sporting events and "created holidays" celebrated at The Piers. The escargot, white fish, and steaks are a favorite of Detroit based yacht clubs. The sea dog with varied taste should try the Pier's seafood platter.

This section has been compiled for the culinary Captain's and crews that wish to expand and create new delights. The recipes are published courtesy of the Junior League of St. Charles, Louisiana, from their cook book the Pirate's Pantry. (Order form included). The cocktails have been assembled from various sources. The Pirate's Guide is most compatible with the bar stool at the Golden Galleon in front of the plaque "Women, Wind and Fortune, Change Quickly."

Pirate's Pantry is by far one of the superior cookbooks by land or sea. The Junior League of Lake Charles, Louisiana allowed the Pirate's Guide to publish a sampling of it's over 800 mouth-watering recipes. During the research of this second edition of the Pirate's Guide, the project wouldn't have been complete without a brief trip to New Orleans. As the world knows, if you want information about automobiles, you come to Detroit. If you want information about Pirate's, you go to Louisiana. During a research visit at the Historic New Orleans Collection, a fascinating and elegant research center and museum, located in the heart of the French Quarter. The Site is a historic landmark, built in Spanish Colonial times, and one of the few survivors of the 1794 fire. The Pirate's Pantry was listed in the card catalogue along with the books regarding Jean Lafitte. (Listed in Publications Section). Pirate's Pantry?, Pirate's Guide? Food & Grog?, where is this book? With the support of Penny Haxthausen, Sheryl Swift (both Chairman's) and their organization, the Junior League, the Pirate's Guide and the Pirate's Pantry headed for the Galley. The cookbook is in it's 5th printing, with no end in sight. The Table of Contents lists 12 chapters: 1. Roux, Gumbos, Soups, 2. Rice 3. Seafood 4. Wildlife 5. Beverages, Wine, Hors D'Oeuvres 6. Eggs and Cheese (Breads) 7. Meats 8. Poultry 9. Vegetables 10. Salads 11. Sauces (Accompaniments) 12. Desserts and a new section of "Fast and Fabulous" including quick and easy recipes marked through-out the book with treasure chests. A new recipe for Blacken Fish battens down this Jean Lafitte treasure found.

The editorial review of the 377 pages of Creole, Cajun, Louisiana delights, almost caused a quick flight to Lake Charles for samples. The Official cookbook of "Contrabrand Days," includes detailed illustrations of historical surrounding and how to prepare, clean and cut many types of fish and seafood. As stated in the Baton Rouge, Morning Advocate ". . . . a treasure booty of fine recipes includes the richness of the old Majestic Hotel's Blackbottom Pie, a heavenly concoction which starts with a gingersnap crust. The Pirate in the pantry is Jean Lafitte, and the loot from the publication goes to community projects sponsored by the Junior League." The following recipes are a sample of the culinary creations included in this best seller.

Bon Appetit!

THE LEGEND OF JEAN LAFITTE

Some folks say that the spirit of Jean Lafitte, the pirate, still hovers over the dark waters of the Calcasieu River, with its cypress bayous and ghostlike Spanish moss. In the murky gloom of twilight, elusive swamp lights offer a phosphorescent promise of buried treasure just beyond.

It is a proven fact that the gentleman pirate and patriot came often to the Calcasieu country to trade, visit, and seek refuge; and he headquartered near here around the year 1810.

A wanted man, the dashing young pirate sought refuge here from United States war vessels. History relates that he slipped more than once under cover of darkness or fog, into safe harbor at the mouth of the Calcasieu River.[1]

Once, learning from sentinels posted down river that an attack was imminent, he sent ashore a party of his most trusted men to bury a treasure by night. Next morning, he set a large force to building an embankment, behind which he placed cannons. When the warship lay at anchor, a shot from the newly constructed fort sank the schooner and routed the accompanying gunboat.

The old fortification, known for many years as "Dead Man's Lake,"[2] can still be seen on the bank of the lake.

Another oft-told tale relates that Lafitte, pardoned by the U.S. in return for his aid in the Battle of New Orleans, sailed to France, and secretly aided Napoleon, after the Battle of Waterloo, in an attempted escape to America. Sailing with a vast amount of gold and jewels, the "Little Emperor" was apprehended and arrested, but Lafitte escaped with the treasure, which he buried along the Calcasieu River.[3]

Strange tomblike vaults, marked with iron crosses, along the shore of Big Lake[4] housed a treasure of gold Spanish doubloons, some say. Though the encroaching waters of the lake have obliterated all traces of the landmarks, the gold remains undisturbed at its bottom.

Trees marked with Roman numerals are another indication of buried treasure; and Niblett's Bluff[5] is the site where Lafitte's gold is said to be buried under 40 gum trees.

Another story places the gold at the bottom of Contraband Bayou.[6] Still another tells of a schooner, laden with gold coin and jewels gathered along the Spanish Main, which sank in the marshes south of Lake Charles.[7]

And, it is said, that the waters around Lake Charles, still provide sanctuary to the notorious pirate. Legend is that his final resting place is on the eastern shore of the lake.[8] His spirit still guards the gold of Napoleon — and casts a mighty shadow across "the Quelqueshue."

Treasured Recipes of Southwest Louisiana

LOUISIANA GUMBO

½ cup Wesson oil
1 cup flour
4 quarts water
2 large onions, finely chopped
1 clove garlic, chopped
1 cup green onions, chopped
¼ cup parsley, finely chopped
⅛ cup bell pepper, chopped (optional)
⅛ cup celery, chopped (optional)
Salt and pepper to taste
Chicken, goose, duck, smoked pork sausage combination
½ teaspoon file'
Hot fluffy rice

In large gumbo pot, make a roux with oil and flour. Cook over medium heat, stirring constantly until roux is a dark caramel color. Remove from fire and add remaining ingredients, except ½ cup green onions, filé, and rice. Boil for about 2 hours, or until meat is tender and gumbo has thickened. In the last 15 minutes of boiling add reserved green onions. Remove from fire and add filé (too much will make gumbo slimy). Serve over hot rice in gumbo bowls. Serves 5-6.

Shrimp Gumbo is made the same way except that shrimp are not added until last 20 minutes of cooking time, after gumbo has preboiled for 45 minutes.

For *Seafood Gumbo*, follow same procedure as Shrimp Gumbo but add crab meat also. In the last 15 minutes of cooking, add oysters.

Mrs. Paul "Dud" Faulk
(Rena Lantz)

COMMANDER'S FAMOUS IMPERIAL CRAB SPECIALTY

1 pound backfin lump crab meat
½ bell pepper, minced
1 small jar pimientos, minced
1 egg, beaten
⅓ cup mayonnaise
1 teaspoon dry mustard
¼ teaspoon black pepper
½ teaspoon salt

Preheat oven to 350°F. Carefully cull any shell pieces from crab meat. Mix all ingredients and toss lightly. Put in shells and bake for 15 minutes. Serves 4.

J. Gilbert Scheib

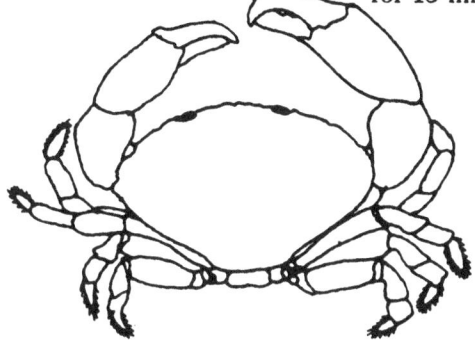

FRENCH CRÊPES

4 eggs
1 cup flour, sifted
1 teaspoon salt
1 cup whole milk
½ teaspoon vanilla
3 Tablespoons butter

FILLINGS

For breakfast: Cover with syrup. For brunch: Fill with creamed crab meat. For dessert: Fill with mixture of cream cheese and sour cream, roll, and top with strawberries heated in pan with sugar and a little strawberry liqueur.

Beat eggs, flour, and salt in bowl. Add milk, vanilla, and butter that has been melted in crêpe pan. (If made the night before serving, omit butter and part of milk from mixture until ready to cook.) For each crêpe, spoon only enough batter into hot crêpe pan to spread thinly and evenly over bottom when tilted. Brown lightly on one side. Roll with desired filling. Freezes well between sheets of wax paper.

Recipe has been in my family for 5 generations.

Mrs. Maurice L. Tynes
(Pam Lennox)

LOUISIANA CREOLE OKRA WITH MEAT BALLS

2 pounds ground round steak
2 eggs
Bread crumbs
Salt and black pepper to taste
Cooking oil
2 pounds fresh okra, sliced ½ inch thick
1 large white onion, chopped
2 cloves garlic, chopped
1 small bell pepper, chopped
2 ribs celery, chopped
2 cans peeled tomatoes
Red pepper to taste

Make small meat balls from mixture of meat, eggs, bread crumbs, salt, and black pepper. Brown in cooking oil in small Magnalite roaster or fryer and drain on absorbent paper. Using drippings, cook okra until tender, stirring often. Add chopped vegetables and sauté until soft. Add tomatoes and mix well before adding meat balls. Cook slowly for about 30 minutes adding hot water as needed to keep meat balls covered. Add pepper. Freezes. Serve over rice with crowder peas, cucumber salad, and corn sticks. Serves 6-8.

A great dish in the summer when fresh vegetables are plentiful. My own original recipe for quick entertaining.

Mrs. Evelyn C. Thompson

CLEANING AND COOKING OF CRABS

SOFT SHELL

Clean soft shell crabs by raising the tips of the "shell", removing lungs and other inedible parts, and finally lifting the back of the "shell" and removing stomach and other parts between the halves. Then remove the eyes and mouth, rinse cleaned crab in vinegar or salt solution (described in section on fish), and place on ice immediately to avoid deterioration.

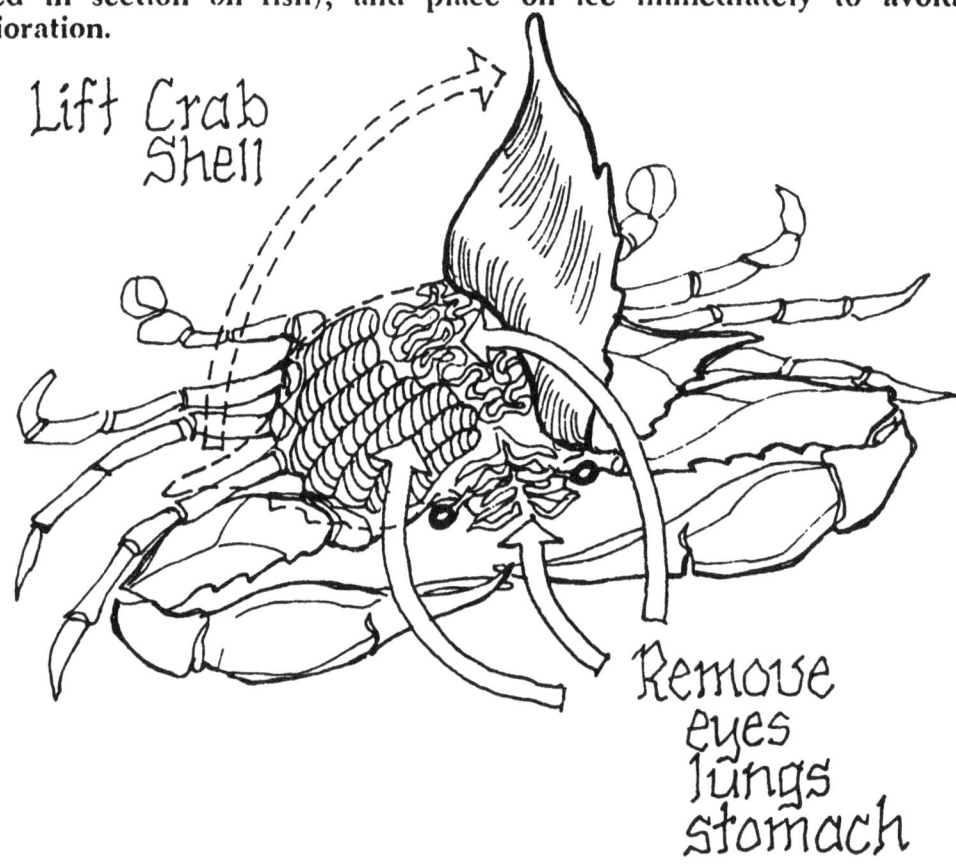

FRIED SOFT SHELL CRABS

Soft shell crabs
2 cups milk
2 eggs, slightly beaten
Flour
Salt, black and cayenne pepper to taste
Oil for deep frying

Clean crabs. Soak in milk and egg mixture for 1 hour before frying. Mix flour and seasonings in brown paper bag. Shake crabs in seasoned flour. Redip crabs in milk mixture and reflour. Fry in deep hot oil until golden brown. Serve 1 large or 2 small crabs per person.

Mrs. Charles S. Ware, Jr.
(Jan Allen)

CREOLE FRIED OYSTERS

1 egg, beaten
¾ cup tomato ketchup
2 Tablespoons Worcestershire sauce
1¼ teaspoons Tabasco
1 teaspoon celery salt
½ teaspoon each black and red pepper
1 quart oysters, drained
Corn meal
Oil for deep frying

In a deep bowl mix well the egg, ketchup, Worcestershire, Tabasco, celery salt, and pepper. Soak oysters in this sauce for 1 hour in refrigerator. Roll oysters in corn meal and fry, uncovered, in deep hot oil. Serves 4.

Mrs. L. Ron Futrell
(Sandra Allen)

GEORGIA FRIED CHICKEN WITH CREAM GRAVY

2 cups flour
½ teaspoon red or black pepper
1 teaspoon salt
½ teaspoon paprika
1 large fryer, cut up, salted and cooled overnight
Shortening or corn oil

CREAM GRAVY
Drippings from fried chicken
2 cups, or more, milk

Shake flour, pepper, salt, and paprika in a paper bag. Drop in several pieces of chicken at a time and shake to coat thoroughly. Heat 4 inches of shortening in iron skillet until very hot. Cook chicken pieces about 15-20 minutes, until brown on both sides, turning only once. Use tongs, not a fork, to turn chicken. After chicken has been removed from skillet, pour off excess fat, leaving only the drippings, which should be golden brown, not burned. Add 2 cups milk, or more if necessary, stirring constantly until desired thickness.

Mrs. G. Lock Paret, Jr.
(Beverly Bowers)

SHRIMP CREOLE

4 Tablespoons flour
5 Tablespoons shortening
1 large onion, chopped
6-8 green onions, chopped
1 small clove garlic, chopped
½ cup celery, chopped
¼ cup bell pepper, chopped
1 can (8 ounces) tomato sauce
1 can water
Salt, red and black pepper
1 Tablespoon Worcestershire sauce
1 teaspoon hot sauce
3-4 pounds raw shrimp, peeled, deveined

Add flour to shortening in preheated deep skillet or cooker kettle and cook on medium heat until a rich, dark brown, stirring constantly to prevent scorching. Add remaining ingredients, except shrimp, seasoning to taste. Simmer for 30 minutes, cover, bring to boiling point, and add shrimp. Cook for 15-20 minutes. Serve over steamed rice. Freezes. Serves 4-6.

Mrs. Allen J. Rhorer
(Mildred Hamilton)

CREOLE JAMBALAYA

- 1 Tablespoon shortening
- 2 Tablespoons flour
- 1 pound pure pork sausage, smoked, or loose uncased sausage
- ½ cup bell pepper, chopped
- 3 cups raw shrimp, peeled, deveined, and chopped
- 5 cups tomatoes, diced and peeled
- 2½ cups water
- 1 large onion, chopped
- 1 clove garlic, chopped
- 2 Tablespoons parsley, chopped
- 2 cups raw rice
- 2 Tablespoons Worcestershire sauce
- 1¼ teaspoons salt
- ½ teaspoon thyme
- ¼ teaspoon red pepper

Melt shortening in large heavy Dutch oven. Add flour and stir until blended; then add sausage (cut into bite sized pieces) and bell pepper. Cook 5 minutes. Add shrimp, tomatoes, water, onions, garlic, and parsley. Bring to a boil; add rice; and stir in Worcestershire sauce, salt, thyme, and red pepper. Cover and simmer for 30 minutes, or until rice is tender. Stir occasionally. Sprinkle with parsley. Does not freeze well. Serves 8.

Typical South Louisiana dish.

Pat Tessier
Baton Rouge, La.

Aliska Castel *of New Orleans uses 1 cup ham chopped instead of sausage in her jambalaya.*

SNAPPER LUZIANNE

- 1 medium or large red snapper
- Salt and pepper
- ¾ cup onion, chopped
- ¾ cup celery, chopped
- 1 clove garlic, finely chopped
- 1½ Tablespoons cooking oil
- 1 can stewed tomatoes
- 2 Tablespoons sugar
- 2 Tablespoons prepared mustard
- 1 Tablespoon Worcestershire sauce
- ¼ cup dry white wine
- 2 bay leaves
- Pinch of thyme
- ½ teaspoon each oregano and pepper
- ½ Tablespoon salt
- Dash of Tabasco
- ½ cup water

Scale and clean snapper. Wipe dry and rub lightly inside and out with salt and pepper. Sauté onion, celery, and garlic in oil until clear. Add remaining ingredients. Bring to a boil and simmer for 5 minutes. Spoon inside and over fish. Bake, uncovered, at 325°F for 25-30 minutes. Baste during cooking. Remove fish and thicken sauce with flour and water.

Mrs. Richard J. Chafin
(Carolyn Corley)

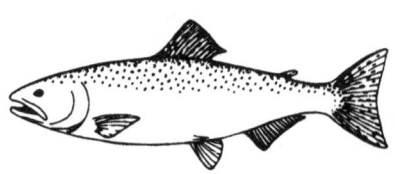

PIRATES'S PANTRY COOK BOOK

MAKO PUBLISHING CO.
35552 GRAND RIVER, SUITE 151
FARMINGTON HILLS, MI 48024

Send _____ copies of *PIRATE'S PANTRY* at $15.95 per copy

MAKE CHECKS PAYABLE TO **MAKO PUBLISHING CO.**

Enclosed is my check or money order for $ _____

NAME _____

STREET _____

CITY _____ STATE _____ ZIP _____

PROCEEDS FROM THE SALE OF **PIRATE'S PANTRY** WILL BE USED FOR COMMUNITY SERVICE PROJECTS APPROVED OR SPONSORED BY THE JUNIOR LEAGUE OF LAKE CHARLES, INC.

THE CRACKED CRAB
112 W. Washington
Ann Arbor, MI

For those of you that long for treasures from the Chesapeake, salt water and fresh water, pull out your north'easter and tie up at the the Cracked Crab. You can only reach this port 'o call by boat, if it is on a trailer. If salt water is in your viens and you can't fly off to Annapolis or New Port immediately, head for the Cracked Crab.

Divided into two sections with bar and booths on one side for dinner, drinks and raw bar, dining room on the other. The bar section sparkles with white Chesapeake white tiles (not formica, the real thing) and artifacts from Marine to Marblehead. The owner is not only a skilled restauranteur, but avid collector of maritime treasures. The oil paintings are excellent, the food is excellent. The owner scours the east coast from lobster shops to ship chandeleries for the authentic prizes to lace walls and ceilings. Where else can you glance at an east coast dingy while enjoying your favorite seafood. Rich dark wood enhances the sensation of ships, sea and salt air. The menu is the most complete seafood menu on the Great Lakes. Daily lunch and dinner specials fit for Captain Ahab. A dining experience that will satisfy and cure all salt water withdrawal symptoms. The only other restaurant/saloon that has the same effect for me, was the Black Pearl in New Port, R.I. It is built on the dock and the ocean rushes under and through the floor boards. Prices are very reasonable - a true seafood bistro. If your dry docked or in winter storage and the cold sweat, chills and salt water delirium's start to set in, Medi-vac yourself and crew to the Cracked Crab. Highly recommended, Salty.

DRINK RECIPES

PIRATE'S GOLD
½ jigger (¾ oz.) Southern Comfort
½ jigger Bacardi light rum
Juice and rind ¼ lime
3 oz. orange juice

Squeeze lime over ice cubes in 8 oz. glass, add rind. Add liquors and orange juice; stir. Add cherry.

BANANA DAQUIRI
In a blender blend 1/3 ripe banana, 1 tsp. sugar, ½ oz. lime or lemon juice, jigger of rum, ½ cup crushed ice. Blend, strain and serve.

NAVY GROG
Use Navy grog mix, or put 1 oz. each of fresh lime or lemon juice, orange juice, pineapple juice and passion fruit nectar, ½ oz. Falernum in a blender. Then add 2/3 jigger Bacardi light, 1-1/3 jiggers Bacardi dark and 1/2 cup finely cracked ice. Mix, pour unstrained into large Old Fashioned glass half filled with cracked ice. Garnish with mint sprigs and serve with straws.

RARE ADMIRAL
2 oz. Rare Scotch
1 oz. lime juice
2 teaspoons grenadine
Slice lime

Shake Rare Scotch, lime juice and grenadine with lots of ice. Pour unstrained, into large Old Fashioned glass. Sip, and add more grenadine, if desired. Garnish with lime slice.

SAILOR'S TODDY
1½ oz. Scotch
Hot fragrant tea
Sugar, to taste
Stick cinnamon, 1" piece

In a large cup or mug, pour Scotch; add hot tea and sugar, to taste. Stir. Garnish with cinnamon stick and lemon twist.

WHALER'S GROG
1½ oz. Scotch
Strong coffee chilled
Sugar to taste
Whipped cream

Over ice in a highball glass, pour Scotch. Add coffee, stir in sugar. Top generously with whipped cream.

Pirate's Guide
1½ shots Mt. Gay or Bacardi Amber Rum
Tonic (bottled)
One slice lime
½ slice orange

CAPTAIN HOOK
2 oz. Scotch
Juice of ½ lemon
1 teaspoon sugar
Club soda, chilled
Cherry or Orange slice

Over ice in a tall glass, pour scotch and lemon juice. Add sugar and stir well. Add club soda, stir quickly.

PIRATE'S PUNCH
1 Bottle Scotch
1 lg. can (46 oz.) grapefruit juice chilled
1 lg. can (46 oz.) pineapple juice chilled
1 can (16 oz.) crushed pineapple, chilled

Just before serving mix all ingredients in a large punch bowl over ice. Float thin slices of lemon on top. When serving dip a bit of the pineapple into each portion.

BAHAMA MAMA
Equal parts
Grand Marquis
Rum
Tequila
Appricot Brandy
Papaya juice
Orange juice

ANCIENT MARINER
Pour equal parts of Anejo rum and Grand Marnier liqueur over ice in a rock glass. Stir.

FISH HOUSE PUNCH
In a large container mix 8 oz. simple syrup, 24 oz. lemon or lime juice, 1½ qts. water. Stir. Add 2 qts. Bacardi light rum, 1 qt. Bacardi dark or Anejo brand rum, 4 oz. peach brandy. Stir. Chill 2 hours. Stir occasionally. To serve, pour mixture over block of ice in punch bowl. Serves 22 people twice.

SUNKEN TREASURE
Amareto and strawberries.

SALTY DOG
Vodka & Grapefruit juice.

STARBOARD LIGHT
Vodka & Green Creme de Menthe.

GOLDEN BIRD
Galliano, Rum and Orange juice.

 Recommended, But Not Reviewed

 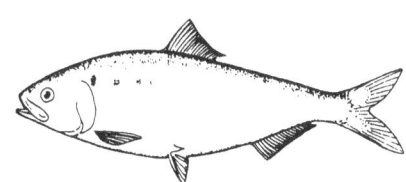 

A STATE OF MIND
FABULOUS
ENTERTAINMENT
& VIDEO
GREAT FOOD
911 WALKER RD.
WINDSOR. ONT.

County Road #2. Rochester Township
Deerbrook, Ontario

39504 Jefferson
Mt. Clemens, MI 48043
Telephone: 465-1003

Chapter 2

NAVIGATION & SEAMANSHIP

"I find the great thing in this world
is not so much where we stand, as
in what direction we are moving.
— Oliver Wendell Holmes

Nautical Charting

A nautical chart shows coastlines, water depths, reefs, rocks, lights, huoys, landmarks, and other details needed for safe navigation, it is a working tool for the mariner and ship navigator in planning voyages, and determining the safest and most efficient courses. Effective foreign and domestic maritime trade depends on the availability and quality of our nautical charts. And these services are also vital to the success of expanding offshore engineering and resource development projects, and the continued growth in the recreational boating industry.

Congress has charged NOS with the charting responsibility for U.S. oceanic coastal waters and the Great Lakes and connecting waterways, amounting to about 2.5 million square nautical miles; and in meeting this requirement NOS has on issue today about 980 different charts covering this great expanse. Different users require different chart scales and formats. Scales of charts vary from the small scale sufficient for sailing between coastal ports and the open ocean, to the large scales needed to navigate in harbors and restricted channels. Complimenting the charts are the nine Coast Pilot volumes which provide supplemental information needed by the mariner on port facilities, harbors, docks, tidal characteristics, piloting, weather statistics, regulations, and landmarks.

Hydrographic and photogrammetric surveys are carried out to provide the basic data needed to produce C&GS charts and maps. Hydrography is the science that deals with the measurement and description of the bottom features of oceans, lakes, rivers, and adjoining coastal areas. These surveys are carried out by ships of the NOAA fleet from C&GS project instructions. Photogrammetry is the science of obtaining reliable measurements by means of photographs. Aerial photographic methods are employed to position landmarks and aids to navigation for nautical charting and to map the shoreline and adjacent features. Over the years, C&GS photogrammetric mapping capabilities have been applied to other environmental problems dealing with the coastal zone such as boundary determinations, the effects of hurricanes and storms and multiple use problems. Bathymetric Maps are topographic maps of the sea floor, the size, shape, and distribution of underwater features are portrayed by means of detailed depth contours. These maps are the basic tools for engineering and scientific studies and the management and develop-

R.P. "Spike" Neesley

MARINE INSURANCE

Call me for Assistance or Prompt Quotation

962-4300

ALLIED UNDERWRITERS, INC. *Insurance*

28 W. Adams, Detroit 48226

ment of offshore energy and living resources.

How To Order C&GS Marine Charting and Mapping Products

Catalogs which describe these publications and list authorized sales agents throughout the United States are available from the Distribution Branch, N/CG33, Office of Charting and Geodetic Services, National Ocean Service (NOAA), Riverdale, Maryland 20737. Hydrographic survey sheets, digital data, topographic and photogrammetric shoreline maps, and aerial photographs are important by-products which arise out of the data acquisition and processing phases that produce these charts and maps. Information on their availability can be obtained by writing to the Nautical Charting Division, N/CG2, Office of Charting and Geodetic Services, National Ocean Service, (NOAA), Rockville, Maryland 20852.

CHARTING PRODUCTS FOR THE MARINER
U.S. Department of Commerce
National Oceanic and Atmospheric Administration
National Ocean Service

Safe Navigation

One of the most important tools used by boaters for planning trips and safely navigating waterways are NAUTICAL CHARTS. Most boaters look to the NATIONAL OCEAN SERVICE (NOS) and organizations such as the Safe Boating Council to provide leadership in safe boating. To meet the needs of the boating public, NOS produces a variety of nautical charts and chart related products.

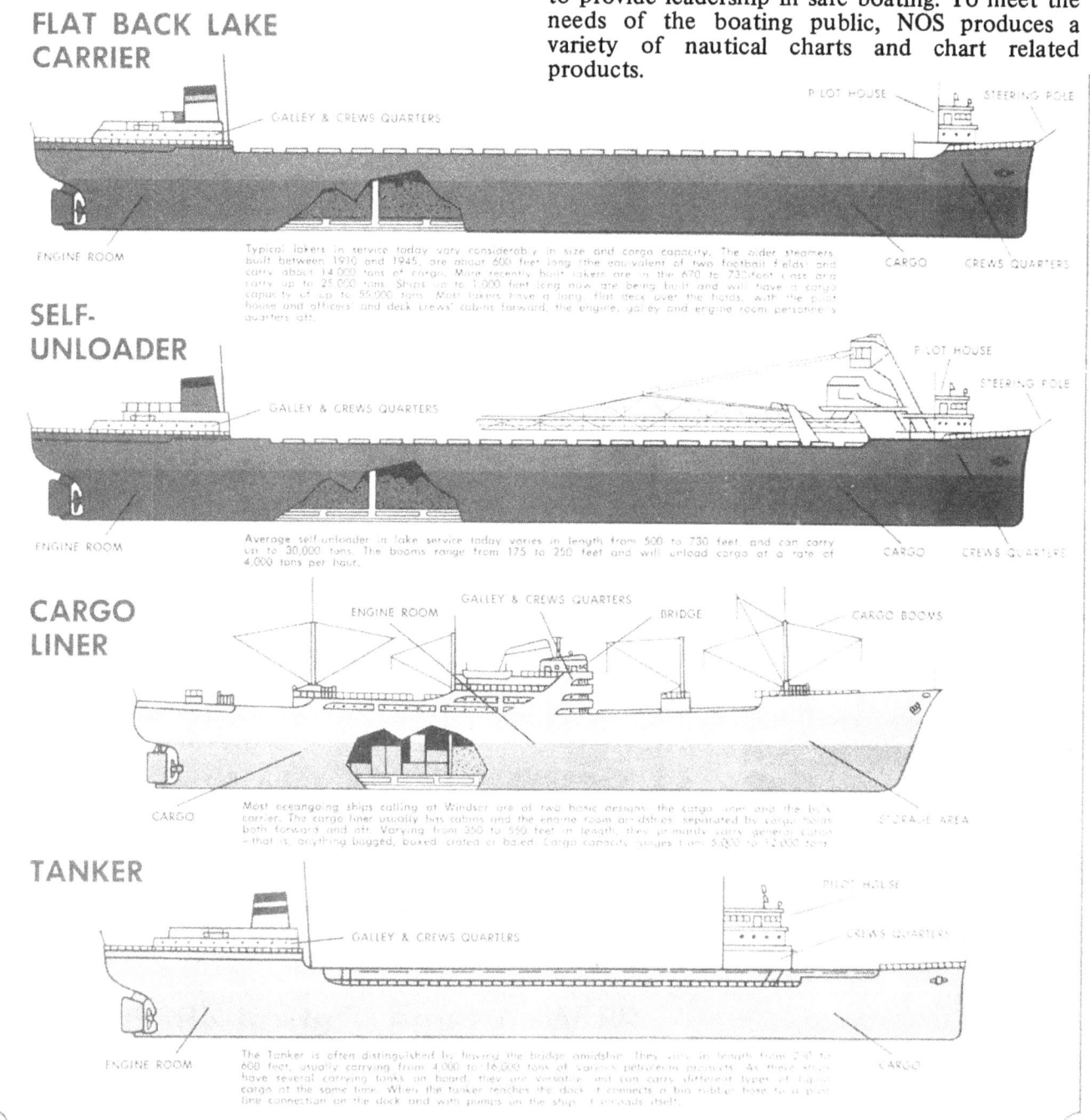

Algoma-Central Railway

Branch Lines Ltd.

Canada Steamship Lines

Hall Corporation

Hindman Transportation Co.

CANADIAN FLAG LAKERS

Imperial Oil Ltd.

Papachristidis Co. Ltd.

N. M. Paterson and Sons

Quebec & Ontario Transportation Co.

Reoch Transports Ltd.

Scott Misener Steamships Ltd.

Shell Canada Ltd.

Texaco Canada Ltd.

Upper Lakes Shipping Ltd.

Yankcanuck Steamships Ltd.

U.S. FLAG LAKERS

American Steamship Co.

Cleveland Cliffs Steamship Co.

Hanna Mining Co.

Interlake S.S. Co.

U.S. Steel Corporation

OCEAN-GOING SHIPS

Black Star Line (Ghana)

Arne Blystad (Norway)

Th. Brovig (Norway)

Louis Dreyfus (France)

Federal Commerce & Navigation Co. (Canada)

Great Lakes Trans Caribbean Line (Germany)

Odd Godager & Co. (Norway)

Manchester Lines (United Kingdom)

Mitsui-OSK Line (Japan)

Orient Mid-East Lines (Greece)

Scindia Line (India)

States Marine Lines (U.S.A.)

Alfred C. Toepfer (Germany)

Volkswagen Line (Germany)

Zim Israel Navigation Co. (Israel)

FLAGS YOU WILL SEE

Belgium | Brazil | Canada | France | Italy

Germany | Greece | India | Japan | Sweden

Liberia | Norway | United Kingdom | U.S.A. | Netherlands

WHEN THE WIND BLOWS

Small Craft Warning

Gale Warning

Whole Gale Warning

WHAT THE WHISTLES MEAN

1 Blast
I am directing my course to Starboard (right)

2 Blasts
I am directing my course to Port (left)

Danger Signal
Several short and rapid blasts, not less than five

Ship's Salute
3 Long, 2 Short
Underway in Fog
3 Short

Anchored in Fog
1 Short, 2 Long, 1 Short
Leaving a Dock
1 Long Blast

NATIONAL OCEAN SERVICE
Office of Charting and Geodetic Services

The Office of Charting and Geodetic Services (C&GS) is one of the four principal line offices of the National Ocean Service (NOS). The NOS, in turn, is one of the five major line components of the National Oceanic and Atmospheric Administration (NOAA). Staffed by scientists and engineers, C&GS has developed significant capabilities and contributed many scientific advances over the years in the fields of geodesy, astronomy, hydrography, nautical and aeronautical cartography, photogrammetry, marine engineering, and data management.

thereby placing additional duties and responsibilities on the organization. Although the first geodetic surveys were not begun until 1816, considerable field work had taken place. By 1836 field work had doubled and the name of the organization changed to the U.S. Coast Survey. In 1871, a geodetic connection between the Atlantic and Pacific coasts was officially authorized by Congress and the name changed in 1878 to the U.S. Coast and Geodetic Survey. In 1926, Congress directed the agency to produce aeronautical charts to meet the growing requirements of the new air age. Geodetic measurements provide the baseline from which all aeronautical and nautical charts,

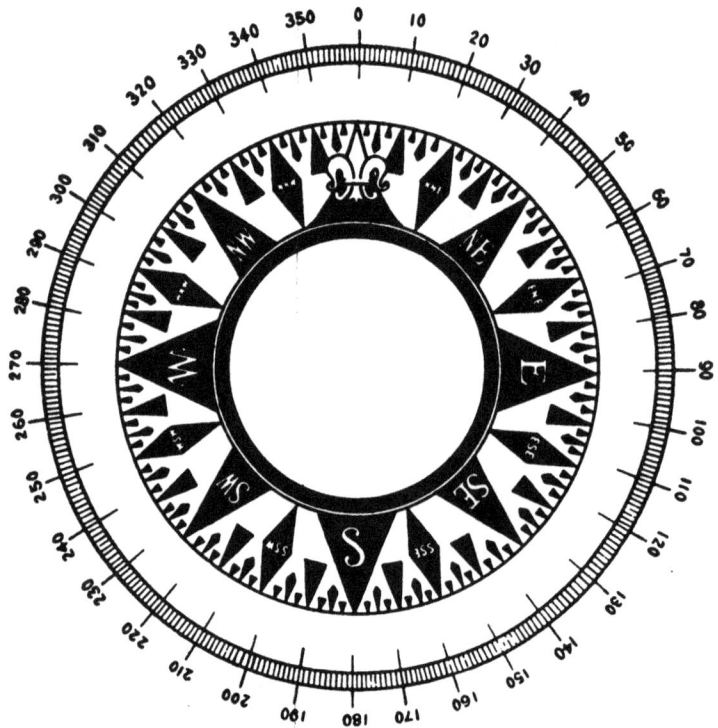

The C&GS product line includes nautical, aeronautical, coastal mapping, and geodetic products and technical services to support safe and efficient air and marine transportation, offshore operations and to meet national positioning and elevation control requirements for cartographic applications, engineering projects, land-use planning, and space and defense systems. Making such important contributions to both the governmental and private sectors of the economy, C&GS touches the lives directly and indirectly of nearly all Americans.

Nation's First Science Agency

C&GS is the oldest scientific organization in the Federal Government, dating from 1807 when President Jefferson recommended to Congress the establishment of a national "survey of the coast." In the ensuing years Congress passed additional legislation to meet scientific and engineering needs of a growing national population and economy

coastal, and bathymetric maps are referenced. Hydrographic survey depth measurements and the interpretation of aerial photogrammetric surveys must be based on the national geodetic networks. In this way, all C&GS programs are dependent on one another. The name of the agency was changed to the National Ocean Survey when NOAA was formed in 1970, broadening the nautical charting mission to include charts of the Great Lakes, previously administered by the U.S. Lake Survey. In December of 1982 the Office of Charting and Geodetic Services within the new National Ocean Service was created to better focus on charting and geodetic services.

SURVEYS – MAPS – CHARTS

Maps and charts are compiled and updated using aerial photographs and field surveys as a basis. Charts are a smaller scale portrayal of field survey sheets and reflect selected portions of surveys. Critical and extreme features are shown, but for clairity purposes all data obtained on the survey cannot be shown on the charts or maps.

Planetable and, in later years, photogrammetric surveys of the coastal area, and hydrographic surveys of the adjacent waters have been in progress by the Bureau for the production and maintenanace of nautical charts since 1835. Consequently, over 23,000 individual surveys are on file in the Bureau Archives and copies are available to the public and to other agencies as needed. These represent a unique and comprehensive record of our coastline and the adjacent waters, showing conditions existing at a particular date over more than a century, and providing a quite detailed record of the changes that have occurred from both natural and man-made causes. These records are used extensively by the public and other agencies of the government for research, engineering, and development purposes. They are often referred to in property disputes where shoreline, that is, the mean high-water or mean low-water line, represents a boundary, and certified copies are frequently presented as evidence in the courts. Topographic and hydrographic surveys are made and recorded separately. For studies of water depths, hydrographic surveys should be requested; each hydrographic survey is identified by a number with the prefix "H". For studies of the shoreline and adjacent land areas, topographic surveys should be requested; such surveys are identified by a number with the prefix "T". Letter size indexes are available for both hydrographic and topographic surveys along the coast, and will be furnished on request. Because of the need for resurveys for chart maintenance, most places along the coast are covered by two or more surveys. Only selected portions of hydrographic surveys are used in the compilation of nautical charts.

The area covered by any individual hydrographic or topographic survey is indicated approximately on the index. The area of coverage varies depending upon chart needs at the time of surveys.

Topographic surveys vary not only in coverage but in content. Many show only the shoreline and planimetric features immediately adjacent thereto. Others are complete planimetric maps covering from the shoreline inland for as much as five or more miles of up to the seven and one-half minute quadrangle limit. The indexes show the type of information as well as the coverage.

From 1835 to 1927 practically all of the topographic surveys were made by planetable and the original planetable sheets are filed in the Archives. Photographic copies, film positives or bromides, are furnished of these. Since 1927, aerial photographs and photogrammetric methods have been utilized increasingly to provide the required topographic information along the coast and most of the

---

Distinctive Vinyl Boat Names

FREE BROCHURE
We'll work with you to develop the right graphics for your boat's name. Custom Designs, Standard Typestyles, Graphic Images hand cut from the best adhesive vinyls. Easy Application. 20 colors. Free Brochure.

Write or Phone
(313) 855-3525

BOAT GRAPHICS INC.
Suite 314, Dept. PG, 19777 W. 12 Mile, Southfield, MI 48076

topographic surveys in recent years are recorded in the form of manuscript maps compiled from aerial photographs and around survey data. Photographic copies of these are furnished as ozalid prints. The survey indexes show whether a topographic survey was made by planetable or by photogrammetric methods.

Scales of the original topographic and inshore hydrographic surveys are nearly always at 1:10,000 or 1:20,000. A limited number in harbor areas are at 1:5,000. Offshore hydrographic surveys are on smaller scales.

Scale Equivalents

Scale ratio	Feet to one inch	Inches to 1 statute mile
1:5,000	416.67	12.67

NAUTICAL CHARTS show the nature and shape of the coast, depths of water, general configuration and character of the bottom, prominent landmarks, port facilities, cultural details, aids to navigation, marine hazards, and other pertinent information. Changes brought about by people and nature require that nautical charts be constantly maintained and updated to aid safe navigation. Conventional and small-craft nautical charts vary in scale and format. For coastal navigation, boaters should use the largest scale chart available.

Related Publications

Nautical charts are the critical element to safely navigate the coast. There are, however, additional chart related publications produced by NOS to assist the mariner:

Small-Scale Charts available through the Canadian Hydrographic Service, Department of the Environment, Ottawa, Ontario K1G 3H6
Lake Michigan U.S. Chart from U.S. Lake Survey chart catalogue.

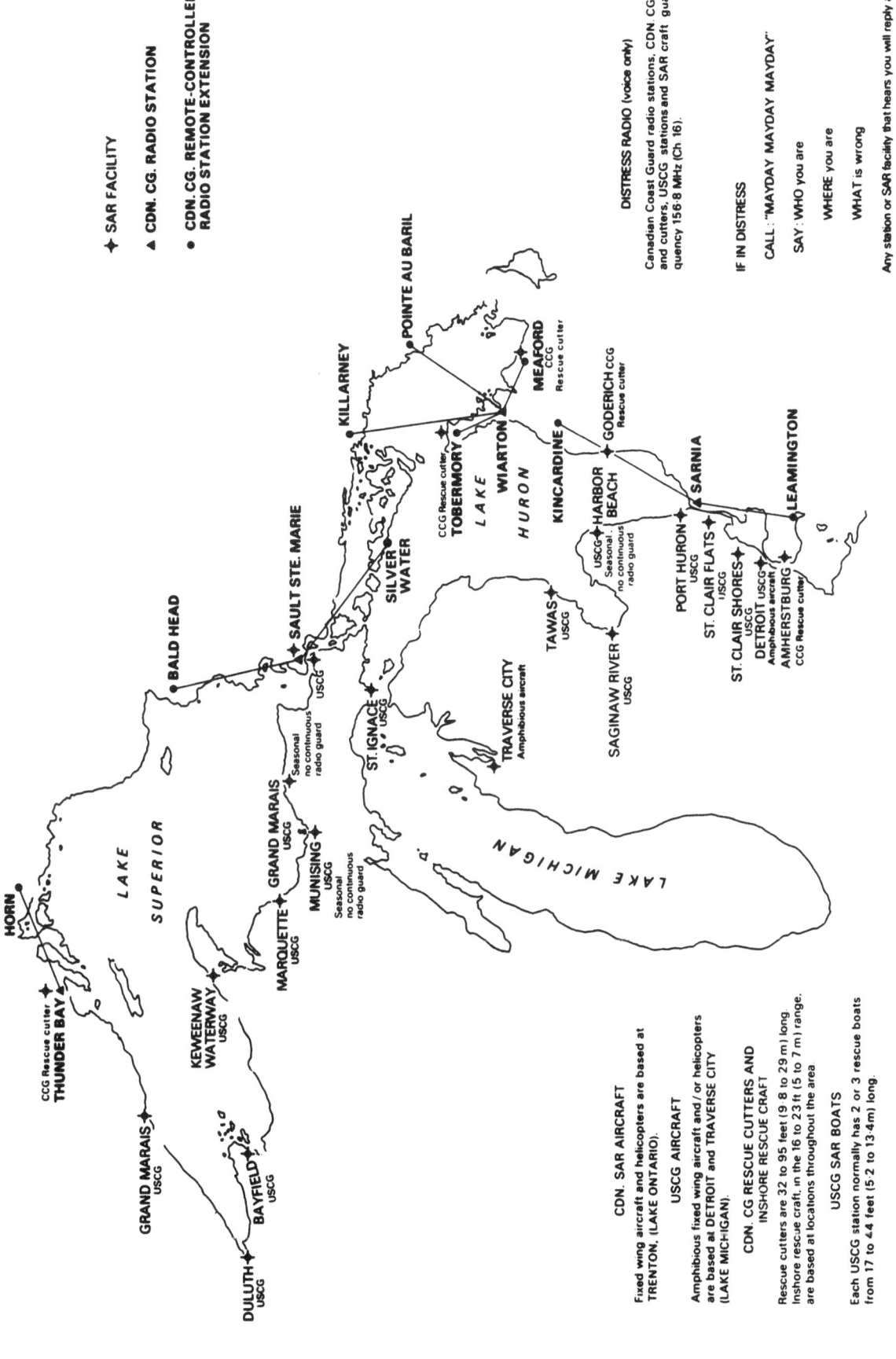

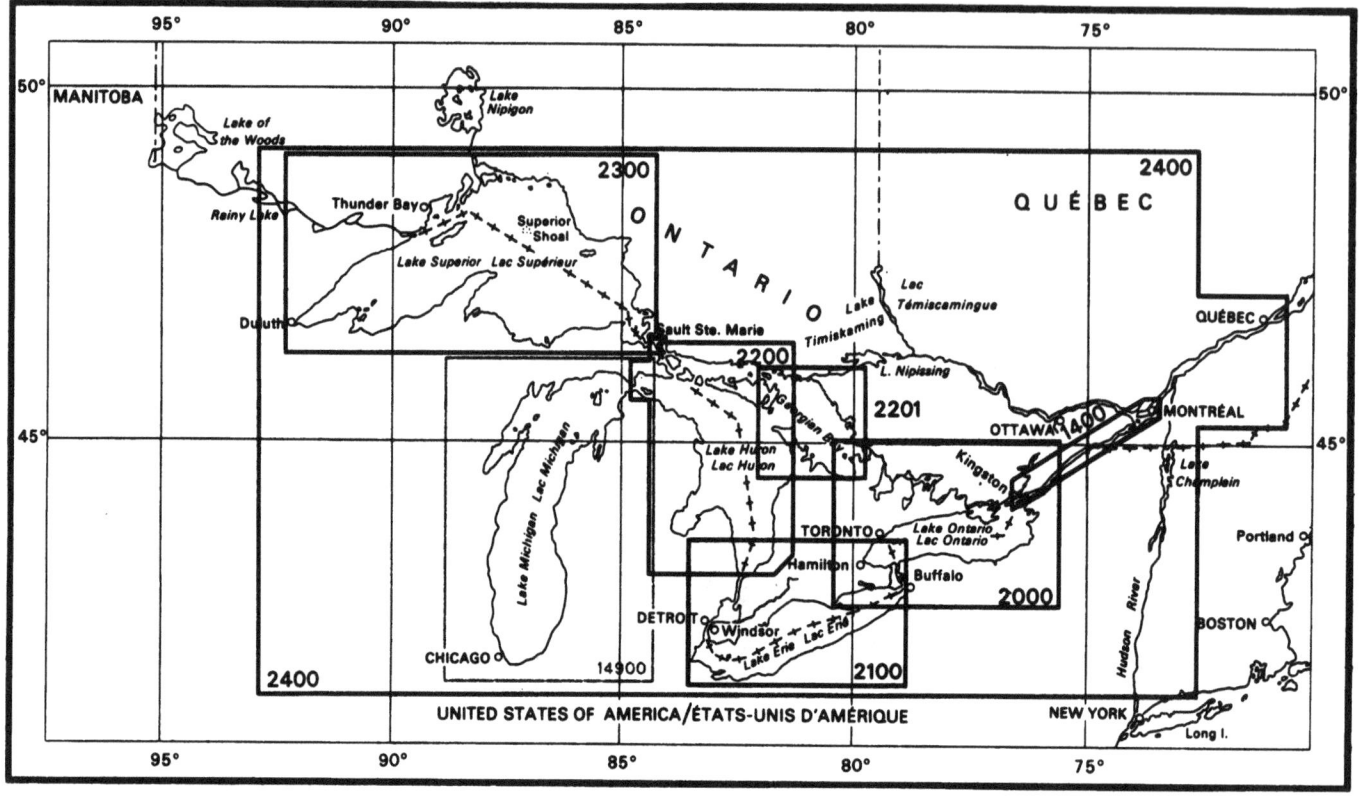

* COAST PILOTS
* TIDE TABLES
* TIDAL CURRENT TABLES
* TIDAL CURRENT CHARTS

The date of a nautical chart is critical to the boater. Only up-to-date charts should be used for navigation. Current chart editions are listed in the free quarterly NOS pamphlet "Dates of Latest Editions – Nautical Charts."

NOS also produces NAUTICAL TRAINING CHARTS for various coastal areas. These charts are particularly useful as educational aids for people enrolled in boating safety courses sponsored by the U.S. Power Squadron and the Coast Guard Auxiliary. A sample of nautical symbols and abbreviations are shown on the reverse of these training charts. For a complete compilation of these symbols, boaters should refer to CHART #1 – NAUTICAL CHART SYMBOLS AND ABBREVIATIONS.

National Ocean Service nautical charts may be purchased either directly by mail from the NOS Distribution Branch or through an authorized agent. There are more than 1,700 nautical chart agents that sell NOS charts. To obtain a list of the agents near you, request a free catalog.

U.S. and Canadian charts are available from the following places:

U.S. Charts
Distribution Division (OA/C44)
National Ocean Survey
Riverdale, MD 20840
Telephone: 301-436-6990

NATIONAL OCEAN SERVICE
Distribution Branch, N/CG33
Riverdale, Maryland 20737

#1 Atlantic and Gulf Coasts, including Puerto Rico and the Virgin Islands
#2 Pacific Coast including Hawaii, Guam, and Samoan Islands
#3 Alaska
#4 Great Lakes and adjacent Waterways
Dates of Latest Editions, Nautical Charts

These catalogs depict each nautical chart by area and provide complete price and order information for purchasing charts directly from NOS. Members of the U.S. Power Squadron and Coast Guard Auxiliary may receive a 10% discount for NOS products if accompanied by a request on letterhead stationary. No discount is available for Training Charts.

Canadian Nautical Charts and Publications
Hydro-Graphic Chart Distribution Office
Department of Fisheries and the Environment
1675 Russell Road
P.O. Box 8080
Ottawa, Ontario K1G 3H6
Telephone: 613-998-4931

SAILING PLAN

Canadian Coast Guard

VESSEL NAME AND NUMBER	☐ SAIL	☐ POWER

NAME AND ADDRESS	TELEPHONE

VESSEL SIZE AND TYPE		

COLOUR ▶ HULL	DECK	CABIN

TYPE OF ENGINE(S)	OTHER DISTINGUISHING FEATURES

RADIOS AND CHANNELS MONITORED ▶ HF CHANNEL	VHF CHANNEL	CB CHANNEL

LIFE RAFTS	SKIFF DORY OR SMALL BOAT (COLOUR)

OTHER SAFETY EQUIPMENT		

FLARES (NUMBER)	LIFEJACKETS (NUMBER)	OTHER

WHERE TO CALL FOR SEARCH AND RESCUE
CALL COLLECT BY DIALING "0" + THE AREA CODE + THE NUMBER

EAST
R.C.C. HALIFAX TELEPHONE NO.
902-426-4730
902-426-2412

M.R.S.C. ST. JOHN'S TELEPHONE NO.
709-772-5151
ZENITH 07021

CENTRAL
R.C.C. TRENTON TELEPHONE NO.
613-392-2811
LOCAL 3870 or 3875
or 1-800-267-7270

M.R.S.C. QUEBEC CITY TELEPHONE NO.
418-694-3599
1-800-463-4393
(FOR 1-800 PLEASE DIAL DIRECTLY)

WEST
VANCOUVER TELEPHONE NO.
604-732-4141

R.C.C. VICTORIA TELEPHONE NO.
604-388-1543

R.C.C. EDMONTON TELEPHONE NO
403-973-8402

POLICE	
OTHER	

Canada

TRIP NO. 1
DATE	TIME		NO ON BOARD
LEAVING FROM		GOING TO	
PROPOSED ROUTE AND TIME OF ARRIVAL			
RETURNING ON-DATE		ROUTE AND TIME OF ARRIVAL	
CALL SEARCH AND RESCUE AT ▶	TIME		DATE

TRIP NO. 2
DATE	TIME		NO ON BOARD
LEAVING FROM		GOING TO	
PROPOSED ROUTE AND TIME OF ARRIVAL			
RETURNING ON-DATE		ROUTE AND TIME OF ARRIVAL	
CALL SEARCH AND RESCUE AT ▶	TIME		DATE

TRIP NO. 3
DATE	TIME		NO ON BOARD
LEAVING FROM		GOING TO	
PROPOSED ROUTE AND TIME OF ARRIVAL			
RETURNING ON-DATE		ROUTE AND TIME OF ARRIVAL	
CALL SEARCH AND RESCUE AT ▶	TIME		DATE

TRIP NO. 4
DATE	TIME		NO ON BOARD
LEAVING FROM		GOING TO	
PROPOSED ROUTE AND TIME OF ARRIVAL			
RETURNING ON-DATE		ROUTE AND TIME OF ARRIVAL	
CALL SEARCH AND RESCUE AT ▶	TIME		DATE

TRIP NO. 5
DATE	TIME		NO ON BOARD
LEAVING FROM		GOING TO	
PROPOSED ROUTE AND TIME OF ARRIVAL			
RETURNING ON-DATE		ROUTE AND TIME OF ARRIVAL	
CALL SEARCH AND RESCUE AT ▶	TIME		DATE

NOTIFY THE PERSON HOLDING THIS SAILING PLAN OF ANY CHANGES ESPECIALLY LATE ARRIVAL PLANS

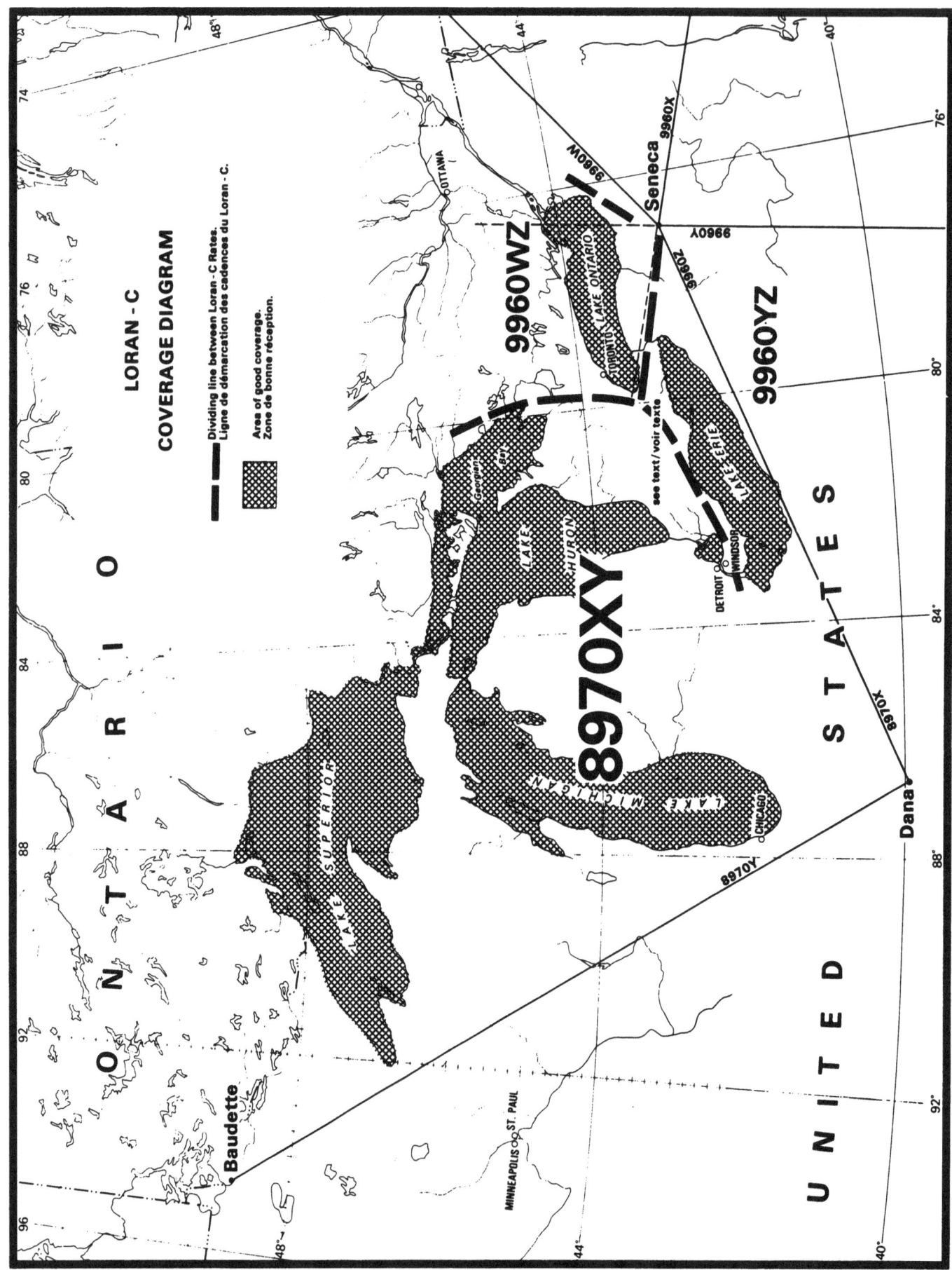

GREAT LAKES WATER LEVELS

ANNUAL MEANS

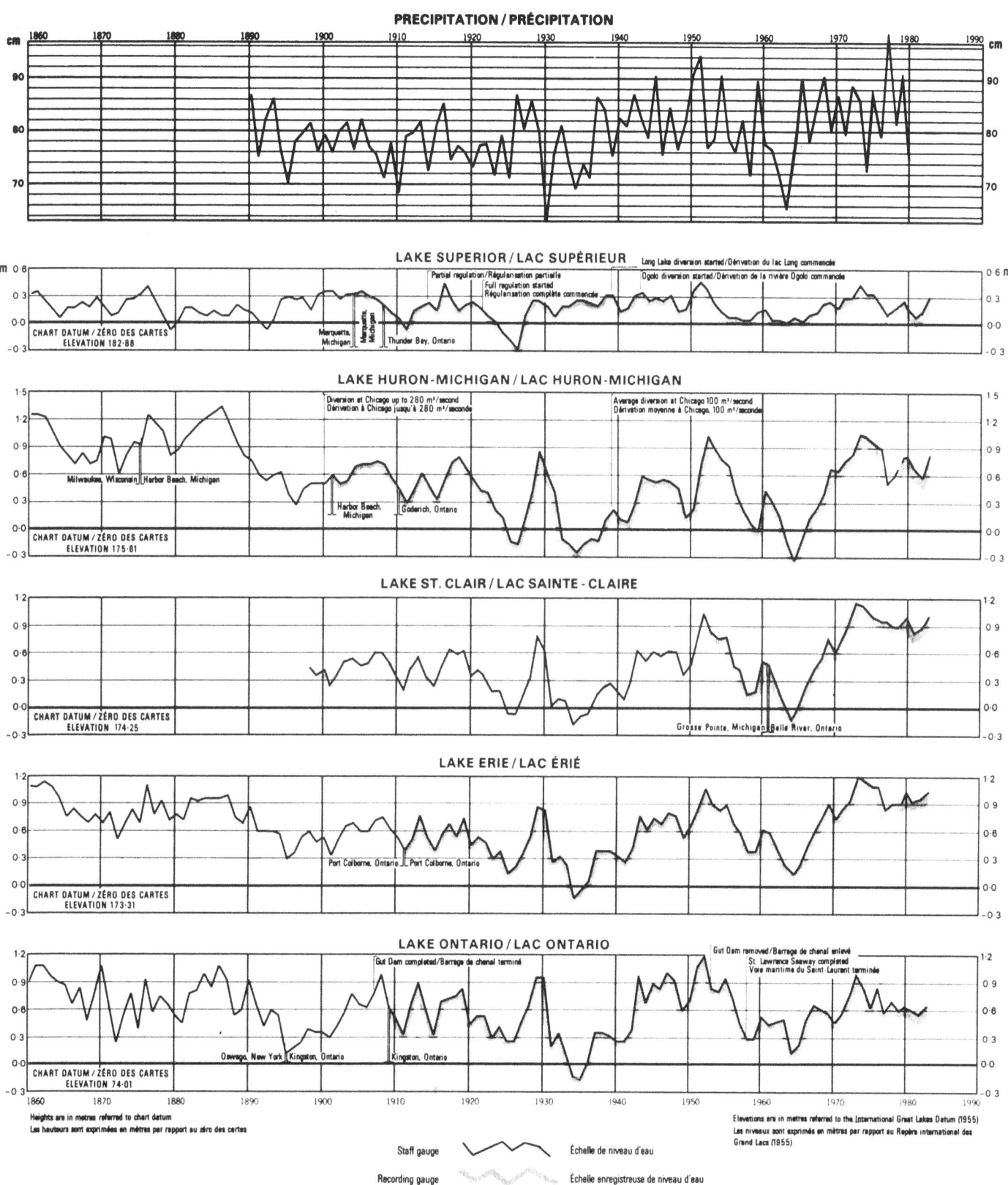

Table II — DISTANCES BETWEEN POINTS ON LAKE HURON AND ST. MARYS RIVER

		2	3	4	5	6	7	8	9	10	11	12	13	14	15	16	17	18	19	20	21	22	23	24	25	26	27	28	29	30	31	32	33	34	35	36	37	38
		Old Mackinac Point	Sault Ste. Marie	De Tour	Port Dolomite	St. Ignace	Mackinac Island	Cheboygan	Rogers City	Stoneport	Rockport	Alpena	Au Sable	East Tawas	Bay City	Saginaw	Harbor Beach	Port Sanilac	Goderich	Kincardine	Southampton	Wiarton	Owen Sound	Meaford	Collingwood	Penetanguishene	Midland	Victoria Harbour	Depot Harbour	Parry Sound	Byng Inlet	Key Harbour	French River	Killarney	Little Current	Gore Bay	Algoma Mills	Thessalon
1	Port Huron[a]	215	234	195	208	215	211	202	169	158	144	136	102	103	141	152	55	29	56	82	105	198	207	209	224	230	231	232	211	215	199	202	195	185	196	217	207	207
2	Old Mackinac Point[b]		78	39	59	5	6	16	47	68	72	100	142	142	167	194	162	187	183	194	180	197	215	210	215	221	215	232	201	204	178	178	170	145	117	101	88	60
3	Sault Ste. Marie[c]			39	59	78	73	73	73	83	93	119	143	161	202	214	181	207	203	185	180	199	208	210	225	231	231	233	207	210	175	168	160	135	114	92	76	42
4	De Tour				20	38	34	34	35	44	53	80	104	122	162	175	143	168	164	146	141	161	169	171	186	192	193	195	172	175	149	142	134	109	88	66	50	21
5	Port Dolomite					24	23	27	41	61	66	98	124	142	179	190	165	189	176	159	153	189	190	191	202	207	201	211	187	189	172	173	171	164	117	94	78	50
6	St. Ignace						5	17	48	57	60	72	124	124	180	195	188	207	188	155	180	197	208	210	215	219	214	233	201	213	182	177	169	144	123	100	87	59
7	Mackinac Island							15	43	67	69	96	122	138	191	182	160	184	182	164	162	184	192	195	209	216	216	218	196	199	177	173	165	140	119	96	83	55
8	Cheboygan								35	57	60	88	112	129	180	149	150	176	172	155	153	177	185	188	202	209	209	210	189	192	171	169	162	136	116	92	80	55
9	Rogers City									23	27	53	78	96	136	116	116	142	140	123	121	147	154	158	173	179	179	181	159	162	143	142	136	120	99	76	64	55
10	Stoneport										8	42	66	84	123	134	113	137	127	104	100	131	142	143	157	162	164	165	156	144	144	142	139	127	137	129	117	93
11	Rockport											27	54	71	123	123	92	115	108	93	96	143	129	143	155	161	164	165	170	159	158	156	153	142	152	146	135	69
12	Alpena												43	60	101	112	89	109	108	93	85	157	114	146	161	167	168	169	149	151	132	131	126	114	124	137	118	93
13	Au Sable													18	60	11	50	75	81	74	85	96	165	154	164	175	176	177	156	159	144	142	139	127	137	129	117	93
14	East Tawas														47	59	52	76	83	82	133	152	133	169	182	189	189	191	170	173	158	156	153	142	152	146	135	129
15	Bay City																89	125	131	118	145	209	206	221	235	242	242	243	222	224	210	210	206	194	204	198	188	174
16	Saginaw																100	28	41	49	69	152	198	163	178	184	185	186	165	169	153	153	149	138	149	166	155	155
17	Harbor Beach																		41	61	84	174	133	185	200	206	207	208	187	190	175	175	170	161	171	190	180	180
18	Port Sanilac																			31	95	109	136	146	161	167	168	169	147	162	163	163	161	150	147	143	144	144
19	Goderich																				25																	
20	Kincardine																											62										
21	Southampton																						25															
22	Wiarton[d]																							31	46	63	64	66	62	64	70	69	76	82	96	123	137	163
23	Owen Sound[d]																								25	60	61	62	65	69	77	84	84	90	103	132	145	171
24	Meaford[d]																								21	45	46	48	59	62	75	83	83	91	105	133	147	174
25	Collingwood[d]																									47	48	50	66	70	84	93	94	104	120	149	162	189
26	Penetanguishene[d]																										9	6	60	63	83	91	92	104	117	149	162	195
27	Midland[d]																												61	63	75	83	93	105	122	150	163	196
28	Port McNicoll[d]																												62	65	84	92	94	106	123	151	165	197
29	Depot Harbour[d]																													5	54	62	63	76	93	122	135	168
30	Parry Sound[d]																														56	65	67	79	96	124	137	171
31	Byng Inlet[d]																															23	27	43	61	89	103	135
32	Key Harbour[d]																																19	36	54	82	96	129
33	French River[d]																																	29	46	75	88	121
34	Killarney[d]																																		21	49	63	96
35	Little Current																																			29	42	75
36	Gore Bay																																				23	53
37	Algoma Mills																																					37
38	Thessalon																																					0

EXPLANATION

Explanation generally applicable to all tables is published in table I.

Points in this table are arranged in geographical sequence proceeding from St. Marys River southward along the west shore, and returning northward up the east shore, around Georgian Bay, and westward through North Channel.

[a] From foot of Grand River Ave.
[b] From sailing course point north of Old Mackinac Point.
[c] From abreast east end of U.S. centre pier, and (except those marked e) via Middle Neebish and Detour; distances downbound through West Neebish are 1 mile less.
[d] Distances to Georgian Bay ports (except those marked e, f, g, h) are via the bay entrance from Lake Huron and St. Marys River points and via Little Current from North Channel points.
[e] Via False Detour and North Channel.
[f] Via Mississagi Strait and North Channel.
[g] Via Lake Nicolet, St. Joseph, and North Channel.
[h] Via Potagannissing Bay and North Channel.

Table I — DISTANCES BETWEEN POINTS ON GREAT LAKES

	2	3	4	5	6	7	8	9	10	11	12	13	14	15	16	17	18	19	20	21	22	23	24	25	26	27	28	29	30	31	32	33	34	35	36	
	Two Harbors	Duluth	Ashland	Houghton	Marquette	Sault Ste. Marie	Escanaba	Green Bay	Milwaukee	Chicago	Gary	Muskegon	Ludington	Alpena	Bay City	Goderich	Collingwood	Midland	Port Huron	Detroit (Woodward Ave.)	Toledo	Lorain	Cleveland	Fairport	Ashtabula	Conneaut	Erie	Buffalo	Port Colborne	Rochester	Oswego	Toronto	Kingston	Ogdensburg	Montreal	
1 Thunder Bay	149	169	143	101	149	237	428	487	540	596	607	510	466	356	439	440	461	468	471	525	572	603	618	633	655	667	691	751	737	839	883	785	899	952	1062	
2 Two Harbors		23	62	136	208	322	513	573	626	682	693	595	551	441	524	525	547	554	556	610	657	688	703	720	740	753	776	837	822	924	968	870	984	1038	1147	
3 Duluth			81	156	227	342	534	593	646	702	713	616	571	462	545	546	568	574	577	631	679	709	724	739	761	773	797	857	843	945	989	891	1005	1058	1168	
4 Ashland				114	185	303	494	554	607	663	673	576	532	422	505	507	528	535	537	591	638	670	685	700	721	733	757	818	803	905	949	851	965	1018	1128	
5 Houghton					73	192	382	442	495	552	562	465	421	311	394	395	417	424	426	480	527	559	573	589	610	622	646	706	692	793	838	739	853	907	1017	
6 Marquette						138	328	388	441	498	508	412	367	258	340	342	363	370	373	427	474	505	520	535	557	569	593	653	639	740	785	686	800	854	964	
7 Sault Ste. Marie							190	250	303	360	370	273	229	119	202	203	226	232	234	288	335	367	381	397	418	430	454	514	500	601	646	547	661	715	825	
8 Escanaba								88	175	212	295	157	113	250	327	295	327	334	335	381	428	459	474	490	511	523	547	607	593	693	739	640	754	808	918	
9 Green Bay									156	222	236	149	107	272	354	355	386	393	387	441	487	519	534	549	571	583	607	667	653	754	799	700	814	868	978	
10 Milwaukee										74	90	70	84	325	407	408	439	446	440	494	541	572	587	602	624	636	660	720	706	807	852	753	867	921	1031	
11 Chicago											22	99	136	381	464	465	495	502	496	550	598	628	643	659	680	693	716	776	762	864	908	810	924	978	1087	
12 Gary												105	145	392	474	475	506	513	507	560	607	639	653	669	691	703	726	786	773	874	919	820	934	988	1098	
13 Muskegon													49	295	377	378	409	416	409	463	510	541	556	573	594	606	629	690	675	777	821	723	837	891	1000	
14 Ludington														250	333	334	364	371	365	419	466	497	512	527	549	561	585	645	631	733	777	679	793	846	956	
15 Alpena															101	108	161	168	136	190	237	269	283	299	321	333	356	416	402	504	548	450	564	618	727	
16 Bay City																119	223	230	141	195	242	273	288	303	325	337	379	421	407	508	553	454	568	622	732	
17 Goderich																	180	183	56	110	157	189	203	219	241	253	276	336	322	424	468	370	484	538	647	
18 Collingwood																		48	224	278	325	356	371	388	408	421	444	504	490	592	636	538	652	706	815	
19 Midland																			231	285	332	363	378	394	415	428	451	511	497	599	643	545	659	713	822	
20 Port Huron																				54	101	132	148	163	185	196	220	280	266	368	412	314	428	481	591	
21 Detroit (Woodward Ave.)																					47	79	94	109	130	143	166	227	212	314	358	260	374	428	537	
22 Toledo (river mouth)																						63	83	103	125	136	161	221	206	308	352	254	368	421	531	
23 Lorain																							24	46	70	83	108	171	156	258	302	204	318	372	481	
24 Cleveland (main entrance)																								29	51	63	89	153	139	241	285	187	301	355	464	
25 Fairport																									26	38	63	127	113	215	259	161	275	328	438	
26 Ashtabula																										13	39	103	90	192	236	138	252	306	415	
27 Conneaut																											29	93	80	182	226	128	242	295	405	
28 Erie																												68	56	158	202	104	218	272	381	
29 Buffalo																													19	121	165	67	181	235	344	
30 Port Colborne																														102	146	48	162	216	325	
31 Rochester																															51	83	77	129	239	
32 Oswego																																126	48	94	203	
33 Toronto																																	140	194	303	
34 Kingston																																		55	164	
35 Ogdensburg																																			109	
36 Montreal																																			0	

[a] From abreast east end of U.S. centre pier.
[b] From foot of Grand River Ave.
[c] From intersection Seaway-Ship Channel. Montreal Harbour.

EXPLANATION

Distances are expressed in nautical miles and have been converted from the statute mile values given in U.S. Government publications. Because of the round-off error in the statute mile tables of up to 0.5 statute mile and of the round-off error after the conversion to nautical miles, distances can be as much as a full nautical mile in error.

Measurements are by the shortest marked or safe direct courses, starting (unless otherwise noted) from the main entrances between pierheads of breakwaters or piers, or from the principal landings of open roadsteads. Where landings are appreciably remote from protected entrances, the appropriate further distances, if desired, may be ascertained from the harbour descriptions or from charts.

Points in this table are arranged in the order of their location on the several lakes in the following sequence: Lake Ontario, Lake Erie, Lake Huron, Lake Michigan, and Lake Superior.

The distance between any two points appears in the line extending horizontally from the point first in order in the list and in the column headed by the other point.

The Future of Charting and Geodetic Services

During the past few years, major emphasis has been placed on the conversion of aeronautical and nautical operations from manual to computer-assisted automated systems. Hydrographic data acquisition and processing have also been made more productive by the use of improved echo sounding equipment and the automated logging and plotting of survey data. The introduction of Bathymetric Swath Survey systems and the use of side scan sonar has given C&GS the capability of performing more complete hydrographic survey coverage in more areas. The C&GS now employs an automated analytical plotter which greatly facilitates photogrammetric analysis of aerial photographs. A computer-assisted automated distribution system for aeronautical and nautical

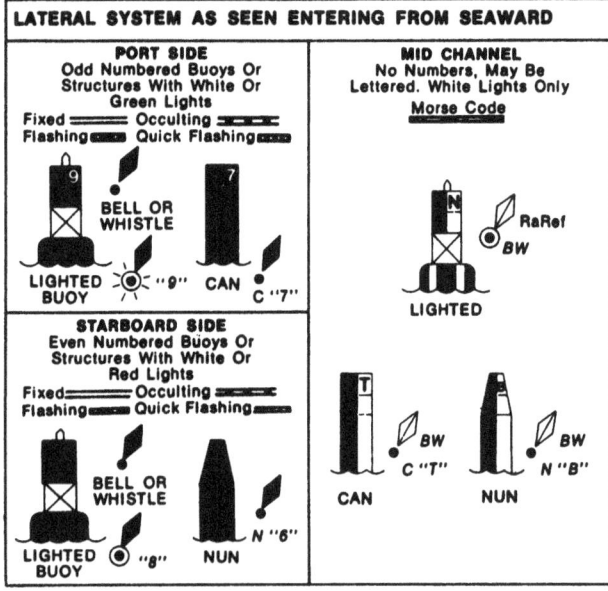

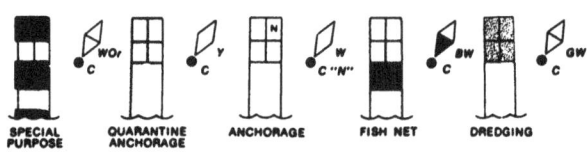

charts have been installed.

Over the past few years, a major effort has been devoted to the adjustment of the National Networks of the Geodetic Control. The network adjustments will result in new datums — the North American Datum of 1983, and the North American Vertical Datum of 1988 — which will improve the accuracy of the entire horizontal and vertical networks.

Conventional geodetic surveying techniques are being replaced by new systems which have been adapted from satellite and space technologies such as the Global Positioning System (GPS) and Very Long Baseline Interferometric (VLBI) survey technique. In the future, this office will convert its field operations to these new systems. Polar motion measurements have undergone a complete technological change with the recent installation of a three-station VLBI receiving array of radio telescopes in the United States. Radio signals received from extragalactic sources (quasars) are observed to monitor Earth rotation and polar motion. These observations provide a primary frame of reference from which all geodetic measurements and positions are compared and also information which is essential in crustal motion monitoring and analyses. Crustal motion data are required for the siting of nuclear power plants, for determining areas of submergence or earthquake hazards, and for other sensitive situations. GPS is a satellite system which will allow C&GS to achieve 2- to 3- centimeter accuracy for determining the coordinates of any point on the Earth.

The C&GS stands on the threshold of a new era in user products providing greater accuracy and improved delivery systems in supporting the nation's economic growth.

Our tall ships are standing tall.

There's nothing in the world like Mystic Seaport. It's America's largest maritime museum, with magnificently restored sailing ships, small craft, indoor and outdoor exhibits and lively demonstrations.

Come early, there's a lot to see and do.

Mystic Seaport

Relive America's Great Seafaring Past

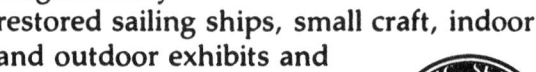

Exit 90, I-95 Mystic, CT (203) 572-0711
OPEN YEAR-ROUND, FREE PARKING

"Sailing across the Atlantic we observed oil pollution on 43 out of 57 days"

Thor Heyerdahl, Ra Voyage

"When I was sailing across the Atlantic on a reed boat I had my nose literally in the water. I saw things no one can see who travels by fast boat.

"Fifty miles off the bulge of Africa we found we could not brush our teeth in the seawater — it was covered with oil. We sailed through this mess for two days, and a week later ran into more.

Oil pollutes the fish we eat

'On a second raft trip we sailed through water filled with lumps of oil *for 43 out of 57 days*.

Great whales and many fish which swim with their mouths open, filtering their food, are swallowing this pollution. Some of those fish we shall eat.

The seas will suffocate

"There are people who tell you that oil does not matter, that the sea can absorb and recycle all this pollution. I call them the Sandmen—they want to put you to sleep with calming words. *Don't listen!*

"Unless you and I—all of us—act now to stop the seas being overloaded with poisonous refuse, they will suffocate and die."

That was 1970, but it goes on today — Nantucket, Cape Cod and Delaware Bay — and you don't see it, except in the press.

That is why World Wildlife Fund is campaigning to save the life and resources of the seas — for our own sakes and those of our children.

You can help

Send for our free information kit or send your tax-deductible contribution to: World Wildlife Fund, Department PH, 1319 18th Street, Northwest, Washington, D.C. 20036.

World Wildlife Fund

Chapter 3

FISHING

"He's a big, smart fish, he's gone under the boat."
— Quint, from the movie *JAWS*

GREAT LAKES FISHING
by David Wallace Johnson (Fishing Guide)

Michigan Department of Natural Resources
Fishery Department © (Fish Line Drawings)
by Ned Fogle.

The following is a thumbnail sketch of just a few of my favorite people, places and fish of this water wonderland.

Top dog in the wet and wonderful world of the Great Lakes is the import from east and west, the Salmon. One species has singlehandedly turned the tourism industry around in our state and two Canadian provinces. The Coho (or silver), the King (or Chinook), the Pink (or humpback), the Steelhead (or lake run rainbow), and the recent addition from the east, the Atlantic Salmon, make it possible for people to pass up the farm pond bullgill and stack stock a really big fish.

Two years ago at one of my favorite fall fishing haunts, Elk River, I ran across a fellow from an Iowa farm. The farmer, had been coming here for the past two years. He didn't fly to the Kenai peninsula, to Norway, Scotland, but to Michigan for the King Salmon. He came for the big fish, and managed to take some home. During his visit the local motel, tackle shop, gas station, supermarket, three restaurants, and at least four saloons, were pleased he didn't go to Kenai, and so was he.

Originally the Salmon were placed in the Great Lakes to stem the "Red Tide". Each year alewives, small baitfish about two to four inches long, washed up on the beaches of the coast lines, by the millions.

The idea was born. Salmon would feed on them. Feasibility studies were done, followed by research in a controlled environment, finally we

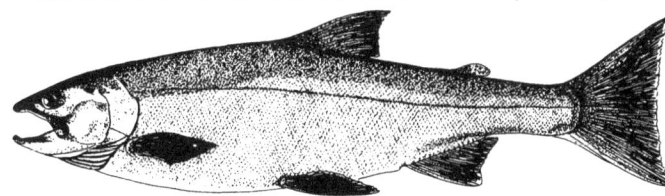
Coho Salmon

had salmon. The first plants were the Coho, or Silver Salmon, and they loved their new home. In their natural environment of Washington and Oregon these small cousins of the Chinook would average eight to ten pounds. After just a few years in their new home, it is not uncommon to see Coho of fifteen to twenty pounds. Great Lakes Coho fever was born.

And fever it was. Fishermen who never had a two pound smallmouth on the line were now able to tangle with the silver fury called "Coho". I still recall the two weeks spent in the Upper Peninsula of Michigan, and the journey over to Thompson with my mother. It was fall, and both of us wanted to see this fish called salmon. We were greeted by trucks, busses, and campers, stacked up and down the highway waiting to launch everything from prams to small cruisers. The harbor was filled with wall to wall boats and shoulder to shoulder wader clad salmon seekers.

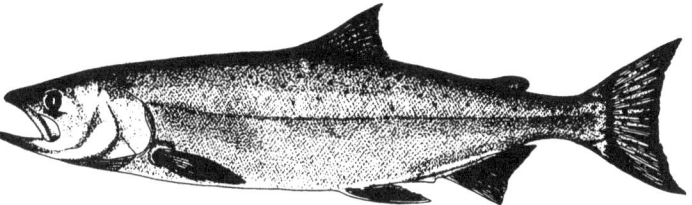
Chinook Salmon

Coho only took a back seat, when the Kings arrived. Kings are the giants of the salmonids. In Alaska the hook and line record is over ninety pounds. Commercial fishermen have unofficially taken specimens to one hundred and twenty three pounds. When the Kings were first stocked in the Great Lakes the DNR hoped to commonly see samples to sixty pounds. Lake Ontario is currently yielding the largest salmon. The real "brutes" will surpass forty pounds. From Michigan, Huron, Superior, and (in the spring) St. Clair, a big salmon will tip the scales between twenty five and thirty pounds. This doesn't mean that larger specimens aren't caught. What it does mean is that these are the averages. There is hope today that we will have salmon in the sixty pound plus catergory. The University of Michigan originally was the catalyst for stocking salmon in the Great Lakes and now working on a new strain. These salmon would spawn, but they would not die. Normally salmon spawn and then immediately die. This would mean that there would be a geometric increase in the life cycle. If salmon could life longer it would mean they would grow to much larger sizes. If you have ever tangled with a twenty-pound salmon, you can dream what it would be like to tangle with a sixty pound salmon.

The smallest of the salmonids is the Pink, or Humpback salmon. The average size of this prize is only around three pounds, but on ultra light tackle these smallest of the salmon can certainly uphold the family honor. They are the latest to be stocked in the Great Lakes. Many consider them to be the best table fare. They were considered to be the most fragile, and therefore were stocked with the greatest fear and trepidation. The fears were unfounded. It seems that in the many tributaries where the "humpies" have been stocked they are flourishing.

The "Atlantic" is another recent addition to the Great Lakes salmon smorgasbord. The Indians of the Pacific Northwest thought the salmon of the region were Gods. The Atlantic salmon is treated in a most civilized and godlike manner by sportsmen/women who seek him in the wild native streams of extreme eastern Canada and the

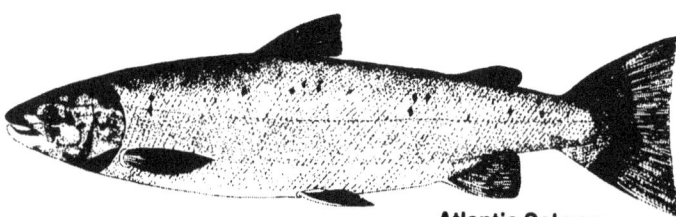
Atlantic Salmon

United States. The Atlantic does not grow to the extreme size of his western cousins. Once so plentiful in Europe that they were table fare for servants and workers at least once, and possibly three times a week. Those were the glory days of Atlantic salmon fishing when they swarmed up rivers in Canada, Europe, Scandinavia, and the United States. Their number along the Atlantic coast of North America have been depleted by heavy commercial and sport fishing pressure and pollution. Their introduction into the Great Lakes may have signaled their rise from the ashes. Unlike their western brethren the Atlantic has one major distinction. Atlantics do not spawn and then immediately die. Their outer appearance does darken as they make their way upstream to spawn, but many do make their way back out to the sea or the lake after they have spawned, to feed and spawn again.

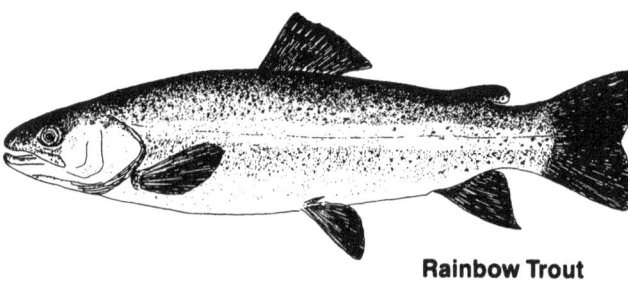
Rainbow Trout

The steelhead is a rainbow trout. Depending upon your predisposition to accept our Great Lakes variety as a true steelhead will determine if you will say that the Great Lakes are an acceptable substitute for the sea.

Note: This is a current controversy. If a salmon or trout normally must migrate to salt water and then back again to fresh water, then if these species migrate to a large body of fresh water (such as the Great Lakes) can they be true representations of their species? This question has been asked most often of the steelhead trout. Many west coast anglers believe that we do not possess a true "Steelhead" trout because we lack salt water. Those on the other side of the question happen to believe that the salinity of the body of water makes no difference. It only matters that the fish swims from a stream into a large body of water with a rich food supply that helps it to grow larger than its cousins which remain landlocked in a stream. The steelhead in the Great Lakes grow to the same proportions as the steelhead of the west coast that happen to migrate into the ocean.

In the Great Lakes they are sought with many techniques and methods borrowed from the west coast. Drift boats are most commonly used during the early spring. The double bowed vehicles are floated downstream and held in place with anchor or oars while a line with a deep driving plug is used to search out the holes around rocks, known haunts for the trout. Strikes are joltingly savage. Dick Swan is known as the father of "noodlerodding". He developed and perfected the midwestern technique of long rods and light lines. Rods range from ten to fifteen feet in length and are extremely supple. They are coupled with lines in the two to six pound class. This enables anglers to take advantage of the superior shock absorbing capability of supple rods with the invisibility of very light lines. Dick currently holds the world record for a variety of trout and salmon trophies.

In the fall you'll find many of the same conditions which I found during my first encounter with "Coho Fever". The Salmon are ascending the spawning streams. If you have never fished for Salmon, pick up a local newspaper, read some of the magazines listed at the end of this chapter, and find an area which interests you. I happen to be very lucky. My wife loves to fish. She is perhaps better at the game than I. (Psychologists tell me that women are always more patient than men.) I send her to do my scouting.. If you are seeking Salmon don't overlook fishing at night. Most fish are nocturnal. Many of the largest will be caught between dusk and dawn. Many fishermen contend that the mere lack of fishing pressure during the hours of darkness contributes to the success during those hours. That premise has validity. I've caught more fish at night than at any other time. This certainly holds true during fall Salmon season. You'll battle fewer anglers, have fewer lines tangled and have a better chance to land a trophy if you fish at night. During the summer the Salmon are deep in the Great Lakes. It starts early in St. Clair. As spring turns to summer, they move further out into deeper water. On calm summer days you'll see small aluminum boats outfitted with low cost, clamp on, manual downriggers searching for Kings and Cohos. All of the Great Lakes are treacherous. They can turn ugly and nasty with only a moments

To catch some great fishing, just say the word.

Say yes to Michigan for pan-fishing fun for the whole family or the thrill of sport fishing for the serious minded.

For once in your life, you won't get caught with an empty stringer. For once in your life, you'll catch "the one that got away."

Michigan lakes and streams serve up everything from perch to trophy trout and the opportunity for first-timers and old-timers to go for the thrill of catching king and coho salmon.

And when the fish aren't biting, there are flea markets and county fairs, boutiques and antiques to get hooked on.

Charter boat services are available on the Great Lakes that surround us. And public access sites to launch your own boat are plentiful.

For round-the-clock reports on current fishing conditions, special events and festivals, call toll free 800-292-5404 in Michigan. Elsewhere, call 800-248-5708.

Big-game trophies can be taken off our 3,000 miles of Great Lakes shoreline.

Sport fish and panfish are abundant in our 11,000 lakes.

Michigan boasts 14,400 miles of prime trout water.

notice. In a large craft they can be dangerous. In a small one they can be deadly. Treat them with respect and they will be your friend.

At most Great Lakes Salmon ports during the summer you will see anglers with trailerable sixteen to twenty one foot boats, bringing in their limits of bright, fresh, Salmon and Trout. This is the time when the weather is warm, the days are long, and the fish are deep and firm of flesh.

If you don't possess a Great Lakes fishing machine, take a Charter! During a charter you can gain information which might otherwise take you years to accumulate. You can learn how to use a graph (depth sounder) and also valuable information about how to locate and catch fish in a variety of difficult conditions. It is always best to shop for a charter. Have a specific date in mind. If you are comfortable with a particular captain, try to lock in your date. Some of the best charter captains will be booked well in advance. One charter captain I know, books his summer weekends by the end of January. If you haven't booked a charter during the winter months, it doesn't mean that all is lost. I have gone fishing on a "wing and a prayer" and managed to be successful. My wife Robin caught a twenty-seven pound King (which now hangs on the kitchen wall) on just such occasion. We decided to take a long weekend in August. We had never stayed in Leland and decided to give it a try. We arrived and checked into the possibility of a charter. Most charter captains insist on a minimum of four people. If there are two of you, your chances are increased because it is more likely that you may be paired with another couple. Costs range between fifty and ninety dollars, per person, per half day, and seventy five to one hundred and fifty dollars per person for a full day. Generally, a half day is four to five hours, and a full day is eight to nine hours. We were able to fish with one of the best captains in the area, Bill Carlson, of Carlson Fisheries. Bill only takes charters on rare occasions, when other captains are full. We had two Captains on board, Bob White was also a full charter captain, and served as first mate. You will find that one captain will help a competitor, in this homogeneous community.

The afternoon was sunny. We took a total of thirteen fish. There were browns, lakers, and Kings in the cooler by the time we headed for port. The largest was Robin's, twenty seven pound King, taken on an outrigger and diving planer. One lake trout was taken on a squid and all others were taken on spoons in sixty to eighty feet of water. Each couple paid one hundred dollars for the afternoon. We also tipped our Captains. For two hundred dollars we had over one hundred pounds of choice Salmon and trout. To see your wife, girlfriend, or friend tie into their first real trophy, it's better than your favorite team winning the Championship, and the cheers are louder!

Good charter Captains work hard. The tackle on board a well equipped boat, and the amount of time and energy expended changing lures, raising and lowering downriggers. Most charter boats have between thirty and one hundred thousand dollars on board in equipment. Even if you have fished a particular area for many years, you'll notice that the charter boats will be trying the latest techniques and tackle. Many experienced anglers consider an occasional charter trip to be a seminar or refresher course, for the new and improved.

Lake Trout are scrappy, bulldogging, lightning fighters, that make excellent table fare. The majority of lake trout from the Great Lakes will weigh between six and twelve pounds. We don't see too many of the monsters such as those caught in some of the remote Canadian and Alaskan lakes. Fly-in Fishing Charters are listed in the nautical publications section. Locally, lake trout are plentiful. It is easy to take your limit in thirty to forty-five minutes at the right spot. Although wire lining for lakers is still popular, you'll find that most will be caught deep trolling with downriggers and sparkle flys behind an attractor called a Dodger. (I tell friends from Los Angeles that I use Dodgers for bait). During the summer, when brown trout are lurking in the depths of the lakes they can be taken with many of the same techinques used for salmon or lakers. We routinely catch browns in the four to eight pound category. During the fall the browns move into the streams and are more concentrated and accessible. However, many streams are closed to brown trout fishing in the fall, check your regulations. (Cooking Note: The careful filleting and

SAVE THE WHALES!

NOVA SCOTIA

Join the North Atlantic Squadron. Great sailing. Fantastic landfalls.

Sailors have been heading for Nova Scotia shores since long before sailing became the great escape. Many of our coves and snug harbours have seen little change from those early days. Other ports of call have everything you need to keep you afloat. One thing that hasn't changed over the years, anywhere that you may drop anchor, is the warmth of the welcome.

Nova Scotians are sea-faring people and have a special place for everyone who goes down to the sea. Don't forget our inland sea, the beautiful Bras d'Or lakes. And if your interest in ships and the sea goes all the way — hang in for the 75th Anniversary celebrations of the Canadian Navy. Ships from 15 nations will assemble in late June. This year, sail on — to Nova Scotia.

Whales are the highest form of life in the sea. Scientists say some whale species have brains larger and more complex than man's, indicating a high intelligence potential. We might someday communicate with them.

But these awesome marine mammals may disappear from Earth soon.

Every 19 minutes another whale suffers an agonizing death, its back blown open by a grenade-tipped harpoon. Most of the ten species of great whales have already been driven to the brink of extinction. The remaining species are now being wiped out.

It is morally indefensible to slaughter these gentle, intelligent creatures. And why are the whales being killed? To make animal feed, fertilizer, lubricating oil, margarine and cosmetics. There are cheap, plentiful substitutes for all whale products.

The chief offenders are Japan and the Soviet Union, whose pelagic (deep-sea) whaling fleets slaughter over 90% of the whales taken in international waters. Other wealthy nations engaging in whaling along their coasts are Australia, Brazil, Iceland and Norway.

THE WORLD IS WATCHING

The International Whaling Commission (IWC) will be meeting June 26-30 in London to decide the fate of the great whales. The IWC will be voting on a moratorium on all commercial whaling.

The whaling nations have repeatedly ignored an appeal for a ten-year moratorium adopted in 1972 by the United Nations Conference on the Human Environment. The vote at Stockholm was unanimous, 53 to 0.

Non-whaling members of the 17-nation IWC strongly outnumber the whalers. How will they vote on the moratorium issue? The non-whalers are the U.S., Canada, Great Britain, France, Netherlands, Denmark, South Africa, New Zealand, Argentina, Panama and Mexico. Will they fight to end the senseless massacre?

YOU CAN HELP SAVE THE WHALES

Only public pressure against the whaling nations will end the slaughter. Write to your newspaper. Tell your friends. Write to President Carter (The White House, Washington, D.C. 20500) asking his help to achieve the moratorium.

Help support the Save The Whales campaign by making a tax-deductible contribution to the Animal Welfare Institute. For a donation of $15 or more, you will receive a beautiful six-color print of the humpback whales (above).

Please give generously. Remember: Extinction is the ultimate crime.

This ad paid for by Friends of Cetaceans.

ANIMAL WELFARE INSTITUTE
P.O. Box 3650
Washington, D.C. 20007
Christine Stevens, President

Please send me more information about how I can help Save The Whales.

☐ Enclosed is my tax-deductible donation of $_____.

Please make check payable to Animal Welfare Institute.

☐ Please send me the Humpback Whale print ($15 minimum donation).

(please print)

Name _____

Address _____

City _____

State _____ Zip _____

The Animal Welfare Institute is a non-profit, educational organization established in 1951 to reduce animal suffering and protect endangered species.
A copy of the Animal Welfare Institute's latest annual report filed with the New York State Board of Social Welfare is available upon written request to the Institute at the address on the masthead, or to the New York State Board of Social Welfare, Office Tower, Empire State Plaza, Albany, N.Y. 12223.

Nova Scotia Tourism,
P.O. Box 130,
Halifax, Nova Scotia.
Canada   B3J 2M7

Please rush me the 270-page Nova Scotia Tourism Guide. Includes 9 fold-out, full colour maps, plus complete information on this unique corner of Canada. Only $1.50 (postage and handling). Please send cheque or money order payable to Nova Scotia Tourism. (Don't mail cash.)   SC1

Name _____

Street _____

City _____

Prov. _____

Code _____

Or call toll free:
From Nova Scotia, New Brunswick and Prince Edward Island, dial 1-800-565-7105. In Halifax-Dartmouth area, 425-5781. From Newfoundland and Quebec, dial 1-800-565-7180. From Central and Southern Ontario, dial 1-800-565-7140. From Northern Ontario, Manitoba, Saskatchewan and Alberta, dial 1-800-565-7166. From British Columbia only, dial 112-800-565-7166.

trimming of all belly fat, and then cooking the fillets on a covered charcoal grill with the skin side down. Brush your fillets liberally, and often, with lemon juice and white wine. You'll find that much of the fat will drip into the fire. Grill until tender, remove the fillet from the skin, if desired. (Serve with California Coolers.)

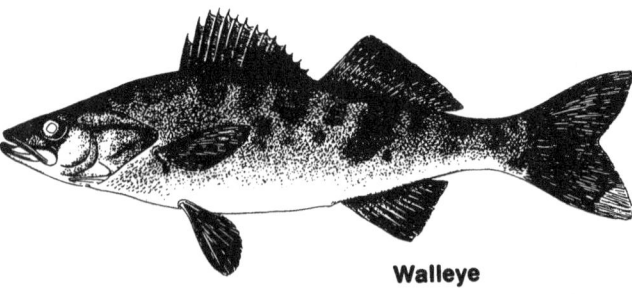
Walleye

Walleye is another prize of the Lakes. They are plentiful, delicious, and in recent years have grown to some trophy-plus sizes. The western basin of Lake Erie and the Detroit River (Lake St. Clair) are now known as the foremost Walleye fishery in the country. An airline pilot recently reported seeing a school of walleye in Lake Erie two miles long and a mile wide. Most are in the two to four pound category, but ten to twelve pounders have been recorded. Many are caught from shore. Some anglers still drift, or cast to a school using a weight foreward spinner tipped with a night crawler. The planer board, downrigger and outriggers are some of the newest weapons in the walleye catching arsenal. The planer board carries your lines as much as one hundred yards out to the side of the boat. That's where the fish are. This new technique has resulted in some phenomenal catches.

Local bass pro, author, and radio/television personality, Tony Prainito has fished for bass all over the country. He contends that Lake St. Clair offers the finest for smallmouth bass fishing. Tony is presently working to bring a major national tournament to the Lake. St. Clair is also noted for its musky, back in the fifties and sixties one or two was a gift. Today, it is four a day.

To locate a particular area, or species, a wealth of information is available. Tony Prainito, Babe Winkelman and Hank Parker all have weekly television shows. (Check local listings) Michigan Outdoors broadcasts on public television. In addition to the outdoor sections in your major dailies. The local papers in fishing/resort communities highlight fishing areas.

SOME MAGAZINES INCLUDE:

Great Lakes Fisherman
P.O. Box 20286
Columbus, Ohio 43220

This monthly publication gives you some of the latest techniques for everything from pan fish to pike. It also gives you an area action guide each month. Specifics on each of the Great Lakes including charter information, comparisons of catches from previous years, the hottest lures, and some tips on areas that are currently being underfished. A valuable resource tool when seeking new areas to fish.

Michigan Fisherman
P.O. Box 977
East Lansing, Michigan 48823

Michigan Fisherman concentrates on action within the state and surrounding Canadain waters. Good features, to keep you updated on new developments. Published bi-monthly.

Fishing Facts
P.O. Box 609
Menominee Falls, WI 53051-9984

Information on everything from structure fishing to how to use chart recorders. You'll find many articles geared toward the serious Bass fisherman. Published monthly.

The IN-Fisherman
P.O. Box 999
Brainerd, MN 56401-9989

Probably the slickest, most colorful fishing publication on the market. Al Linder started about ten years ago. His yearly television specials are a "must see", and the IN-Fisherman radio reports are broadcast nationally. Illustrator, Larry Tople creates some of the most realistic and beautiful portraits and covers in this bi-monthly publication. Includes international techniques and fishing news.

Local AAA offices compiles a weekly fishing report, published in some local papers. If not contact your AAA office.

To begin, refine and hook the trophies, knowledge is the key. The more you know, the better fisherman you will become. Fishing is certainly becoming more scientific, but never a science. It will always be an art. Even though we know more about habitat, migration patterns, and the elements of structure, we still make assumptions. Although we have modern graphs and Loran to find the fish, once they are found it is still up to us to catch them. Suppose that's the reason it's so much fun!

God bless ya, good fishing, and GOOD LUCK!

DWJ

MAP 1
(INCLUDES DIVISIONS 1, 2, 3, 4 AND 5)

Determine what division you will be fishing in and then consult the open season and catch limit guides on the following pages for details.

• Indicates exception to species season listed below   • Indicates open season

	1	2	3	4	5
PIKE	•	•	•	•	•
YELLOW PICKEREL (WALLEYE) and SAUGER	•	•	•	•	•
BASS (LARGEMOUTH and SMALLMOUTH)	•	•	• •	•	•
MUSKELLUNGE	•	•	•	•	•
BROOK TROUT	•	•	•	•	•
BROWN TROUT	•	•	•	•	•
RAINBOW TROUT	•	•	•	• •	•
LAKE TROUT and SPLAKE	•	•	•	•	•
STURGEON	•	•	•	•	•

Species	Season
PIKE	All year
YELLOW PICKEREL (WALLEYE) and SAUGER	May 10 (2nd Sat.) to Mar. 31 All year May 10 (2nd Sat.) to Mar. 31
BASS (LARGEMOUTH and SMALLMOUTH)	June 28 (last Sat.) to Dec. 31 June 28 (last Sat.) to Nov. 30
MUSKELLUNGE	June 7 (1st Sat.) to Dec. 15 June 21 (3rd Sat.) to Nov. 30
BROOK TROUT	Apr. 26 (last Sat.) to Sept. 15 Apr. 26 (last Sat.) to Sept. 30
BROWN TROUT	All year Apr. 26 (last Sat.) to Sept. 15 Apr. 26 (last Sat.) to Sept. 30
RAINBOW TROUT	All year Apr. 26 (last Sat.) to Sept. 15 Apr. 26 (last Sat.) to Sept. 30
LAKE TROUT and SPLAKE	All year Jan. 1 to Oct. 10 Jan. 1 to Mar. 15 May 10 (2nd Sat.) to Oct. 5
STURGEON	All year June 15 to May 14

▲ EXCEPTIONS TO THE OPEN SEASON GUIDE

Brook Trout, Brown Trout, and Rainbow Trout
County of Bruce (Division 4)—Cameron Lake, Gillies Lake, Cyprus Lake and County of Grey (Division 4)—Bells Lake, Eugenia Lake, Wilcox Lake, McCullough Lake, Wilder Lake, Bass Lake, Williams Lake, and Irish Lake; Jan. 1-Mar. 31 and Apr. 26 (last Sat. in Apr.) to Sept. 30.
Pinery Park Pond (County of Lambton): Jan. 1 to Mar. 31 and Apr. 26 (last Sat. in Apr.) to Sept. 15.

Lake Trout and Splake
Lake Huron (Division 2): Dec. 1-Sept. 30.
Lake Ontario (Divisions 2 and 8) Jan. 1-Sept. 30.

Whitefish
Lake Simcoe (Division 5): Jan. 1 to Mar. 15 and May 11 to Oct. 15.

Simcoe County
The Talbot River and its tributaries and the Trent Canal System in the Township of Mara are now part of Division 6.

Bruce, Grey and Huron Counties
All fishing except commercial bait fishing is **prohibited** from Oct. 1 to Apr. 25 (Fri. preceding last Sat.) in:
a) all of the streams and rivers in the counties of Bruce and Grey, excluding the waters mentioned in Schedules IV and XXIII, of the Ontario Fishery Regulations.
b) Bayfield River, Nine Mile River, Maitland River and an unnamed Creek known locally as Naftels Creek and their tributaries in the County of Huron, excluding the waters mentioned in Schedules IV and XXIII, of the Ontario Fishery Regulations.

Regional Municipality of Durham
All fishing is prohibited in all streams (including Duffin Creek) located in the Regional Municipality of Durham from Nov. 16 to Apr. 25 (Fri. preceding last Sat.) This restriction does not apply to those designated streams having an all year open season or a special extended season for rainbow and brown trout.

These exceptions are listed on page 16 under Fall Fishing For Rainbow Trout And Brown Trout and under Stream Mouths Having An All Year Open Season On Rainbow Trout And Brown Trout.

Note: Fishing for sturgeon is open all year in the County of Simcoe.

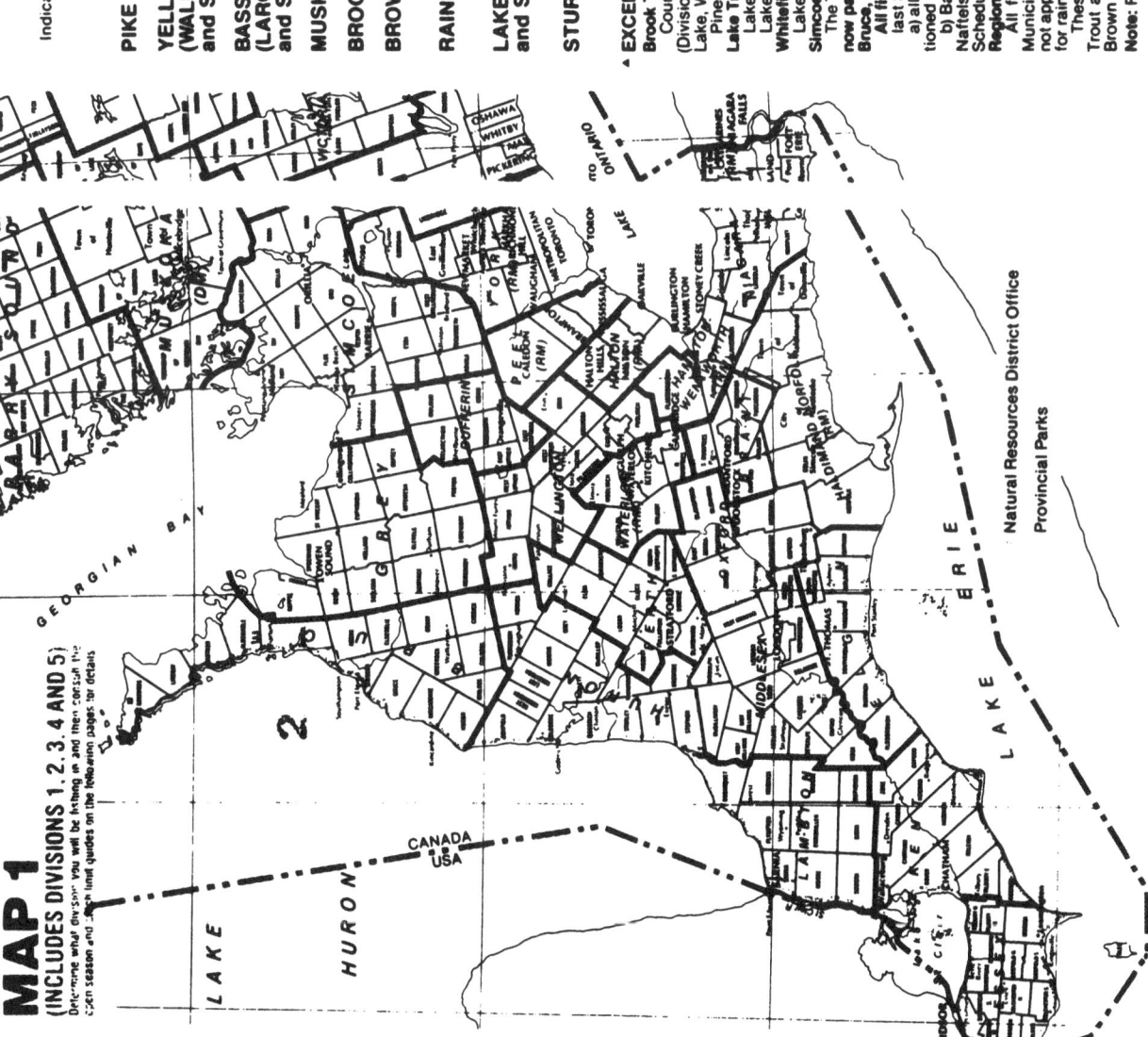

— — — Natural Resources District Office
▬▬▬ Provincial Parks

FOR CLIENTS WHO DEMAND AND APPRECIATE
SUPERIORITY
IN A BOAT — THE

M/V SHORTY BAIRD

IS
DESIGNED
ENGINEERED
AND
CONSTRUCTED
TO BE A
SUPERIOR
BOAT

SUPERIOR BOAT WORKS, INC.

P.O. BOX 326   GREENVILLE, MISSISSIPPI 38701

LEA BRENT   CONTACT AT   HOWARD BRENT

601-378-9100

Chapter 4

CITIES, TOWNS & HARBORS

"I told you bout the swans
that live in the park"

Eric Clapton

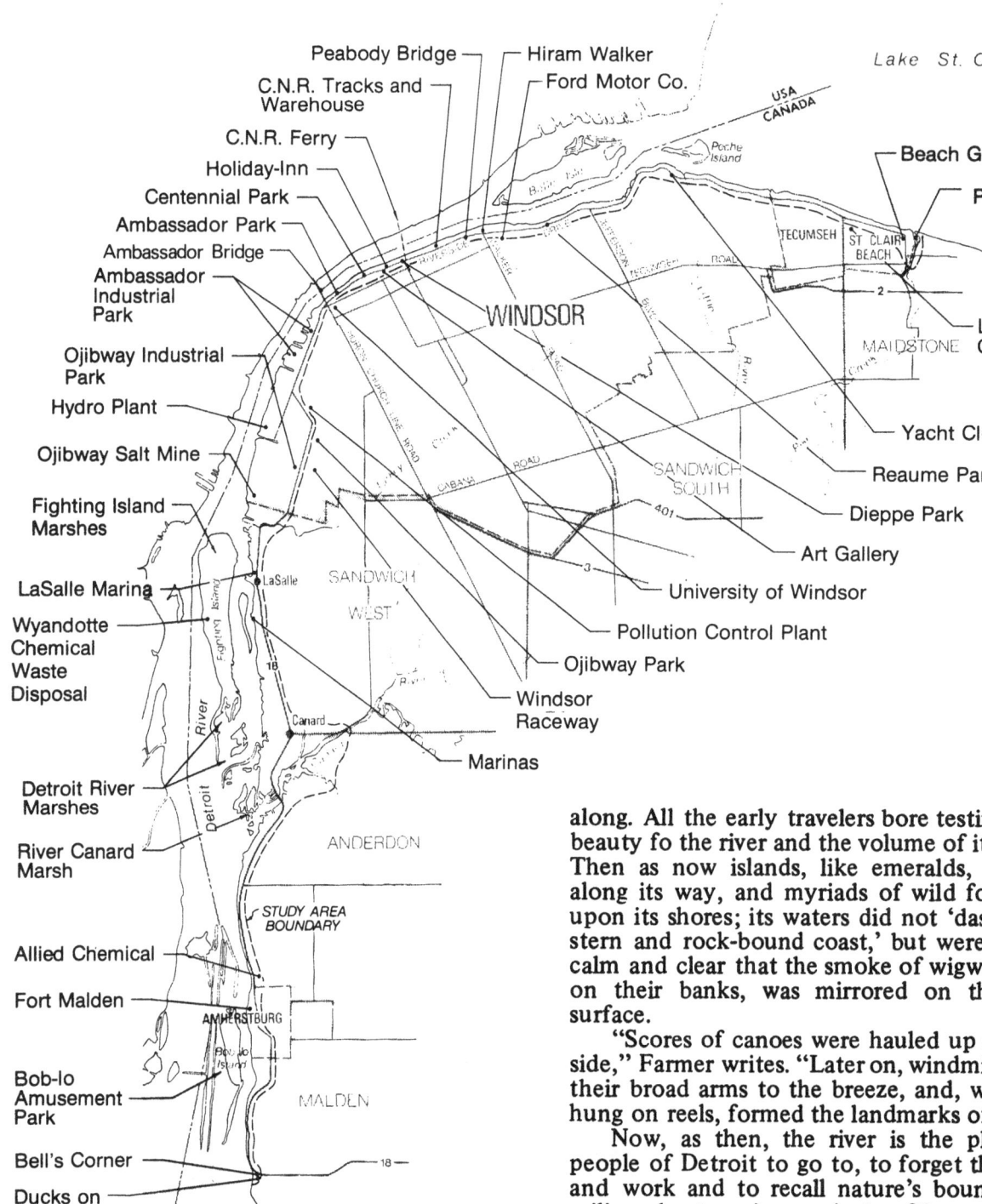

THE DETROIT RIVER

"London has its Thames, Paris the Seine, Rome the Tiber, and New York the Hudson; but in everything the Detroit (River) excels them all." So wrote Silas Farmer in his voluminous History of Detroit and Wayne County and Early Michigan, first published in 1890. He continues: "It is no wonder that the first visitors came by water when such a stream flowed by them and beckoned them along. All the early travelers bore testimony to the beauty fo the river and the volume of its waters. .. Then as now islands, like emeralds, were strung along its way, and myriads of wild fowl then fed upon its shores; its waters did not 'dash high on a stern and rock-bound coast,' but were so still and calm and clear that the smoke of wigwams, nestled on their banks, was mirrored on their smooth surface.

"Scores of canoes were hauled up on the riverside," Farmer writes. "Later on, windmills stretched their broad arms to the breeze, and, with fish-nets hung on reels, formed the landmarks of their day."

Now, as then, the river is the place for the people of Detroit to go to, to forget their troubles and work and to recall nature's bounty. Fishing, sailing, boat racing or just rafting up to a half dozen friends' vessels for a social afternoon next to Peche Island, still occupy Detroiters during the fair months of the year. During the winter, when the flow slows to a freeze, skaters and ice fishermen dot the shore and some winters, as in February, 1855, Farmer reports "the river was so completely frozen that a little shanty was erected in the middle, in which liquors were sold."

The river forms the boundary between the U.S. and Canada, which is due south, with the line about midway of the stream. Congress declared it a public highway on December 22, 1819. Its length is 27 miles, 1515 yards from the Windmill Point

Light, at the foot of Lake St. Claire, to Bar Point, where the Detroit empties into Lake Erie. Its greatest width is three miles, its narrowest, just opposite downtown Detroit, is just over a half mile wide. Its average is one mile wide. The river's depth varies from 10 to 60 feet, averaging 34 feet.

But that says nothing about the great rivers flow, which is incomparable the world over. The fresh, clear waters of Lakes Superior, Michigan, Huron and St. Clair, of the Green, Saginaw and Georgian Bays and countless streams, flow into the Detroit and rush past the shores of the city. It's estimated that some 12,000 cubic feet of water pass the city each second, coming from 82,000 square miles of northern lake surface and 125,000 square miles of land.

Its islands offer boaters plentiful resting spots from the first, Peche Island, a Canadian property kept entirely natural which was once the home of the Ottowa Chief Pontiac, to Belle Isle, a giant Detroit city park, to smaller cays known as Fighting, Mud, Grassy, Gras, Mama-Juda, Grosse, Turkey, Stoney, Slocum's, Humbug, Fox Elba, Calf, Snake, Hickory, Sugar Bois Blanc, Horse, Cherry and Tawa.

THE CITY OF DETROIT

. America has just a few cities that can accurately be called old and Detroit is one of them. Before New York, New Orleans, Philadelphia or Boston was settled, France's Sieur de Champlain had almost reached the city's present border and the Indians had described the site and named it Yon-do-ti-ga (A Great Village).

Silas Farmer, in his 1890 History of Detroit and Wayne County and Early Michigan, tells us that when Cadillac first came to Detroit to settle the area, the East India Company had still not been heard of and there was not yet a newspaper or post-office in the United States.

"The first colony here established was like a bit of France in the wilds of the New World and no city in the Eastern States, and but one or two in the South, have anything in common with our earlier life," Farmer writes. "Some of the old records (of Detroit) read like a passage of Froissart, and visions of medieval scenes and pictures of savage life are strangely intermingled in the records of our past."

From the early 1600s, the French government claimed the region of Detroit as its own, calling it New France. Farmer tells us: "During French rule, no less than three kings and three regents exercised authority over Detroit and its surroundings."

Those early French settlers first stayed close to army forts, but later ventured off to dig "ribbon farms" in narrow strips from the water's edge to the plains and forests north to streets such as the one they named "Gratiot," which remains a major thoroughfare in Detroit today. They had no need for wells, engines or pumps for water, as Silas Farmer tells us: "Each farmhouse had its single rough-hewn log or plank projecting into the stream and barefooted maidens, morning by morning, 'walked the plank,' dashed a bucket into the river and with the rope to which it was attached drew out the water for their daily needs. There were no assessors to inquire how many the family included. Shut-offs were unknown. The supply was literally 'as free as air,' and whosoever would, might draw or drink."

The French struggled valiantly to keep hold of New France throughout wars with English and Indians. But the city fell during the reign of France's King Louis XV, then only 13-years-old. Detroit was surrendered by French Commandant Bellestre to the great Major Robert Rogers and

England's George III became Detroit's fourth king under the 1763 Treaty of Paris.

The city had five names before settling on its current appelation. The Algonquin Indians called it Yon-do-ti-ga, and later named it Wa-we-a-tun-ong, meaning the Circuitous Approach because of the bending river. The Wyandott Indians called the area Toghsaghrondie, which was modernized into Teuchsa Grondie in early Colonial Documents. To the Huron Indians, the place was Ka-ron-ta-en, meaning the Coast of the Strait.

Farmer tells us the location was first called Fort Pontchartrain by the French, in honor of their Colonial Minister of Marine. "As the number of inhabitants increased, and the settlement grew into a village, it received its present name from the word d'etroit, or strait," Farmer writes. Finally it was designated by Act of January 18, 1802 as "The Town of Detroit."

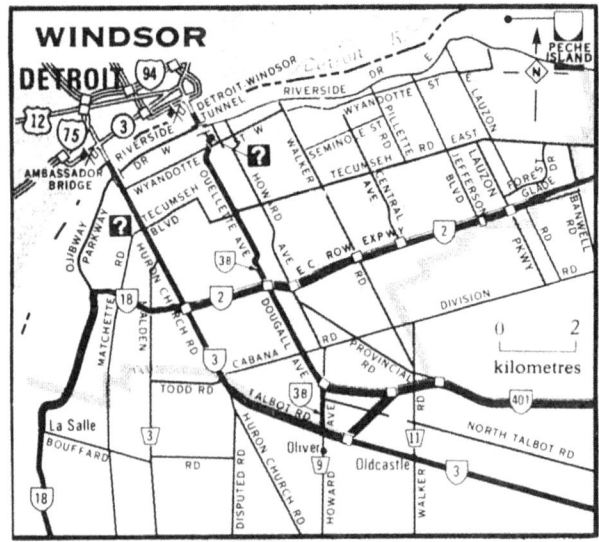

CANADA

Visiting our foreign neighbor Windsor, Canada, is easy and enjoyable if you follow the guidelines established by Canadian Customs.

When crossing the Ambassador Bridge (41), located off I-75 between Porter and Howard Streets, or the Detroit-Windsor Tunnel (11), west of the Renaissance Center, be prepared to present identification papers such as birth, baptismal, voter's or naturalization certificates or alien registration card.

Most establishments will accept American currency, but to receive the most accurate exchange rate, change your money at a bank or trust company on either side of the border.

With proof your Canadian visit was at least 48 hours, American citizens may bring $300 worth of personal household merchandise across the border once every 30 days. Not more than 100 cigars, one carton of cigarettes and 32 ounces of alcoholic beverages for personal consumption may be included in the $300 exemption.

The Province of Ontario requires all automobile drivers and passengers to use seatbelts at all times. Canadian road distances and speed limit signs are indicated in kilometers.

The Windsor-Detroit Tunnel Bus makes traveling between the neighboring lands simple. Buses run every half-hour beginning at 5:30 a.m. Monday-Saturday and 8 a.m. Sunday. Downtown Detroit stops are Fort St. and Woodward Ave. and the Tunnel entrance next to the Renaissance Center. For further details, contact Transit Windsor at 944-4111.

Additional information on Canadian attractions is available through the Windsor and Essex County Tourist and Convention Bureau, 80 Chatham St. E., Windsor, Ontario, Canada N9A

Port of Windsor, Ontario, Canada, which is on the shore of the Detroit River, connecting Lake Erie and Lake St. Clair, the busiest waterway in the world. Traffic passing this vantage point in Windsor averages around 14,000 cargo vessels carrying a total of over 207 million tons of cargo. Commercial ships that call at Windsor-Detroit are owned by companies scattered throughout the world. For general purposes, however, they can be separated into two groups: Lake ships that usually trade almost exclusively within the five Great Lakes; and oceangoing ships (these, of course, make virtually every steamer track in the world). When an ocean-going ship arrives in our Harbour from the Atlantic, she has climbed 572 feet above sea level — the equivalent of scaling a 50-story building. Lifted by locks in the St. Lawrence Seaway and the Welland Canal, ships make the 610 mile run from Montreal entrance of the Seaway to Windsor in an average of 3 to 4 days.

During a typical Great Lakes navigation season (from early March through late-December), the port handles over 3 million tons of cargo. Shipments of bulk agricultural products, coal, steel, salt, stone, building material, grain, alcoholic beverages, canned goods, petroleum products, tobacco, etc. represent the major volume through the Port of Windsor. In addition to the foregoing there are thousands of tons of more novel and specialty items such as; computer parts, playing cards, cucumbers, footwear, malt, olives, onions, scales, spark plugs, beer, wine, drugs, mobile homes, rice, rubber, etc. Approximately 1,100 commercial ships call at the Windsor Harbour every season. In addition to the regular commercial vessels we had approximately 4,500 railroad ferry entries accounting for 3,000,000 additional tons to make the total annual volume within the harbour over 5,600 entries with 6 million tons.

The Windsor Harbour has more to offer a boat-watcher, however, than commercial shipping. Over 133,000 pleasure craft, both engine driven and under sail, abound in the Detroit River area. And there are the Coast Guard Cutters, the tugboats, the dredges, the excursion boats, the mail boat, the various work scows, the fire boats and the police boats. The sounds of the harbour complement the sights. The ships' whistle signals are a very common sound, and the rumbling of trains and trucks, the helicopters, the squawking of sea gulls and the flocks of ducks (some of which stay year round in the river).

WINDSOR
City of Roses   (Pop. 240,000)

The first permanent settlement on the south shore of the Detroit River in 1750. Incorporated 1854 and achieved city status in 1892. Roses with 500 varieties flow thru-out Windsors spotless 900 acre park system. Jackson Park in the heart of the city acquired royal status in 1984 and renamed Queen Elizabeth Gardens to commemorate the Queens visit. The famous sunken gardens also include the Windsor Memorial Lancaster Bomber, commemorating Royal Canadian Air Force flyers who lost their lives in World War II. The Windsor Peace Fountain in the Detroit River at Coventry Gardens is the beautiful park visible by boats on the Detroit River. Operating from May through October, it is North America's largest floating fountain. It is made up of 34 computer controlled spray patterns, divers hook up the power lines connecting the fountain to its on-shore controls each spring. The fountain covers 180 feet in diameter, and sprays up to 80 feet in height. The hidden beauty is the computer programmed 27 minute rotation cycle, with a spectacular flow of all four jets, pumping 12,000 gallons of water per minute, with colored lights, exposing a liquid lightshow that is awesome at night. If the Queen granted Jackson Park the roayl seal, the Pirate's Guide grants the Peace fountain our royal seal. The creative blend of high-tech, H2o and Mother Nature, what City planners should look at before picking up a pencil, names withheld, but we know.

Thru-out these Vignette's the similarities of New Orleans and the Detroit/Windsor areas will surface. Both cities are located on peninsulas, and all surrounded by water, ports of entry and French origination (the unique dialect still spoken by a few Windsor people influenced the French dialect of the Mississippi Valley). The city of New Orleans was after the regent of France Duc d' Orleans, also the name of the St. Clair River pleasure boat DUC D'ORLEANS which was originally produced by the MAC CRAFT Corp., which began operations in Wallaceburg, Ontario, August 8th, 1938.

In 1834, the city had been called La Traverse, Sandwich Ferry, Richmond and South Detroit. A meeting took place in one of the local pubs and the city was graced with the name Windsor, after the Windsor Castle.

Ministry of Tourism and Recreation provides free map, trip ticket and a complete up to date free library of publications ranging from Fly-In Fishing Services (name, address, phone number and facilities available) to Bed and Breakfast Inns, Homes and Cottages thru-out Canada, all free and all totally complete. When they say "YOUR'S To Discover" they really mean it's Your's! The following will help you Yachtsmen, Dockboy and inquisitive minded, come or go to its many sights.

Chamber of Commerce
500 Riverside Drive West

Tourist & Convention Bureau
of Windsor and Essex County
80 Chatham Street East (City Maps)

Emergencies: 911

Information for the Disabled
March of Dimes Office
1695 University W.
Suite C, Windsor

Points of Interest WINDSOR
Art Gallery of Windsor
445 Riverside Drive West

A Gallery of galleries, permanent and traveling displays, childrens, workshops, with cafeteria and gift shop. Open Tues.–Sat. 10-5, Wed. 'til 10, Sun. 1-5.

Hiram Walker Historical Museum
254 Pitt St. West
(519) 253-1812

The traditions of Hiram Walker and historical museum including Windsor and region. Symbolizing the end of the Pioneer Period and the beginning of the Industrial revolution. A wood carvers dream, beautiful wood beams and surrounded by immaculate grounds.

Windsor City Market
Chatham Street West
(519) 255-6260

For the chef afloat this is the place to start, over 500 stalls of treats that include fresh vegetables, poultry, eggs, meats and on and on, push rare seasoned meats and unique cheeses, even flowers for the gimble table or that special mate. I'd start here!

Windsor Raceway
P.O. Box 998
(519) 969-8311

From surf to turf, considered one of the best all-weather surfaces in North America. Ambro Vibrant set a world record for two-year-old fillies, completing the one mile circuit in 1:58 flat in 1979.

Dieppe Gardens (foot of Quellette)
A great view of the Detroit Skyline accepted by the Udine Fountain donated to the city by its twin city in Italy and the Spirit of Windsor, a steam locomotive.

Colio Wines of Canada Limited
P.O. Box 372, Colio Drive, Harrow
(519) 726-5317

WINDSOR TRIVIA

John and Horace Dodge, auto tycoons, first established their careers in Windsor. They worked for the Canadian Typetheic Company in 1890. Horace became plant supervisor and the two brothers invented the Evans and Dodge bicycle (E&D) and leased the plant to manufacture the two wheeler. A machine shop was opened in Detroit in the early 1900's and attracted the attention of the automobile makers.

Windsor had the first mile of concrete pavement in North America.

The Detroit Red Wings played their first home game in the Windsor's Border City Arena (now Windsor Arena) on November 18, 1926. Olympia Stadium wasn't finished, but the Wings were — the Boston Bruins won 2-0.

Windsor opened the first joint YMCA-YWCA in the world, 1937. The world's first palm and turn safety top was instigated by the late Henri Breault.

The pediatrician was head of the Poison control center and saw two accidental poisonings a day. The International Tool Company of Windsor came up with the invention poisonings were down 90 per cent. These results led to the passing of legislation in 1974 regarding safety containers for prescribed drugs.

The first bottle of Canadian Club whiskey was produced by Hiram Walker & Sons Ltd. in 1858.

There are 250 acres of land under glass and plastic in the Sun Parlor (Windsor) of Canada — nearly half of the greenhouse area in Canada. These greenhouses produce 25 million dollars worth of cucumbers and tomatoes annually.

The development of the St. Lawrence seaway and the rail system account for the population boom that errased the French ribbon farms that met on the shores of the Detroit River and Lake St. Clair. The history is expansive and futile like the prized soil, still farmed today. For additional historical information the following publications are available: The Windsor Border Region (Documentary) by Ernest J. Lajeunesse, C.S.B., University of Toronto Press, Toronto, Ontario. Garden Gateway to Canada, One Hundred Years of Windsor and Essex County—1854-1954, by Neil F. Morrison, M.S., Ph.D., The Ryerson Press, 299 Queen West, Toronto 1, Ontario. A Brief Historical Sketch of Windsor and Area, by R. Alan Douglas, Curator, Hiram Walker Historical Museum, Windsor.

1 Canadian Rock Salt Co. Ltd.
2 Morton Terminal Ltd.
3 J. Clark Keith-Hydro Electric Power Corp.
4 Consolidation Coal Co.
5 Canadian Salt Co. Ltd.
6 Canada Steamship Lines
7 J.J. Kovinsky Ltd. (Hill St.)
8 Windsor Harbour Commission - Imperial Dock
9 Windsor Harbour Commission - Confederation Dock
10 Adams Cartage
11 Pyramid Aggregates
12 Premier Concrete Products and Lake Ontario Cement Co.
13 Canadian Pacific Railway
14 Dieppe Park Dock
15 Canadian National Railway
16 Hiram Walker and Sons Ltd.
17 Ford Motor Co. of Canada Ltd.
18 Windsor Yacht Club
19 Southwestern Sales

THE AMBASSADOR BRIDGE

Officiallly opened to traffic on November 11, 1929. The 2½ years of construction under the guidance and heartache of Detroit financier Joseph A. Bower. The final cost $23,500,000. The longest international suspension bridge in the world. One and three-quarter miles between terminals, 7,490 feet long, clearance above the water is 152 feet at the center. Each tower is 386 feet above the ground. 37 strands, with each strand having 216 wires compile the two suspension cables. Concrete anchorages 22½ feet wide and 100 feet long fasten the cables to bedrock 105 feet down. An average of 14,000 vehicles per day and approximately 5,000,000 cross the Bridge annually.

The SS Columbia and her sister ship the SS Ste. Claire, the largest passenger steamships in the World, ferry vistors to Boblo Island from their dock in downtown Detroit. Boblo is located on the Detroit River near Lake Erie in Ontario, Canada. Boblo is owned by the Automobile Club of Michigan. Boblo, 151 W. Jefferson, Detroit, Michigan 48226.

BOBLO
More Than an Amusement Park

Whether they purchase a ticket to Boblo Island Amusement Park, for an evening of dancing or a cruise on Detroit's spectacular river with the Boblo boat, people buy much more. They buy a small chunk of history.

Boblo Island and its two large steamships are steeped in history. Boblo, located in Canada and situated in the Detroit River near the entrance to Lake Erie, first opened as a recreational destination in 1898. The SS Columbia and SS Ste. Claire, both on the National Historic Registry for the United States travel the Detroit River between Canada and the States along the world's largest unprotected border between two foreign countries carrying Boblo's visitors to the amusement park.

Boblo's original name was "ETIOWITEEN-DANNENTI" and was coined by the Huron Indians who once lived there. It meant "Peopled Island of White Woods Guarding the Entrance." The term white woods referred to the white wood poplar trees that covered the Island. Because of its strategic location near the entrance to Lake Erie, several different groups inhabited the 272-acre Island. When the French and British were there, it was the French who renamed the Island "Bois Blanc", meaning white wood. During the War of 1812, the Chieftain Tecumseh staged tribal council meetings on the Island. Fifty years later at the outbreak of the Civil War, runaway slaves found refuge in the wooded areas on their way to Canada.

One of the two blockhouses built by the British for fortification may still be seen on the south end of the Island. The lighthouse, built in 1837 by the Government of Upper Canada to facilitate navigation on the river is still standing.

In mid 1800, Bois Blanc was developed as a picnic and park area with ferries transporting visitors from Amherstburg, Ontario. Small Boblo ferry boats maintain that tradition today. Unable to pronounce Bois Blanc properly, the visitors originated the name "Boblo". The Island was officially christened "Boblo" in 1929. An enormous dance pavillion constructed in 1931 dominates the Island. Known as the largest dance floor in North America, it has been closed temporarily because of deterioration of its roof in recent years.

The two historic vessels, SS Columbia and SS Ste Claire, have a capacity of 2,500 people each and weigh 969 tons. The Columbia was built in 1902 by the Detroit Shipbuilding Company of Wyandotte and the Ste Claire was built in 1910 by the Toledo Shipbuilding Company.

Moonlight cruises with live bands and dancing have become another tradition for Boblo. Special memories have been created through these evenings and several marriages and receptions have taken place on the boats.

Owned by the Automobile Club of Michigan since the spring of 1983, Boblo is currently undergoing additional changes to enrich family entertainment. A new participatory children's area opened in 1984; a major new ride, The Falling Star, also made its debut in 1984. New walkways, improved food service, increased landscaping and a comprehensive five year plan helps insure Boblo's future.

Boblo provides a brief oasis of family fun in today's frenetic lifestyle. It is a place for quiet thoughts and picnics, renewing family ties and just having an exciting carefree day of fun. One can watch the shows on the Island, ride the miniature railroad, reserve a picnic area for a large group, thrill to the action-packed rides offered. And there is the river . . . that incredible Detroit river that has carried Indians, British troops, steamers, freighters from around the world, smaller pleasure craft and the stately Boblo boats. Today at Boblo you can be a part of yesterday in the nicest possible sense.

MICHIGAN HISTORY

Michigan was admitted to the union as its 26th state on January 26, 1937. Steven T. Mason was acting governor proclaimed with a toast "Our country always right — right or wrong, our country." The Great Lakes system, historically, was the resource that charged the growth and development we experience now. The link up with the Erie canal in the 1820's ignited the population and commerce flow into the Great Lakes system.

Michigan Sesquicentennial, 1987

The water ways moved society into the Michigan and Ontario areas. In 1820 Michigan had approximately 9,000 non-Indians, by 1830 the figure had reached 31,000. Steven T. Mason led Michigan into statehood, both Mason and our present Governor Blanchard received the "Boy Governor" designation. As historian Jean Frazier stated of Mason "a progressive thinker, astute politician, precocious thinker, social charmer — and a historical surprise.

The Constitutional Convention of 1835 had adopted the Great Seal of Michigan. The date MDCCCXXXV 1835 and the motto, which remained today "If you seek a pleasant peninsula, look around you."

The next ten years exploded from 31,639 to 212,267.

Immigrants flowed into Michigan for the rich farm soil, the fresh water and as Phillip Shaw did, purchased 160 acres of land on Section 21, township of Novi, for $800.

The many lumber mills honed out the blanks for the emerging state and the many river and lakes supplied the liquid freeway to market. The creation of Paul Bunyan tales still encompass the creative spirit of the lumbermen.

Michigan has 3,251 miles of freshwater shoreline, buckets more than any other state. 38,575 square miles. The glaciers forms the lakes and pioneers connected Mother Natures system with the opening of the Erie Canal from the Hudson River to Lake Erie in 1825, the Soo Locks in 1855 connected Lake Superior to Lake Huron. The portage Lake Canal in 1868 across the Keweenaw Peninsula The Mighty St. Lawrence Seaway in 1959 linking the Great Lakes to the oceans of the world.

SARNIA (Population 82,000)
Beautiful Bluewaterland

Home of Canada's 2nd Prime Minister, Sir Alexander Mackenzie. Sarnia developed from a small settlement known as "The Rapids", to a booming oil town in the mid-1880's. Sarnia's shipping facilities accommodating ocean vessels, were established in the early 1920's. One of the world's leading petrochemical centres and owes its growth as a highly industrialized area to a unique combination of circumstances both natural and man-made. In 1858, oil was successfully produced from a well dug to a depth of 15m (49 ft) in nearby Oil Springs, launching North America's first oil boom. 1871 saw the construction of Sarnia's first oil refinery, the forerunner of what is now known as Canada's Chemical Valley. This fantastic complex of petrochemical industries is an awe inspiring sight by day and a fairyland of lights by night.

For the yachtsman, a great day, weekend or lay over harbour. Over 1,000 berths for dockage, for the yachtless, the Sarnia-Lambton has 35 full service parks and camp grounds. The fisherman can enjoy Lake Huron, St. Clair, Sydenham, AuSable Rivers and the shores of Walpole Island for pike, pickerel, salmon, bluegill, sturgeon and musky. The "Salmon Capital of Ontario" hosts a Salmon Derby, sponsored by the Bluewater Anglers Association. The derby is approximately April 20 thru May 6 (check dates). Organizers expect $20,000 in prizes to be won. There are four categories: salmon, brown trout, rainbow trout and lake trout, 90% of the fish are salmon. For further info call the Visitors Bureau at 336-2400. Fishing charters available.

Lambton Country Music Festival, April 23 thru May 4. Over 12,000 participants from Michigan and Ontario will compete in bands, choirs and solo instrument and voice categories.

Can-Am Championship Highland games: Highland dancing, Piping and Pipe Band competition. The annual event will attract over 10,000 people with 30 bands, 300 dancers and 10 professional heavy weights. Scotland at its finest.

Mackinac Race: A great place to watch the start of the Mackinac sailboat race. The start on Lake Huron, with the party location being the Bridge Park to watch the flow of weekend warriors glide under the Bluewater Bridge. Arrive early for a good spot.

Steam Threshers Reunion: August 17-19. Brigden Fair Grounds, annual event which displays the pioneer ways of farming. Displays, demonstrations, parades and lumber sawing. Fun for the whole family.

The development of the new waterfront area provides the yachtsmen with a water community of shops and restaurants, with a touch of California dreamin'.

Scuba Diving: Interesting wrecks lying on the bottom of the St. Clair river and Lake Huron provide a great diving adventure. For information on charters and facilities, call B&J's Dive Shop.

Canatara Park: 3,000 feet of beach front on Lake Huron. 262 acres located on the shore of Lake Huron. Canatara, was the name by which the Mohawk Indians called Lake Huron, which means The Big Lake. The small lake located in the northeast section of the park is called Lake Chipican which means Lake of Roots and was regarded as sacred waters by the Mohawks.

Centennial Park and Germain Park, both elegant floral parks. Centennial Park is right on the river with picnic tables, benches and playground for children. After seeing the use of Mother Nature' accents, you have to wonder why cement was used at Hart Plaza?

Duc d' Orleans—River Boat Cruise Ship: A cruise ship for one or group charters. Sunday brunch, Sunday afternoon and Monday thru Saturday. The tradition of New Orleans again surfaces.

Indian Pow-Wow: Annual summer event, featuring Indian dancing in full costume, crafts, food. Three Indian reserves: Kettle Point, Chippewas of Sarnia Indian Reserve and Walpole Island Indian Reserve.

Farmer Market open Wednesday and Saturday morning for fresh provisions.

Sombra Township Museum, Sombra. Highlighting early nautical equipment, that was used to travel the river and lakes. Displays of pioneer tools and equipment.

Arkona Lions Indian Artifacts Museum: Contains one of the greatest collections of Indian artifacts in sotuh-western Ontario. The curator has been collecting these articles all his life, and has an outstanding reputation as an expert in this area. There are nine museums in the area.

KENT COUNTY
Museums & Special Features

"Look At Kent" – You will be warmly welcomed into the "Golden Acres" of Kent County. Use this guide to help you explore what Kent has to offer. As you drive through, you will come across both large and small communities noted for their friendliness.

Walking Tours
Chatham offers two mini walking tours for you to enjoy anytime of the year.
    1. Historical Walking Tour
    2. Chatham – King Street
For free brochures contact: Chatham and District Chamber of Commerce

River Cruise
For scaled down nautical fare, Captain Mike's Landing, located on the banks of the Thames River in Chatham is a popular summertime attraction. For families there are paddle boats, while "The Lady Thames" accomodates larger groups. This boat cruise goes up the Thames as far as Lake St. Clair.

Shopping
Chatham & Kent County offers excellent quality and selection. Browse through small town shops, boutiques, antique shops or explore one of the many specialty shops ranging from fine china to saddle shops. You will find many road side stands where you can get the freshest supply of fruit and vegetables. If you are looking for shopping malls. Chatham and Kent have many to offer. There is quite a choice, just look and see.

Dining
Treat yourself to something special today for dinner. In Kent County there are restaurants specializing in foods from around the world. Mouthwatering steak and seafood to ballpark franks the way you like them.

Flea Market
All roads lead to the "Highgate Market". It's open every Saturday and Sunday from 10 a.m. to 5 p.m. In an old country astmosphere, 35 retailers under one roof display something for everyone from doll furniture and cheese to waterbeds and wood burning stoves.

Craft & Antique Shops
There are numerous shops nestled throughout Chatham and Kent County. Discover everything from Indian crafts and weavings to antique shops. A list of specialty shops may be found in the Chatham Chamber office.

Farmers Market
Kent County noted as the "Banana Belt" has an abundance of fresh fruits and vegetables. The Farmers Market – located on Hwy. #3 has several stands offering a variety of produce.

Things To See and Do
CHATHAM CULTURAL CENTRE – Chatham
The Chatham Cultural Centre overlooking Tecumseh Park in the heart of Chatham, offers musical entertainment, live theatre and arts. For details call: 354-8338.

DRESDEN RACEWAY – Dresden – "Onatrio's Little Saratoga", is one of the most up-to-date racing locales in the country, with modern facilities for horsemen and patrons alike.

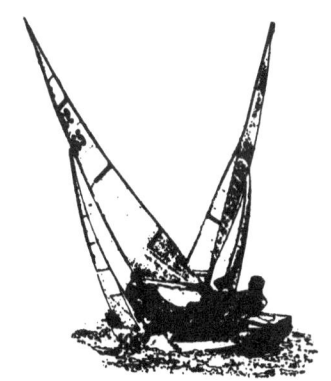

CHARAL WINERY & VINEYARDS INC. – Blenheim. Wines from this winery go to table throughout Ontario. Tours are conducted if production of the wines is taking place.

Museums
CHATHAM-KENT MUSEUM – Chatham – The Chatham Kent Museum overlooks Tecumseh Park. The salute cannon at the front of the Museum was used in the war of 1812 by the Canadians on Niagara Peninsula. Housed in the museum are Indian artifacts and an unusual bird collection as well as other memorabilia.

FAIRFIELD MUSEUM — Bothwell — This museum displays items from the site of the burnt village of Moravian Town, located three miles east of the original site. Bothwell was also the scene of an early oil boom during the American Civil War.

RALEIGH TOWNSHIP CENTENNIAL MUSEUM — North Buxton — This area is noted to be a route for the underground railroad, for the black slaves escaping the South.

RIDGEHOUSE MUSEUM — Ridgetown — A typical middle-class home in the early 1800's. It contains a wealth of items from the Victorian period, and looks as if the family who used to live here will be returning at any moment.

TILBURY WEST AGRICULTURAL MUSEUM — Tilbury — Agrilcultural tools of the past, dating back to 1880 are exhibited at this museum. This museum is located 10 km southwest of Tilbury.

UNCLE TOM'S CABIN — Dresden — In this house lived the Rev. Josiah Henson, whose early life in slavery provided much of the material for Harriet Becher Stowe's novel, "Uncle Tom's Cabin". Born in slavery, Henson escaped to freedom in Canada and established here the British American Institute for fugitive slaves.

PORT HURON/MARYVILLE (Population 70,000)

The City began in 1670 with visits by the French Priests, Fathers Dollier and Gallinee. The area was populated by the Algonquin Indian tribes (Potawatomies, Sauks, Foxes, Miamis, Chippewas, and Ottawas). LaSalle followed in 1679 and Father Louis Hennepin who arrived aboard the "Griffon". In 1686, the explorer, Duluth under order from Louis XIV of France, built Fort St. Joseph on a site just north of the Blue Water Bridge. This was fifteen years before Cadillac founded Detroit. The first permanent settlement was along the Black River in the late 1790's. In 1814 the U.S. Government built Fort Gratiot on the same site as the French had built Fort St. Joseph. The new village of five plats, Peru, Huron, Desmond, Gratiot and Fort Gratiot was incorporated as a village in 1849 and a City in 1857. In the second half of the 19th Century lumbering was the main industry followed closely by shipbuilding. As lumbering and shipbuilding dwindled, the community diversified into railroading, paper manufacturing, salt and metal industries. Regular ferry service across the St. Clair River began in 1836. The world's first electrified underwater international railway connects Port Huron Michigan with Sarnia, Ontario.

Thomas A. Edison, home town boy. Living in a home 800 feet north of the Pine Grove Park "Al" Edison began his career as inventive genius. The home is now located at Greenfield Village. The descriptions of young Edison include: industrious, friendly "one of the boys", untidy, unruly and always doing some crazy things, sound familiar? His laboratory was in the basement of his father's home, depending on whether or not his mother had thrown out his bottles and motors. Experiments that included a steam engine to drive a circular saw, which operated, but the boiler exploded. A battery machine whose charge restored unconscious persons to consciousness. The list goes on, for the next, In Search of Excellence book. Not a good formal student, but a reader. He shot off to make a living developing the practical sense of earning a buck. He became a "News Butcher" on the Grand Trunk Railway between Port Huron and Detroit. Selling papers and farm products. A journey that would explode this young man into the genius that ignited the world. Home Town Boy.

Thomas Edison Monument: located at the foot of Garfield Street at the Coast Guard Station, marks the entrance to the St. Clair River and is the oldest operating Lighthouse on the Great Lakes.

Port Huron's Port: located on the St. Clair River at 2336 Military St. There are 1,400 feet of

---

A NEW SERVICE IN TOWN
PROFESSIONAL DOCUMENTATION
& MORTGAGE SERVICES
YACHTS & COMMERCIAL BOATS

LEONARD A. MATHEWS, INC.
Vessel Documentation Service

10 S. Gratiot, Suite 201
Mt. Clemens, Michigan 48043

CALL US FOR SERVICE & RATES

(313) 468-2628
(313) 468-BOAT

Leonard A. Mathews

dock, 50,000 square feet of warehouse space and open storage with complete loading and unloading facilities, including cranes. The facility is one of the few natural deep water ports on the Great Lakes.

IN THE HEART OF THE
ST. CLAIR RIVER
DISTRICT

The　　　　　information has been included to assist you on entry to a new port. The cities surrounding Lake St. Clair and surrounding waters are as entertaining and unique as the Great Lakes.

MARINE CITY　　　　　(Population 4,423)
In the Heart of the St. Clair River District

A beautiful town settled by the French in 1786. It was known as LaBelle Riviera, Yankee Point, the Belle River, Ward's Landing, and by 1831 — Newport. In 1865, the area was incorporated as "the Village of Marine." Two years later, the name was abbreviated to Marine City. By far one of the richest cities in nautical heritage. More cargo passes Marine City than is shipped through the Suez and Panama Canals combined. Wooden shipbuilding, shipping, and lumber accent a history of boat builders that would evolve into international corporations, they started here. A community that is dedicated to the preservation of that history, with the first exhibit of an outdoor Marine Museum, being the Peche Island Lighthouse. The museum has been proposed by the Michigan Bank of Port Huron.

The city hosts numerous activities directed toward the water lover. Maritime Days is an annual summer festival, with the headline event the ANNUAL ANTIQUE and CLASSIC BOAT SHOW. The exhibit showcases a fleet of boats representing a period of artistic boat building years, from 1910 to the early 1960's, a real treat in the world of planned obsolescence. These mistresses of the Lakes, include steam power, antique outboards, inboard power and sail. An antique boat is one built from 1870 through 1970, each one being unique and built one-at-a-time.

The men and women that started the fine art of wooden boat building established the immortal names of GAR-WOOD, MARINEE BOAT CO., CHRIS-CRAFT, HACKER BOAT CO., CENTURY BOAT CO., GREAVETTE BOAT CO., MAC-CRAFT, and the ONTARIO BOAT & ENGINE WORKS, the Queen of the Waters. A boat parade is included in the Maritime festival with Ed Burch's model boats on display. Between Marine City, Algonac and Wallaceburg, this area is home port for the start of the boating business. For further information contact the Marine City Chamber of Commerce at P.O. Box 521, Marine City, MI 48039.

Blue Water International Bridge: Connects Port Huron, Michigan and Sarnia, Ontario at the foot of Lake Huron. Construction began in 1937 and opened October 19, 1938. Total completion cost was $4,500,000.00. The Canadian approach cost $697,023.29 and the center span, $2,700,000.00 and both were financed by the State of Michigan. The total length of the bridge is 8,021 feet, height above river bottom is 150 feet, to top is 210, and the width is 40 feet.

Beaches:　Lakeside Park, 3781 Gratiot Ave.
　　　　　Lighthouse Park, Conger St.
Maryville City Park: 1440 River Road, has nearly 40 acres of natural beauty, with picnic facilities overlooking the St. Clair River.

Blue Water Festival is held annually in July and accompanies the Port Huron to Mackinac Island Invitational Sail Boat Race, sponsored by the Bayview Yacht Club.

　　　　　Greater Port Huron-Marysville
　　　　　Chamber of Commerce
　　　　　920 Pine Grove Ave.
　　　　　Port Huron, MI 48060

ST. CLAIR PARKWAY

The St. Clair Parkway Commission was established July 7, 1966 by the Legislature of Ontario. In the tradition of using the natural beauty, Canada has again displayed control of the Lake. A couple hours drive along the unseen parts of Lake St. Clair, with very special treats, that are for the finding. Mitchell's Bay in the wetlands giving Lake St. Clair added uniqueness to the explorer. Bring a camera if possible for photos that U.S. urbanites won't believe is Lake St. Clair. Parks all along the route, trailers welcome. A Marine park is located at Mitchell's Bay with launching ramps, restaurant gift shop, tackle and bait shop, Canada Custom's office, land and Marine gas dock, dumping stations and fully serviced camping. When seeking a different weekend, give the Marine Park a try. The difference between a weekend at Metro Beach and Marine Park is the difference between New York City and Brighton. A perfect place for the true boating get-a-way, very low profile, peace and quiet. For those of you that want to enjoy your boat, the water and that special weekend mate, this is the place! Please respect the Canadians' spotless parks.

- - - THE ST. CLAIR PARKWAY
- G   MARINE GAS
- L   BOAT LAUNCHING RAMP
- S   MARINE SEWAGE DISPOSAL FACILITIES
- M   MOORING
- H   BOAT HOIST

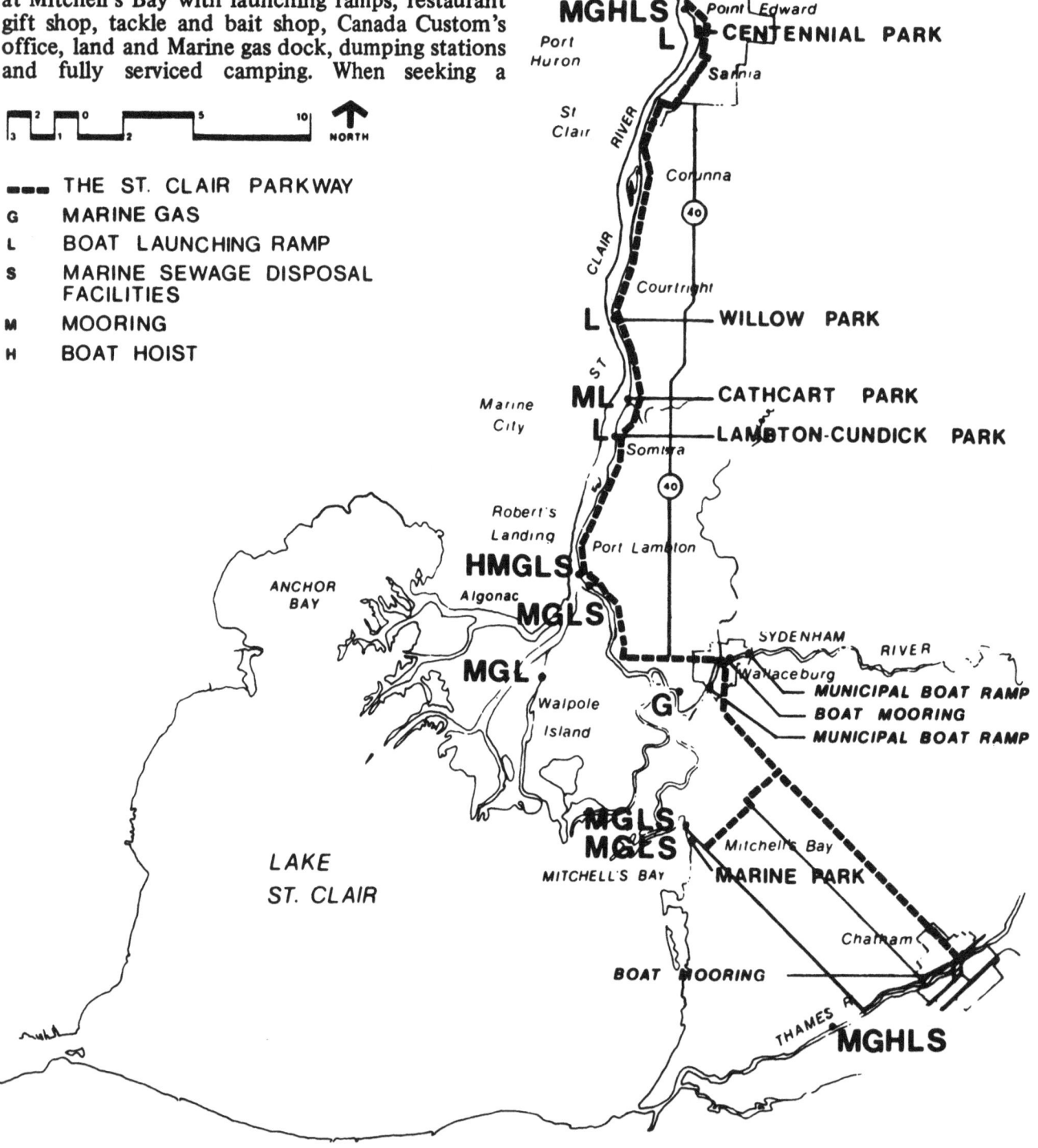

Watching these huge ships mysteriously creeping through the fog almost at your touch is just one of the many moods of the river, which is always fascinating.

Camping

The Parkway offers three campground facilities, each offering many attractive features.

Cathcart Park is situated between the Parkway and the St. Clair River. This older Park has 66 fully serviced sites. Boat launching and Boat mooring facilities are available.

Lambton Cundick Park is a newer park set back from the Parkway, still with an excellent view of the river. It has 50 fully serviced sites, a beach area, a boat launching facility, and lots of open space.

Marine Park on Mitchell's Bay offers a pleasurable setting for your camping-fishing holiday. This new facility has 80 fully serviced sites, boat mooring and boat launching facilities, and much more.

Cetennial Gardens

The gardens at Sarnia Centennial Park on Sarnia Bay are planted with 50,000 annuals each year, providing a colourful highlight to the park. A casual stroll along the riverfront walkway bestows an excellent view of the bay and its activities.

The park also features an outdoor skating rink, concession, amphitheatre, open play areas, boat launching facilities, and a meeting place at the MacLean Centre.

Parkway Golf Course

The most challenging course in southwestern Ontario

The Parkway's 18 hole championship golf course provides a challenge to the weekend golfer as well as the professional. Play a fully irrigated course with its large tees, greens, and well landscaped fairways. You will enjoy this interesting course layout, playing amid manmade lakes and bunkers on the fairways guarding the greens.

After a round of golf, drop into our dining room for something to eat or relax with friends in the pleasant atmosphere of our fully licensed lounge. Shower and change facilities are available in the clubhouse. Before leaving, make a point to visit our well equipped pro shop.

Marine Park

A different recreational experience for the whole family

Marine Park provides both land and water recreational facilities. Located at Mitchell's Bay, one of the best pan fishing areas in Ontario, this exciting new complex has 8 boat launching ramps, marine and land gas bars, Canada Customs, 240 boat wells, marine and land dumping stations, boat and motor rentals, bait and tackle shop, restaurant, serviced campsites, showers, laundry facilities, and plenty of parking for both car and car and trailer combinations. This is the ideal spot for your camping and fishing holiday, which the whole family can enjoy.

Things to See ...

This beautiful example of Victorian architecture, built in 1882 has been restored and redecorated to fit its era and now serves as head office for the St. Clair Parkway Commission. Located north of Corunna this unique building is just one of the many complimenting the Parkway.

These plaques can be found in Alexander Park, Sarnia, in honour of the second Prime Minister of Canada (1873-1878). Prior to being elected to represent Lambton County in the Legislative Assembly in 1861, Alexander MacKenzie was a well known building contractor in the Sarnia area.

The Chippewa/Ojibway nation was one of the largest populations of Indians in North America. This area of Ontario was a major crossroads of these people before European settlers arrived. A Pow Wow held annually in July attracts contestants from across Canada and the United States.

The Parkway

The St. Clair Parkway Commission operates a joint programme of parks development with the province of Ontario, the counties of Lambton and Kent, and cities of Sarnia and Chatham. Since its inception in 1966, the Commission's principal goals have been the creation of a scenic drive along the beautiful St. Clair River, to acquire as much of the natural shoreline as possible for public access to the river, and to encourage tourism to "Blue Water Country."

The Commission's efforts to preserve this natural beauty is evident in the chain of well landscaped parks bordering the river where visitors may pull off to relax and observe the pleasant view and the changing scenes of river traffic. The bright blue colour of the St. Clair River has always been a memorable experience for Parkway visitors.

For further information, Please Write:
The St. Clair Parkway Commission
Corunna, Ontario N0N 1G0
Phone: (519) 862-2291

CHATHAM (Pop. 40,952)
The Maple City

A naval dockyard in 1793, like its namesake in England, Chatham sits near the mouth of the River Thames. The history of this area has deep roots including a major battle in the War of 1812, John Brown's plotting raid on Harper's Ferry, helping to trigger the American Civil War and the establishment of a location for the "Underground railroad." Tecumseh Park named for the Shawnee chief who died in Canada's defense in 1813. The Chatham Mineral Water Company was formed in 1900 with the similar asperations that Mt. Clemans was enjoying for mineral springs. On December 15, 1900, the Daily Planet (true) the city's major newspaper, had the following report: Chatham mineral water company received charter, Officers elected. Chatham has the best mineral water in the world, though it is practically the same wate as that used at Mt. Clemens, but slightly superior. The climatic and natural advantages of Chatham over Mt. Clemens, Chatham Mineral Baths will become noted the world over. In the future, Chatham will be noted not for its maple trees but for its mineral baths, to which people will come from all over the world to seek its healing waters. The center is now the Chatham Cultural Centre. One of the hidden treasures for a weekend break. Quiet, peaceful and very civilized. Good restaurants, movie theaths, pleasuret weekend trip, about two hours by boat up the Thames from Lake St. Clair.

THAMESVILLE (Pop. 961)

The site of a Moravian mission to the Delware Indians, a 100 year old village on the Thames River. Surrounded by the ribbon farms of rural Canada, one of the only places you can see a farmer on his tractor with sea gulls perched on the tractor too.

DRESDEN (Pop. 2,550)

Located on the Sydenham River. The Rev. Josiah Henson's early life in slavery inspired Harriett Beecher Stowe's famous abolitionist novel. Uncle Tom's Cabin Museum located here. Rev. Henson escaped to Canada and establsihed the British American Institute, as a refuge and rehabilitation centre for runaway slaves. For a change of pace, the Dresden Raceway is Ontario's "Little Saratoga" for harness racing under the lights with seating for 2,000 (June-October).

MITCHELL'S BAY (Pop. 200)

The government marina is clean, well kept, with small restaurant, showers and over night dockage. It's so nice and peaceful you hate to tell people about it. For the high pressure executive or over worked Pirate that can't make it to Sam Lord's castle in Barbatos, quitely cruise over and disconnect your stereo. Sand beaches for lounging, barbeques and watching the lake roll by. Mitchells Bay is the type of harbor you can't see the Ren-Cen from. After a day or two you may not want to. Fishing and duck hunting guides and rumor has it George Perrot had a private home on one of the islands you could only get to by boat. Gas dock and small cabins scattered about for rent. To the U.S. citizen Lake St. Clair takes on a totally different dimension in these Canadian waters. Good place to turn off and tune out. You, your mate, your boat and the lake. No public nightlife and no sidewalks to roll up. Keep it a secret and keep it clean.

PORT LAMBTON (Pop. 750)

The location of a car ferry to Algonac. The St. Clair Parkway for those of you that don't have a boat or dry dock is where the Henryetta is for a week or so, the drive from Sarnia or Algonac to car ferry and Port Lampton is worth exploring. A two lane road follows the St. Clair River as she wines from small town to small town. No high rises. Fwn Island located in the River has no automobiles, but one tractor, only reached by boat. The little towns have parks, parks and more parks all spotless. Detailed maps and points of interest in this chapter.

LONDON (Pop. 254,280)

On the site of the Thames River, a large industrial city. Many museums, with artifacts dating back to 1853. Street names reminiscent of the other London. To accompany the merry old England history an authentic double-decker bus from London for daily tours of the many art galleries, and historical locations.

WALPOLE ISLAND (Pop. 2,000)

Walpole Island is an unceded Indian reserve made up of five islands. The Chippewa, Pottawatomie and Ottawa are the three tribes that inhabit the 56,000 acres. Rivers, streams flow throughout and provide an ideal habitat for game and fish. The many unique items made by the craftspeople can be purchased at the Cultural Centre in the Highbanks Park. An invitational Celebration is part of Indian culture, therefore, many tribes from the U.S. and Canada come to celebrate in this annual event. Enjoy Indian cooking, dancing, craft displays and sales. A dinner and dance top off this sacred part of our history. The Indians have observed the so called progress of the white man, to bad we didn't observe and incorporate their values and society, prior to polluting the air, water and skyrocketing our progressive violent crime rate. Buffy Ste. Marie echoes our social progress in her blood tipped songs "Now that the Bufflo is gone" and "My country 'tis of Thy people You're dying." "Now that your woundering how can it be real," you force us to send our toddlers away to your schools where there're taught to dispise their tradition, forbid them there languages then further say "that American history really began, when Columbus set sail out of Europe and stress." The sins of our fathers, and sins they are.

WALLACEBURG   (Pop. 11,223)

Located on the Sydenham River the docking and morring locations is similar to the intercostal water. Shops, restaurants, parks a nice trip with the docks right on the main street.

MOORETOWN

Located south of Sarnia the Moore Museum consists of log cabin, Victorian cottage, light house and exhibition hall. Artifacts include social, agricultural and marine development in this area.

CORUNNA   (Pop. 3,100)

The Pilot House Museum (part of a Great Lakes oil tanker centre castle) features exhibits depicting life aboard ship. One of the many small towns on the St. Clair Parkway with parks to watch the freighters go by and then see what life is like on board.

SOMBRA   (Pop. 700)

Sombra'S TOWNSHIP MUSEUM, Marine room, features more nautical exhibits of early St. Clair River ships. Sombra is also the international Port-of-entry for the ferry service crossing to the United States daily.

BELLE RIVER   (Pop. 3,150)

The Muskie capital of the world, as stated in the Guienness Book of Records. Fishing is not the only attraction Belle River offers. Famous during the Rum running days as port of departure this Port-of-call has it all. The city evolves around the river and lake activities. Many very good restaurants, beaches and hotels that offer a variety of night life. The water tower on the chart is the mark to follow. Many sights to take up and beaches with picnic and barbeque facilities. Sieur de Lamotte Cadillac, representing King Louis XIII of France at Fort Ponchartrain (now Detroit) made many voyages opening the shores of Lake St. Clair for settlement. He sent a party of soldiers to survey this region. The soldiers sighted a fairly large river suitable for landing. Commander Papineau spotted this area and stated "Qu'elle Belle Riviere." For those that don't want to get to far from provisions, newspapers and beach parties Belle River has it all.

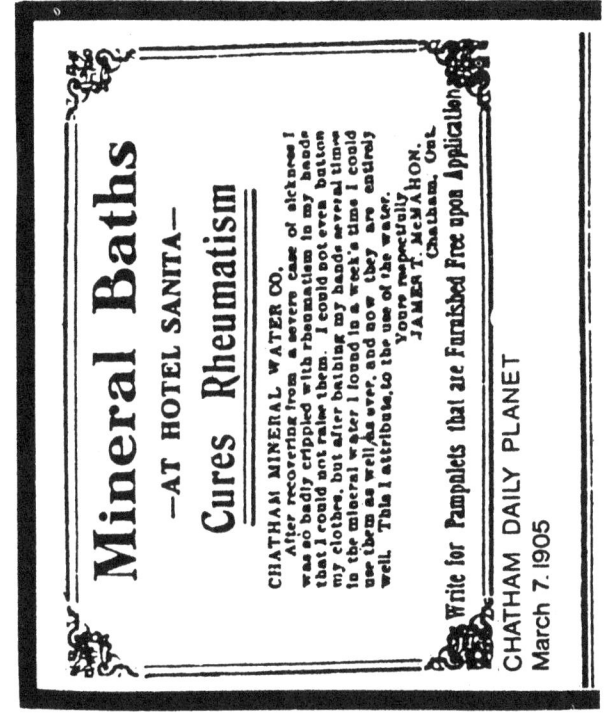

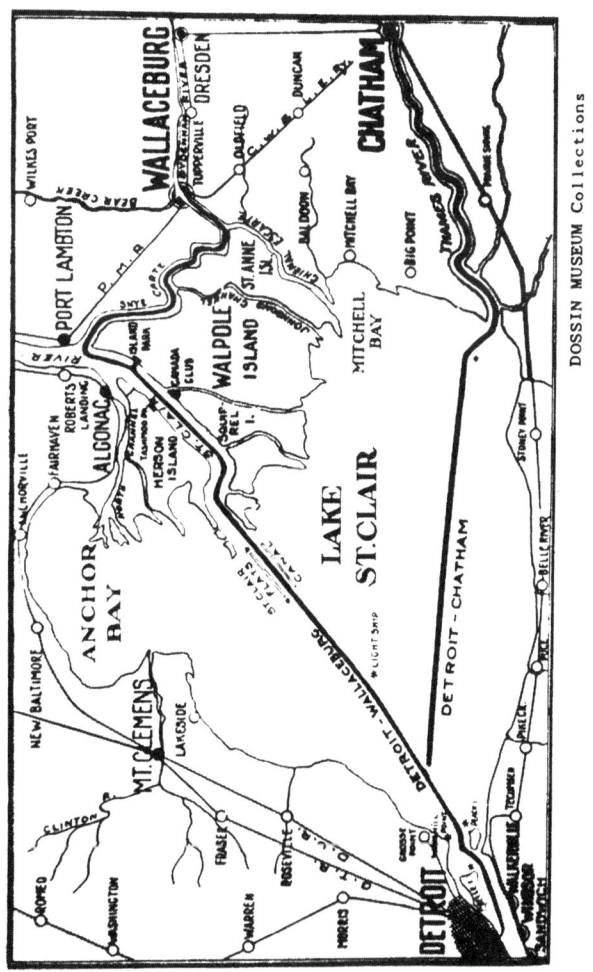

Chapter 5

AERIAL HARBOR PHOTOGRAPHS

"Just a stretch of water, and a stretch of sky,
Where white wings and clouds go scurrying by—
And over and under... there lies between
A watery meadow and a stretch of green.
                From "When Michigan Was New,"
                    Hollands A. Flanagan

ELBA-MAR BOAT CLUB

HUMBUG MARINA

HUMBUG MARINA

FORD YACHT CLUB

GROSSE ILE

FORD YACHT CLUB

WATEREDGE MARINA

WATEREDGE MARINA

RIVEREDGE MARINA   WAYNE COUNTY SHERIFF MARINE BASE
MONITOR CHANNEL 16 OR PHONE (313) 381-8100

WYANDOTTE YACHT CLUB

WYANDOTTE YACHT CLUB

BOB LO ISLAND & HARBOR

GROSSE ILE YACHT CLUB

DETROIT BOAT CLUB

MORTON FREIGHTER TERMINAL

GREAT LAKES STEEL MARINA

LA SALLE

LA SALLE

**PIER 500/MARINA CLUB
HIDDEN BOAT HARBOR/RICK'S COVE**

BAY VIEW YACHT CLUB/GREGORY MARINA

GRAYHAVEN

DETROIT BOAT BASIN

DETROIT MEMORIAL PARK MARINA

DETROIT MEMORIAL PARK MARINA

DETROIT YACHT CLUB

GROSSE POINTE CLUB

GROSSE POINTE CITY HARBOR

GROSSE POINTE PARK HARBOR

**WINDSOR YACHT CLUB HARBOR
RIVERSIDE MARINA**

LAKEVIEW PARK MARINA

GREAT LAKES YACHT CLUB/NAUTICAL MILE

ROOSTERTAIL/SINDBAD'S

KEAN'S DETROIT YACHT HARBOR
Recipient Golden Doubloon Award

BLACK RIVER/PORT HURON

BLACK RIVER/PORT HURON

BLACK RIVER/PORT HURON

SHORE CLUB HARBOR/NINE MILE LIGHT

SHORE CLUB HARBOR

GROSSE POINTE YACHT CLUB

Don't You Want the 240,000 Registered Lake St. Clair Boat Owners, to Know You're Afloat?

Contact:

Pirates Guide

for the right course.

CRESCENT SAIL YACHT CLUB

**GROSSE POINTE FARMS
MINICIPAL HARBOR**

SCHWID MARINA

SALT RIVER

CAPTAIN COVE/SURF SIDE

VELGER MARINA

ADMIRAL HARBOR

SHORE CLUB/MT. CLEMENS

BRIDGEVIEW MARINA

BRIDGEVIEW MARINA

SARNIA YACHT CLUB

SARNIA YACHT CLUB

SUNSET MARINA/HARSENS ISLAND

BLUE LAGOON/BELLE MAER MARINA

BLUE LAGOON/BELLE MAER MARINA

CLINTON RIVER

CLINTON RIVER MARINE SAFETY UNIT

NAUTICAL MILE/ST. CLAIR SHORES

ST. CLAIR MUNICIPAL HARBOR

BLACK RIVER/PORT HURON

SARNIA, ONT.

DRAWBRIDGE INN, SARNIA

DRAWBRIDGE INN, SARNIA

ST. CLAIR/LYLES MARINA

COLONY MARINE

SASSY MARINA

NORTH CHANNEL YACHT CLUB

DECKER'S

FAIR HAVEN

BELLE ISLE COAST GUARD STATION

EDGEWATER MARINE, LTD./ISLAND VIEW

THE RENDEZVOUS

WINDSOR COUNTRY CLUB

PIKE CREEK

PIKE CREEK

PUCE INLET

BELL BUOY

BELLE RIVER

RUSCOM RIVER

STONEY POINT

LIGHTHOUSE, THAMES RIVER

MARINER HARBOR, THAMES RIVER

MITCHELL'S BAY

MARINE PARK

MITCHELL'S BAY

My special thanks to the Wayne County Marine Safety Unit, 4685 W. Jefferson, Ecorse, which monitor Channel 16 or phone (313) 381-8100 and W.J. "Bing" Stroh for their time, knowledge and patience in cataloguing and labeling this section.

Chapter 6

WEATHER INFORMATION

"Red sky at night, sailor's delight, red sky in morning, sailor's take warning."
— Sailors proverb

WEATHER

Investigations still go on about the whys and hows of the sinking of the Edmund Fitzgerald on Lake Superior, November 10, 1975, when all hands were lost in a tragedy so close to the people around the Great Lakes reminding us all of the nightmares and death bad weather can produce. The facts are there, 29 sailors gone, no trace. This chapter I hope will help all of you to become better acquainted with the signs and signals of the weather to insure a pleasurable day, weekend or summer without Mother nature surprising you with her most feared personality, bad weather. The National Weather Service provides mariners with continuous broadcasts of the latest weather information from locations throughout the nation. I will not limit my printing of broadcast stations to Lake St. Clair, due to its importance, Lake St. Clair has its own locale broadcasting stations and they will be emphasized.

The National Oceanic and Atmospheric Administration was established October 3, 1970, in the U.S. Department of Commerce. The purpose of forming NOAA was to create a civil center of strength for expanding effective and rational use of ocean resources, for monitoring and predicting conditions in the atmosphere, ocean, lakes, and space, and for exploring the feasibility and consequences of environmental modification. Formation of NOAA combined the functions of:

— Environmental Science Services Administration of the Department of Commerce;

— Bureau of Commercial Fisheries, Marine Game Fish Research Program, and Marine Minerals Technology Center of the Department of the Interior;

— National Oceanographic Data Center and National Oceanographic Instrumentation Center, both administered by the Navy;

— National Data Buoy Development Project, of the Department of Transportation's Coast Guard;

— Sea Grant Program, administered by the National Science Foundation;

The Michigan Sea Grant Program is a cooperative effort of The University of Michigan and Michigan State University. Also the Michigan Sea Grant Program has a Marine Advisory Agent in St. Clair. That address is:

District Marine Advisory Agent
Cooperative Extension Service
County Building, 9th Floor
Mt. Clemens, Michigan 48043
Tel.: (313) 469-5180

— Great Lakes Survey of the Army Corps of Engineers. I could go on and on about who tells who what or when, but I'm afraid by the time I got done with this agency and that agency, the boating season would be over.

The complete story of NOAA is available by writing:

U.S. Department of Commerce
National Oceanic and Atmospheric Administration
Superintendent of Documents
U.S. Government Printing Office
Washington, D.C. 20402
Stock Number 003-017-100326-4
Price $1.50
(or get for free at the Boat Show)

The National Weather Service provides mariners with continuous broadcasts of the latest weather information. These NOAA Weather Radio transmissions repeat taped messages every four to six minutes. Tapes are up-dated periodically, usually every two to three hours, and amended as required to include the latest information. Messages include weather and radar summaries, wind observations, visibility, sea and lake conditions, and detailed local and area forecasts, as well as information tailored to the needs of boaters and others who use the water for work or recreation. When severe weather warnings are in order, routine transmissions are interrupted and the broadcast is devoted to emergency warning.

NOAA Weather Radio broadcasts on 162.40 and 162.55 MHz can usually be received within 20 to 40 miles (30 to 60 KM) from the transmitting antenna site, depending on terrain and the quality of the receiver used. Where transmitting antennas are on high ground, the range is somewhat greater, reaching 60 miles (100 KM) or more. The VHF-FM frequencies used for these broadcasts require narrow-band FM receivers. The National Weather Service recommends receivers having a sensitivity on one microvolt or less and a quieting factor of 20 decibels.

Some receivers are equipped with a warning alert device that can be turned on by means of a tone signal controlled by the National Weather Service office concerned. Include LOCAL — This signal is transmitted for 13 seconds preceding an announcement of a severe weather warning.

Weather forecasts for boating areas in the United States and Puerto Rico are issued every six hours by the National Weather Service. Each forecast covers a specific coastal area. If strong winds or sea conditions hazardous to small-boat operations are expected, forecasts include a statement as to the type of warning issued and the areas where warnings are in effect.

Similar forecasts and warnings are issued for numerous inland lakes, reservoirs, and river waterways throughout the country. Warnings of coastal and river flooding are also issued as required.

Latest forecasts are available also from commercial radio and television and marine radio telephone broadcasts. When storm and flood warnings are in effect, all stations make frequent broadcasts of these advices as a service to small craft operators, the general public, and other interests.

Broadcast schedules of radio stations, National Weather Service office telephone numbers and locations of warning display stations, are shown on Marine Weather Services Charts, issued periodically for the following areas:

COPY OF MARINE WEATHER SERVICE CHARTS

Copies of these charts are available at local mariners and marine chart dealers, or by ordering from:
>   Distribution Division (C44)
>   National Ocean Survey
>   6501 Lafayette Ave.
>   Riverdale, Maryland 20840
>   Price 25 cents

Prior to departing:

Obtain the latest available weather forecast for the boating area. Where they can be received, the NOAA Weather radio continuous broadcasts (VFH-FM) are the best way to keep informed of expected weather and sea conditions. If you hear on the radio that warnings are in effect, or see flags or lights at warning display stations, don't venture out unless you and your crew are confident that your boat can be navigated safely under forecast conditions of wind and sea.

While Afloat:

1. Keep a weather eye out for: the approach of dark, threatening clouds, which may foretell a squall or thunderstorm; any steady increase in wind or sea; any increase in wind velocity opposite in direction to a strong tidal current. A dangerous rip tide condition may form steep waves capable of broaching a boat.

2. Check radio weather broadcasts for latest forecasts and warnings.

3. Heavy static on your AM radio may be an indication of nearby thunderstorm activity.

4. If a thunderstorm catches you while afloat, you should remember that not only gusty winds, but also lightning poses a threat to safety.

— stay below deck if possible.
— keep away from metal objects that are not grounded to the boat's protection system.
— don't touch more than one grounded object at the same time (or you may become a shortcut for electrical surges passing through the protection system).
— Sailboats drop sails if under strain, use engine or small sail for some control of the craft.

It's estimated that at any given moment, nearly 2,000 thunderstorms are in progress over the earth's surface. Their frequency and their potential for violence make them one of nature's great killers and destroyers.

Thunderstorms, generated by temperature imbalances in the atmosphere, are a violent example of convection. Cooling of cloud tops, or warming of the cloud base, puts warmer, lighter air layers below colder, denser layers. The resulting instability causes convective overturning of the layers, with heavier, denser layers, sinking to the bottom and the lighter warmer air rising rapidly.

Mechanical processes are also at work. Warm, buoyant air may be forced upward by the wedge-like undercutting of a cold air mass, or by flowing up a mountain slope. Winds blowing into the center of a low pressure area may force warm air near that center upward.

In the first stage of thunderstorm development, an updraft drives warm air up to where the water vapor it contains, condenses into visible droplets and a cloud is formed. Continued upward movement produces cumulus formation; rising mounds, domes, or towers. Air flows in through the cloud's sides, mixing with and feeding the updraft. Strong winds above the developing clouds may produce a chimney effect, drawing air upward to augment the updraft.

As the cloud forms, water vapor changes to liquid and/or frozen cloud particles. This results in a release of heat that takes over as the principal source of energy for the developing cloud. Once the cloud has been formed by other forces, this release of heat helps keep it growing.

As the cloud particles grow by colliding and combining with each other, they may become rain, snow, and/or hail. Precipitation begins when they become heavy enough to fall against the updraft.

Having reached its final stage of growth, the cumulonimbus cloud, called a thunderstorm, may be several miles across its base and often towers to altitudes of 40,000 feet or more. Winds shred the cloud top into the familiar anvil form. These cloud towers are sometimes visible as lonely giants, or while moving several abreast in the form of a squall line.

This stage is also marked by a change in wind flow within the storm cells. The previaling updraft which initiated the cloud's growth is joined by a downdraft generated by precipitation. This updraft-downdraft couplet constitutes a single storm "cell." Most storms are composed of several cells that form, survive for perhaps 20 minutes, and then die. New cells may replace old ones and it's possible for some storms to last for several hours.

LIGHTNING

Man has long marveled at lightning. It was the ultimate weapon of the gods of ancient civilization. Today, lightning is subjected to scientific scrutiny, but it is no less awesome, and it still deserved respect. National Center for Health Statistics data for recent years show that lightning kills about 125 Americans per year and injures more than 500. Property loss is estimated in the hundreds of millions of dollars annually.

Lightning is an effect of electrification within a thunderstorm. As the thunderstorm develops, interactions of charged particles produce an intense electrical field within the cloud. A large positive charge is usually concentrated in the frozen upper layers of the cloud, and a large negative charge

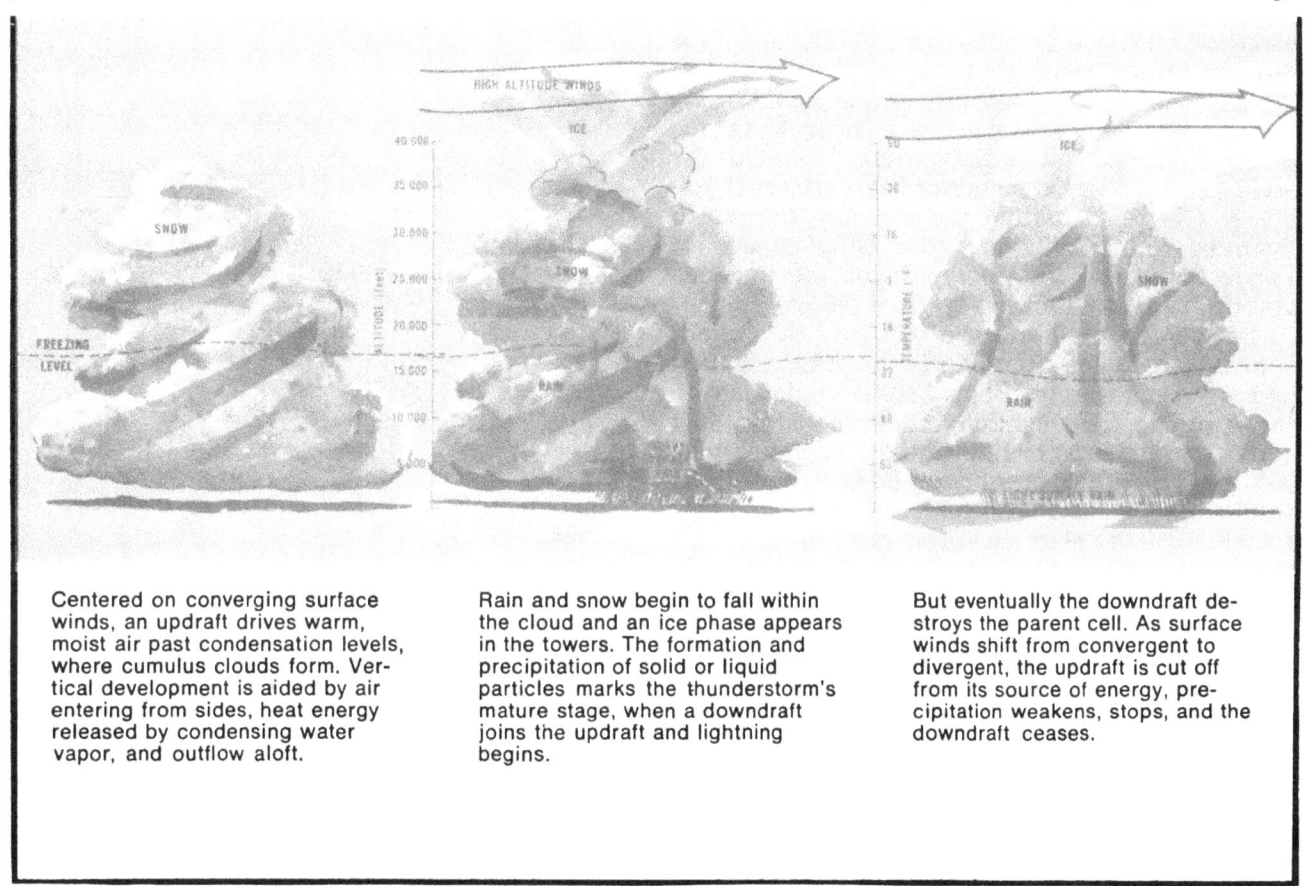

Centered on converging surface winds, an updraft drives warm, moist air past condensation levels, where cumulus clouds form. Vertical development is aided by air entering from sides, heat energy released by condensing water vapor, and outflow aloft.

Rain and snow begin to fall within the cloud and an ice phase appears in the towers. The formation and precipitation of solid or liquid particles marks the thunderstorm's mature stage, when a downdraft joins the updraft and lightning begins.

But eventually the downdraft destroys the parent cell. As surface winds shift from convergent to divergent, the updraft is cut off from its source of energy, precipitation weakens, stops, and the downdraft ceases.

On the ground directly beneath the storm system, this stage is often accompanied by strong gusts of cold wind from the downdraft, or heavy precipitation rain or hail. Lightning always accompanies the thunderstorm. These are nature's warnings that the thunderstorm is in its most violent stage. Tornadoes may also be associated with the thunderstorm.

Even so, the thunderstorm cell has already begun to die. The violent downdraft, having shared the circulation with the sustaining updraft, now strangles it. Precipitation weakens, and the cold downdraft ceases. The thunderstorm cell, a short-lived creature, spreads and dies.

along with a smaller positive area is found in the lower portions.

The earth is normally negatively charged with respect to the atmosphere. But as the thunderstorm passes over the ground, the negative charge in the base of the cloud induces a positive charge on the ground below and for several miles around the storm. The ground charge follows the storm like an electical shadow, growing stronger as the negative cloud charge increases. The attraction between positive and negative charges makes the positive ground current flow up buildings, trees, and other elevated objects in an effort to establish a flow of current. But air, which is a poor conductor of electricity, insulates the cloud and ground charges are built up.

Lightning occurs when the difference between positive and negative charges, becomes great enough to overcome the resistance of the insulating air, and force a conductive path for current flow between the two charges. Potential in these cases can be as much-as 100 million volts. Lightning on the water can be a very dangerous situation. When lightning strikes the water by a boat it can give the same effects of an explosion. If lightning is striking by your vessel, be sure to handle only the parts on the boat that are wood or fiberglass. The metal or aluminum parts will carry the electricity and electrocute you, if you are holding on to any of these parts. Move slowly only when you have to. I have been electrocuted once down in Florida and it was almost death. It was from a break in an electrical cord and once the cord hit the metal toe rail, the power tool froze to my hand and just shot electricity thru my body. The main trouble with this situation is you can't get loose from the current, it locks you to the current. If you hit the water, you die or have a minor heart attack. If you are ever in this situation try and stop the power from its source or swing your body enough to knock the power tool loose. If you see someone and can't get the tool loose, use a piece of lumber to free it, don't grab it, or it will send the current thru both people. Lightning is the same situation and just as dangerous. Boats act like a magnate to the lightning, like lightning rods on barns. Stay away from the mast or flying bridge when lightning is hitting. Electrical storms can be just as deadly as wind storms. I have been told there is a glow that sometimes takes place on sailboats during electrical storms, it is called St. Elmo's fire. The electricity circles the spar and just hovers around the mast throwing off different colors and hissing. The most common advise I can give, is try to get out of the storm region, put things that could catch on fire down below and don't touch the metal objects if possible.

Persons struck by lightning receive a severe electrical shock and may be burned, but they carry no electrical charge and can be handled safely. Even someone "killed" by lightning can be revived by prompt action. When a group has been struck, the apparently dead should be treated first. The American National Red Cross says that if a victim is not breathing, first aid should be rendered immediately to prevent irrevocable damage to the brain. Give mouth to mouth resuscitation once every five seconds to adults and once every three seconds to infants and small children.

If the victim is not breathing and had no pulse, cardiopulmonary resuscitation — a combination of mouth to mouth resuscitation and external cardiac compression — is necessary. This treatment should be administered only by persons with proper training. Victims who appear only stunned or otherwise unhurt may also need attention. Check for burns, especially at fingers and toes, and next to buckles and jewelry.

TORNADOES

The most violent of thunderstorms is the tornado. The one thing I can tell you is you will know when this beast is going to appear. It is a violently rotating column of air which descends from a thunderstorm cloud system. Tornadoes move anywhere from 30 to 200 miles per hour. In

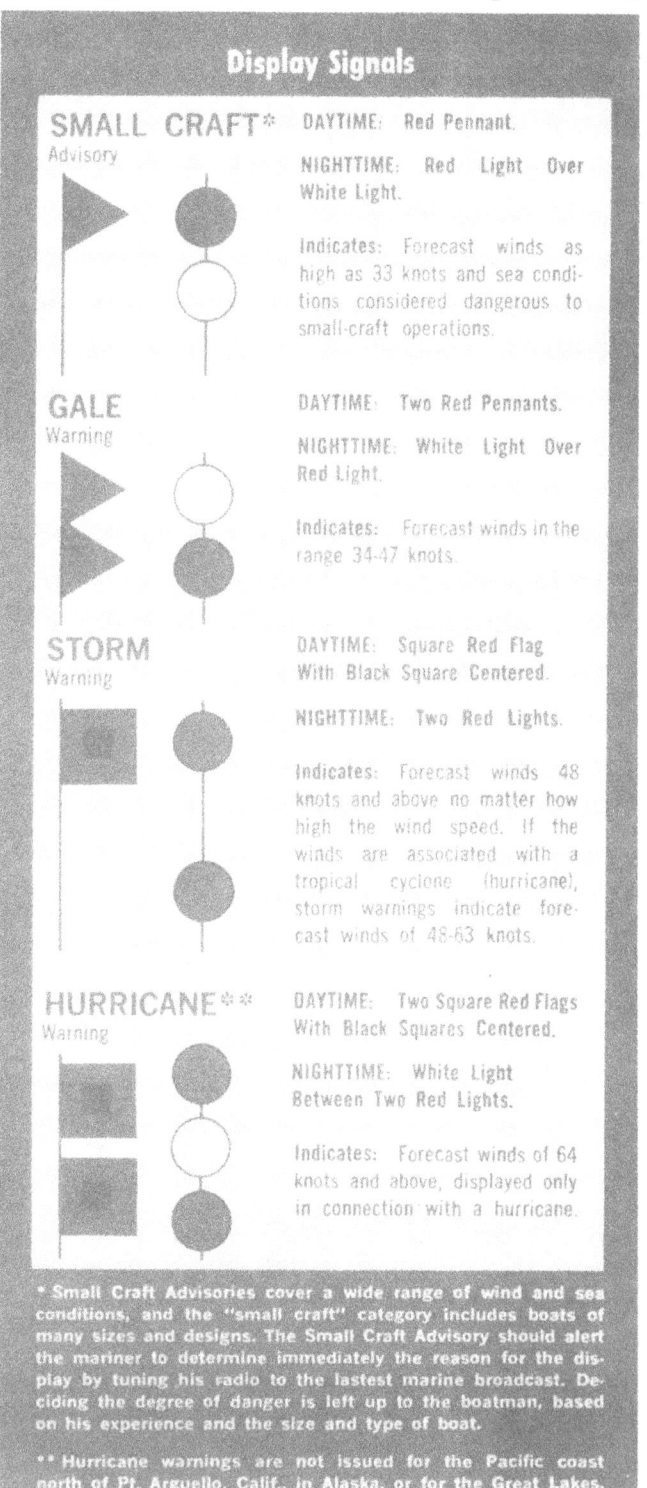

an average year, tonadoes in the United States claim about 100 lives. If you are on the water and in the path of a tornado, the only thing to do is batten down the hatches, take down the sails, and go below. A friend of mine went through a hurricane off the coast of Florida. Once the storm had pased over, seven coats of varnish were gone and only bare wood left on the bright work. The worst time for these storms to hit is at night. If things start to get still and the sky color starts to change, head for home or another safe port, till it blows over.

FOG

Warm air passes over a colder surface and the result is the fog. The main danger in fog is naturally the inability to see. In most cases it is suggested that you move very slowly and try and hear other boats or fog horns, stay out of main traffic flows and follow radar or loran units for navigation.

Distress signals for the water:
1. Wave arms slowly up and down.
2. Wave orange flag.
3. Sound horn, bell or whistle repeatedly
4. Set off orange colored smoke signal.
5. Use red rocket or flare.
6. Display orange and black cloth.
7. Send MAY DAY on radio.
8 Blink flashlight or white light S.O.S.

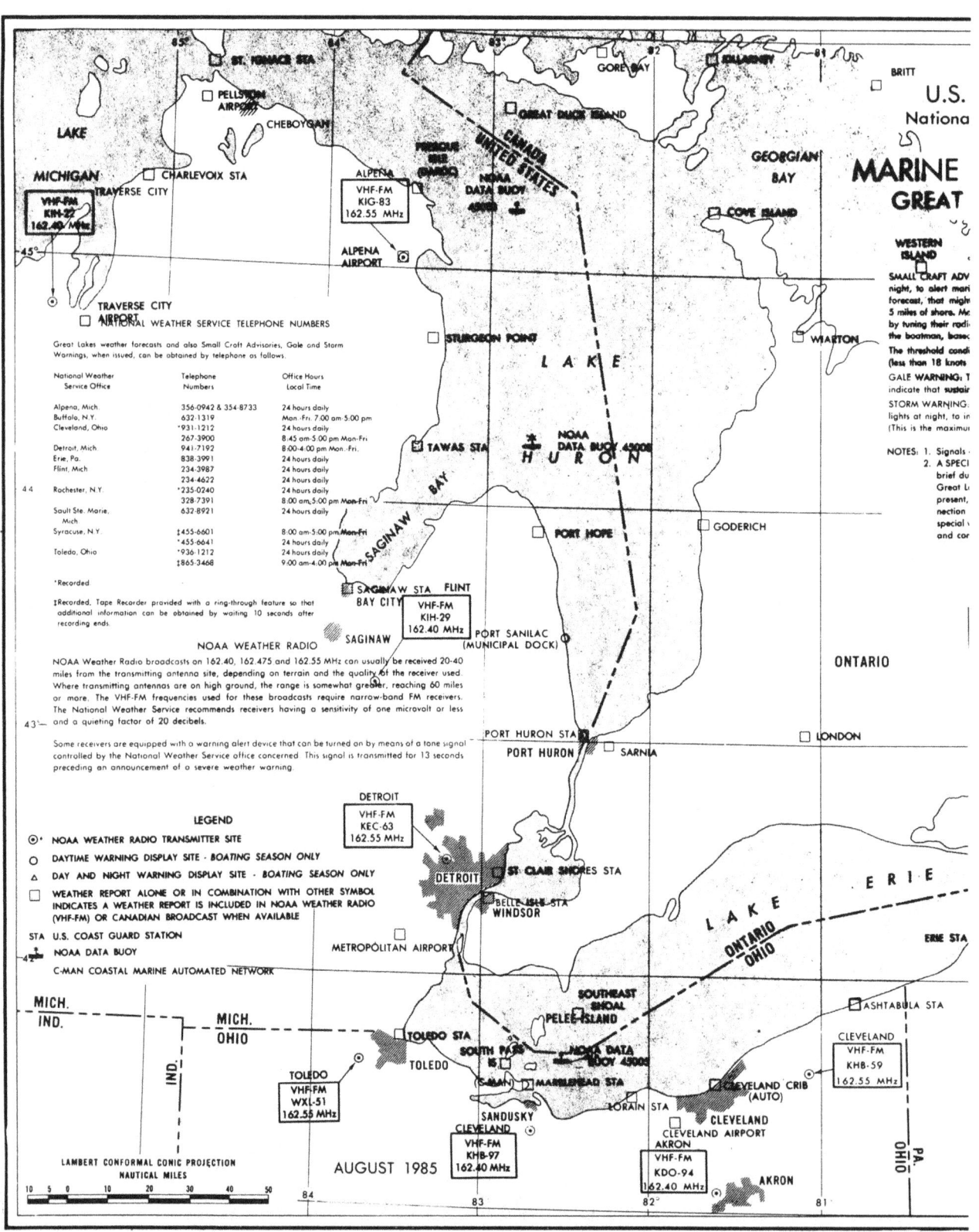

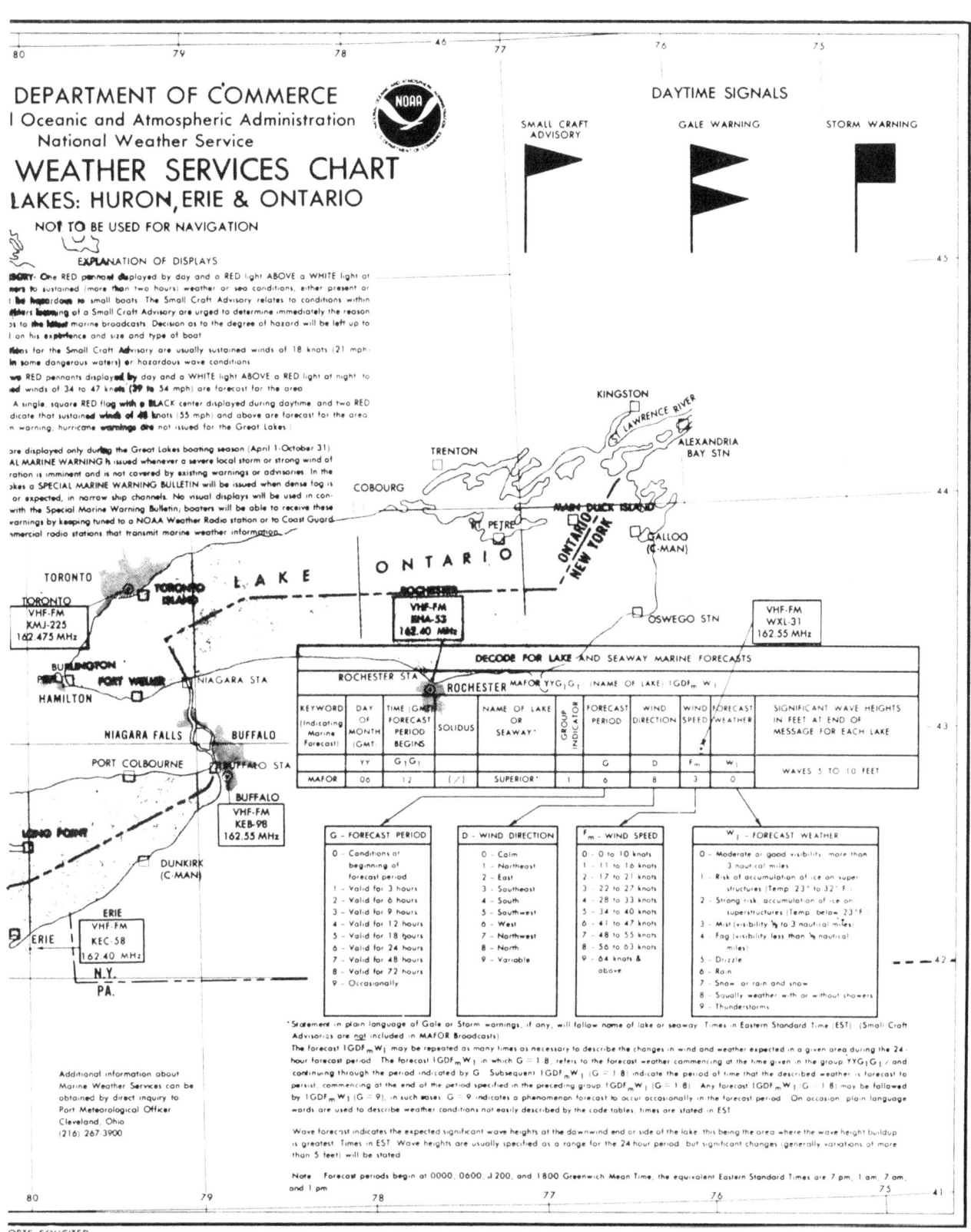

NOAA WEATHER RADIO BROADCASTS

City	Station	Frequency	Broadcast Times
Akron, Ohio	KDO-94	162.40 MHz	24 hours daily
Alpena, Mich.	KIG-83	162.55 MHz	24 hours daily
Buffalo, N.Y.	KEB-98	162.55 MHz	24 hours daily
Cleveland, Ohio	KHB-59	162.55 MHz	24 hours daily
Clio, Mich.	KIH-29	162.40 MHz	24 hours daily
Detroit, Mich.	KEC-63	162.55 MHz	24 hours daily
Erie, Penn.	KEC-58	162.40 MHz	24 hours daily
Rochester, N.Y.	KHA-53	162.40 MHz	24 hours daily
Sandusky, Ohio	KHB-97	162.40 MHz	24 hours daily
Sault Ste. Marie, Mich.	KIG-74	162.55 MHz	24 hours daily
Syracuse, N.Y.	WXL-31	162.55 MHz	24 hours daily
Traverse City, Mich.	KIH-22	162.40 MHz	24 hours daily

These NOAA Weather Radio stations, locations shown on the front, are managed by National Weather Service. Broadcast tapes are updated every 3 to 6 hours and amended as required; contents vary, but in general, contain the following information:

1. Forecasts for the U.S. portion of nearby land areas.
2. Marine forecasts, advisories and warnings for appropriate lake or near shore areas.
3. Weather observations from selected National Weather Service and Coast Guard stations.
4. Radar reports when pertinent.
5. Local weather observations and forecast.
6. Special bulletins and summaries concerning severe weather.

GREAT LAKES WEATHER BROADCASTS

	STATION	CALL SIGN	FREQUENCY (MHz)	LAWEB	MAFOR	GALE & STORM ③WARNINGS	PLAIN LANGUAGE LAKE FORECASTS
LORAIN ELECTRONICS CORP	Ripley, NY	KIL 929	156.850-CH 17	2:30 & 8:30 am & pm EST	②12:02 & 6:02 am & pm EST	On Receipt and every 30 mins for 2 hours	
	Cleveland, OH	KQU 440	156.850-CH 17	"	"	"	
	Lorain, OH	WMI	161.900-CH 26	"	"	"	
	Oregon, OH	KIL 928	156.850-CH 17	"	"	"	
	Algonac, MI	KIL 927	156.850-CH 17	"	"	"	
	Harbor Beach, MI	KIL 926	156.850-CH 17	"	"	"	
	Alpena, MI	KIL 925	156.850-CH 17	"	"	"	
	Pickford, MI	KIL 923	156.850-CH 17	"	"	"	
CENTRAL RADIO	Rogers City, MI	WLC	2514 kHz-CH 57 4369.8 kHz 161.900-CH 26	④8:45 am & pm, 2:45 pm EST	6:17 am & pm, 12:17 pm EST	On Receipt and 45 min past even hours 0500-2200 EST only	
	Tawas City, MI	WLC (SLAVE)	161.900-CH 26	"	"		
	Sault Ste Marie, MI	WLC (SLAVE)	"	"	"		
U.S. COAST GUARD	Sault Ste Marie, MI	NOG	157.100-CH 22			Every 3 hours Beginning at 12:05 am	Every 3 hours following the warnings broadcast
	Buffalo, NY	NMD 47	"			Every 3 hours Beginning at 2:55 am	Every 3 hours following the warnings broadcast
	Detroit, MI	NMD 25	"			Every 3 hours Beginning at 1:55 am	
	Alexandria Bay	NMD 35	"			Every 3 hours Beginning at 2:35 am	
CANADIAN COAST GUARD	Cardinal	VDQ	161.65-CH 21B				Continuous broadcast of forecasts for Lake Ontario and St. Lawrence River; Port Weller, Pt. Petre, Kingston, Trenton, Cobourg, Toronto Island, and Han
	(Kingston)	"	161.775-CH 83B				
	(Cornwall)	"	161.775-CH 83B				
	Toronto	VBG	161.775-CH 83B				Continuous broadcast of forecasts for Lakes Ontario and Erie, and LAWEB obs Toronto I., Pt Petre, Colbourg, Port Dover, Hamilton, Trenton, Kingston, Main Ontario, Erie, and Simcoe.
	(Cobourg)	"	161.65-CH 21B				"
	(Font Hill)	"	161.775-CH 83B				"
	(Orillia)	"	161.65-CH 21B				"
	Port Burwell Sarnia	VBE	161.65-CH 21B				Continuous broadcast of forecasts for Lakes Ontario, Erie, and Huron; weather Dover, Port Colborne; Lake Erie Ships, and Buoy 45005.
	(Port Burwell)	"	161.65-CH 21B				
	(Leamington)	"	161.775-CH 83B				Continuous broadcast of forecasts for Lakes Superior, Huron, and Erie; wec Goderich, South East Shoal, Gt. Duck, Wiarton, Windsor, Port Colborne, Data
	(Kincardine)	"	161.775-CH 83B				
	Sault Ste Marie	VBB	161.65-CH 21B				Continuous broadcast of forecasts for Lakes Huron, Superior and Georgian I., Slate I., Great Duck, Cove I., Sault Ste Marie; and Lakes Superior and
	(Bald Head)	"	161.775-CH 83B				
	(Silverwater)	"	161.775-CH 83B				
	Wiarton	VBC	161.65-CH 21				"
	(Meaford)	"	161.775-CH 83B				Continuous broadcast of forecasts for Lakes Huron, Superior, and Georgia Great Duck I., Wiarton, Goderich, Sarnia, Gore Bay, Data Buoys, and Lak
	(Tobermory)	"	161.775-CH 83B				"
	(Killarney)	"	161.65-CH 21B				"
	(Pt. Au Baril)	"	161.65-CH 21B				"

NOTES: 1. The LAWEB contains plain language reports of wind direction and speed (in knots) and wave heights from shore stations in the Lake Region and ships underway on the Lakes. Ships' positions are given in distance in miles and direction from well-known landmarks; visibility and weather are included in all reports when visibility is less than 5/8 of a mile. Observations are taken 1½ hours prior to the times of broadcast.

MARINER REPORTING PROGRAM

The National Weather Service (NWS) has established a nationwide Mariner Report Program – MAREP – to help improve marine warnings and forecasts.

Through this cooperative effort, professional mariners make radio reports of sea and wind conditions to NWS marine forecasters. If you would like to participate or learn more about this volunteer program, please call:

NWS Cleveland   (216) 267-3900

LAND STATION WEATHER REPORTS BROADCAST DURING GREAT LAKES WEATHER BROADCAST (LAWEB)

LAKE SUPERIOR
- Sault Ste. Marie
- Whitefish Point
- Grand Marais, Mi.
- Marquette
- Copper Harbor
- Portage
- Ontonagon
- Duluth
- Grand Marais, Mn.
- Thunder Bay, Ont.
- Slate Island
- Caribou Island

LAKE MICHIGAN
- Frankfort
- Ludington
- Muskeegon
- St. Joseph
- Michigan City
- Dunne Crib
- Kenosha
- Milwaukee
- Sheboygan
- Gills Rock
- Green Bay
- Escanaba
- Seul Choix Pt.
- Twin Rivers
- Sturgeon Bay

LAKE HURON
- St. Clair Shores
- Port Huron
- Cheboygan
- Port Hope
- Saginaw
- Sturgeon Point
- Presque Isle
- Tawas Point
- Alpena
- St. Ignace
- Detour Passage
- Gore Bay
- Great Duck Island
- Cove Island
- Wiarton
- Goderich
- Sarnia

LAKE ERIE
- Buffalo
- Erie
- Ashtabula
- Cleveland Crib
- Lorain
- Marblehead
- Toledo
- Belle Isle
- Southeast Shoal
- London, Ont.
- Long Point
- Port Colborne

LAKE ONTARIO
- Alexander Bay
- Oswego
- Rochester
- Niagara
- Port Weller
- Toronto Island
- Trenton
- Main Duck Island
- NOAA Data Buoys

WEATHER BROADCASTS BY AIR NAVIGATION RADIO STATIONS

Airways and pilot weather reports, including aviation advices as issued, are transmitted by stations on schedules and frequencies as follows:

City	Station	Freq. (kHz)	Schedules
Cleveland, Ohio	CLE	344	Continuous broadcast
Detroit, Mich.	DTW	388	Continuous broadcast
Sault Ste. Marie,	CPW	400	5:00 am-10 pm

OTHER MARINE WEATHER SERVICES CHARTS AVAILABLE

MSC-1	Eastport, Me. to Montauk Point, N.Y.	MSC-8	Mexican Border to Point Conception, Calif.
MSC-2	Montauk Point, N.Y. to Manasquan, N.J.	MSC-9	Point Conception, Calif. to Point St. George, Calif.
MSC-3	Manasquan, N.J. to Cape Hatteras, N.C.	MSC-10	Point St. George, Calif. to Canadian Border
MSC-4	Cape Hatteras, N.C. to Savannah, Ga.	MSC-11	Great Lakes: Michigan and Superior
MSC-5	Savannah, Ga. to Apalachicola, Fla.	MSC-12	Great Lakes: Huron, Erie and Ontario
MSC-6	Apalachicola, Fla. to Morgan City, La.	MSC-13	Hawaiian Waters
MSC-7	Morgan City, La. to Brownsville, Tex.	MSC-14	Puerto Rico and Virgin Islands
		MSC-15	Alaskan Waters

Copies of these charts are available from:

National Ocean Service
Distribution Branch (N/CG33)
Riverdale, MD 20737
Telephone: 301-436-6990

Nautical charts for navigation purposes for these coastal areas are available from local marinas, marine supply stores and above address.

For information on water levels direct inquiries to Dept. of the Army, Detroit District Corps of Engineers, Detroit, Michigan 48231.

RADIO FACSIMILE	LAKE W	F	REMARKS
① 10:00 am & pm EST	ALL		① Broadcast on public correspondence channels after preliminary call on CH 16.
	"		② MAFOR includes Plain Language Synopsis.
	"		③ All warnings are preceded by call on CH 16.
	"		
	"		
	S, M, H	ALL	④ LAWEB is broadcast over Central Radio Stations in Fall and Winter and during periods of inclement weather in Spring and Summer.
	"	"	
	"	"	
	S, M, H	H, M	⑤ O = Ontario
			E = Erie
	E, O	E, O	S = Superior
			M = Michigan
			H = Huron
	ST.C, E, H		ST.C = St. Clair
			ST.L = St. Lawrence River
	ST.L		
			Warning broadcast on receipt & continuously there after.

LAWEB observations from Main Duck I., ...ilton.

...ervations for Port Colborne, Port Weller, Duck and ship observations from Lakes

...observations from Southeast Shoal, Port

...ther observations from Cove I., Sarnia, Buoys, and Lakes Erie and Huron Ships.

...Bay. Weather observations for Caribou Huron Ships.

...n Bay. LAWEB observations for Cove I., e Huron Ships.

143

Strongest One-Minute Winds as Reported From Anemometer – Equipped Vessels Since 1940
(Source is the Great Lakes Pilot 1970)

Lake	Superior	Michigan	Huron	St. Clair	Erie	Ontario
Record Speed (knots)	81	58	95	61	87	50
Direction	NW	WSW	WNW	S	NNW	WNW
Date of Record	June 25/50	Nov 16/55	Aug 6/65	July 14/63	July 4/69	Nov 12/64

SARNIA, ONTARIO 43°00'N., 82°18'W.

		JAN	FEB	MAR	APR	MAY	JUN	JUL	AUG	SEP	OCT	NOV	DEC	YEAR
Temperature														
Daily Maximum Temperature	°C	-1.9	-0.6	4.4	11.8	17.9	23.5	26.2	25.4	21.7	15.4	7.9	1.1	12.7
Daily Minimum Temperature	°C	-9.4	-8.3	-3.2	2.3	6.8	12.8	15.6	15.0	11.3	5.7	0.4	-5.3	3.6
Daily Temperature	°C	-5.7	-4.5	0.6	7.1	12.4	18.1	20.9	20.3	16.5	10.5	4.2	-2.2	8.2
Extreme Maximum Temperature	°C	11.1	14.5	22.7	28.5	32.1	37.8	36.6	34.4	34.0	29.4	23.3	17.8	37.8
Extreme Minimum Temperature	°C	-28.9	-26.9	-25.6	-10.0	-3.0	-1.1	6.1	4.7	-1.1	-8.9	-12.8	-20.6	-28.9
Precipitation														
Rainfall	mm	22.3	21.6	41.5	75.1	69.2	81.1	65.8	55.3	68.2	54.1	61.8	38.4	654.4
Snowfall	cm	28.8	23.7	22.0	6.1	0.4	0.0	0.0	0.0	0.0	3.8	16.1	38.0	138.9
Total Precipitation	mm	52.4	45.3	61.9	90.6	67.2	67.2	60.6	51.3	62.7	59.9	77.6	81.6	778.3
Greatest Rainfall in 24 hours	mm	24.9	26.7	46.2	49.5	30.0	64.8	34.0	43.7	35.0	63.8	28.2	37.6	64.8
Greatest Snowfall in 24 hours	cm	23.6	15.7	33.3	16.5	T	0.0	0.0	0.0	0.0	17.8	18.5	22.4	33.3
Greatest Precipitation in 24 hours	mm	31.4	26.9	46.2	49.5	30.0	64.8	34.0	43.7	35.0	63.8	28.2	37.6	64.8
Days with														
Rain		4	4	7	11	11	11	10	9	10	9	10	6	102
Snow		11	9	7	2	0	0	0	0	0	1	5	10	45
Precipitation		13	11	13	12	11	11	10	9	10	10	13	15	138
Fog														
Thunder		0.2	0.3	1.1	2.6	3.5	6.1	6.1	4.6	3.6	0.9	0.5	0.4	29.9
Mean Sea Level Pressure kPa		101.7	101.8	101.6	101.6	101.5	101.4	101.6	101.7	101.7	101.8	101.7	101.7	101.7
Relative Humidity %		79	78	77	68	68	70	70	72	72	72	77	80	74
Cloud Amount Scale 0-10														

		JAN	FEB	MAR	APR	MAY	JUN	JUL	AUG	SEP	OCT	NOV	DEC	YEAR
Wind														
Percentage Frequency	N	2.4	5.5	7.2	14.8	15.3	14.5	10.8	8.7	8.6	5.4	2.2	3.1	8.2
	NNE	1.7	4.5	5.0	10.1	10.4	8.5	9.2	8.9	5.7	3.3	1.3	2.3	5.9
	NE	3.1	3.2	4.1	6.2	6.2	4.6	5.7	4.8	4.3	2.0	1.5	1.8	4.0
	ENE	2.1	3.8	2.3	2.6	2.4	1.8	2.3	2.3	2.6	2.3	1.5	3.1	2.4
	E	2.4	4.8	4.4	2.9	2.4	1.7	2.1	2.4	3.7	3.6	3.9	3.1	3.1
	ESE	3.5	2.8	3.8	3.2	2.4	1.4	1.6	2.2	3.4	3.2	3.5	5.2	3.0
	SE	4.2	3.5	5.8	4.9	4.3	2.9	2.2	2.5	3.7	4.1	4.3	4.9	3.9
	SSE	4.7	3.4	6.4	4.0	6.1	6.3	4.4	4.7	5.2	6.2	5.5	4.8	5.1
	S	14.0	13.8	12.6	10.5	11.6	13.5	13.4	15.9	16.5	15.4	14.8	13.9	13.8
	SSW	9.0	7.2	8.2	7.5	7.7	12.5	12.3	11.9	9.9	11.8	11.9	10.4	10.0
	SW	7.5	4.4	4.2	3.9	3.5	7.0	6.7	6.1	5.1	5.9	7.8	7.0	5.8
	WSW	9.4	7.1	4.6	4.1	3.3	4.5	5.1	5.0	5.5	6.7	9.8	9.3	6.2
	W	17.3	12.3	9.6	6.5	5.5	5.5	6.6	5.9	7.3	10.7	14.3	14.2	9.7
	WNW	9.1	10.0	6.7	4.3	3.5	2.7	3.5	3.4	4.9	6.3	6.9	6.7	5.7
	NW	5.1	6.8	6.9	4.4	3.8	2.9	3.0	3.0	4.1	6.1	5.8	5.5	4.8
	NNW	2.3	2.9	4.4	5.2	5.4	4.1	4.1	3.5	4.1	3.5	2.7	2.1	3.7
	Calm	2.2	4.0	3.8	4.9	6.2	5.6	7.4	8.8	5.4	3.5	2.3	2.6	4.7
Mean Speed (knots)	N	10.3	11.9	11.4	11.9	9.2	8.7	8.3	7.9	9.4	10.8	11.5	15.1	10.5
	NNE	9.7	11.4	9.2	9.6	8.6	7.6	7.7	7.5	7.8	8.1	9.5	11.0	9.0
	NE	11.1	8.3	8.4	8.7	7.0	7.1	6.2	6.3	7.4	8.5	7.4	9.5	8.0
	ENE	7.8	6.4	9.0	7.9	7.0	5.7	4.5	4.6	5.7	7.7	6.8	7.0	6.7
	E	11.3	6.0	8.6	6.3	6.7	4.6	3.9	4.4	4.9	7.1	7.7	6.7	6.1
	ESE	7.7	7.0	8.3	11.1	7.5	6.1	5.9	6.5	5.7	6.6	6.9	8.8	7.3
	SE	7.3	8.6	9.6	11.6	8.2	7.0	4.7	4.9	6.0	6.5	7.0	8.0	7.4
	SSE	8.5	7.2	8.7	8.5	7.8	7.5	4.6	5.1	5.6	6.4	7.0	6.7	7.0
	S	8.2	9.3	9.6	8.3	7.7	7.6	5.3	5.3	5.9	7.3	7.9	8.2	7.6
	SSW	9.8	9.4	11.7	9.9	9.0	8.8	7.0	6.9	7.4	8.8	9.1	9.8	9.0
	SW	9.6	10.1	10.8	10.1	8.5	8.3	6.6	7.0	7.3	8.3	9.2	9.4	8.8
	WSW	10.5	9.2	10.0	12.4	9.2	9.2	7.1	6.3	6.6	7.5	9.3	9.2	8.9
	W	10.7	11.1	11.1	11.8	10.5	9.0	7.4	5.9	7.3	8.6	9.7	10.2	9.4
	WNW	13.4	11.6	13.1	11.9	8.4	7.9	7.4	6.3	8.8	10.3	10.7	13.0	10.3
	NW	14.4	11.8	13.2	12.0	8.4	8.1	7.6	8.1	9.3	11.4	13.3	15.0	11.1
	NNW	12.7	10.0	11.7	12.3	7.9	8.3	7.3	8.1	10.1	11.2	12.4	12.8	10.4
	All Directions	9.9	9.4	10.1	9.9	7.9	7.6	6.2	5.9	6.9	8.1	8.9	9.6	8.4
Extremes	Maximum Hourly Speed													
		35.0	29.1	34.0	38.3	32.9	30.2	28.6	23.2	30.2	25.9	44.8	50.2	50.2
		SVL	NW	SW	WSW	N	WSW	WSW	SW	N	N	SW	NW	NW
	Maximum Gust Speed													
		50.2	41.0	54.0	56.1	50.2	46.9	54.0	46.9	41.0	39.9	52.9	58.9	58.9
		SVL	W	SW	W	NNE	W	WNW	WSW	WNW	WNW	SW	NW	NW

Notes: SVL — more than one occurrence of the same speed.
T — trace amount — less than 0.1 mm liquid precipitation or less than 0.1 cm snowfall.
kPa — kilopascals = mb ÷ 10.
Number of days with, under precipitation, indicates days with falls of 0.2 mm or more of rain, 0.2 cm or more of snow and 0.2 mm or more of water equivalent.

Someone told me long ago,
  there's a calm before the storm . .
            Credence Clearwater Revival

Mafor Weather Decoding Chart

DECODE FOR LAKE AND SEAWAY MARINE FORECASTS

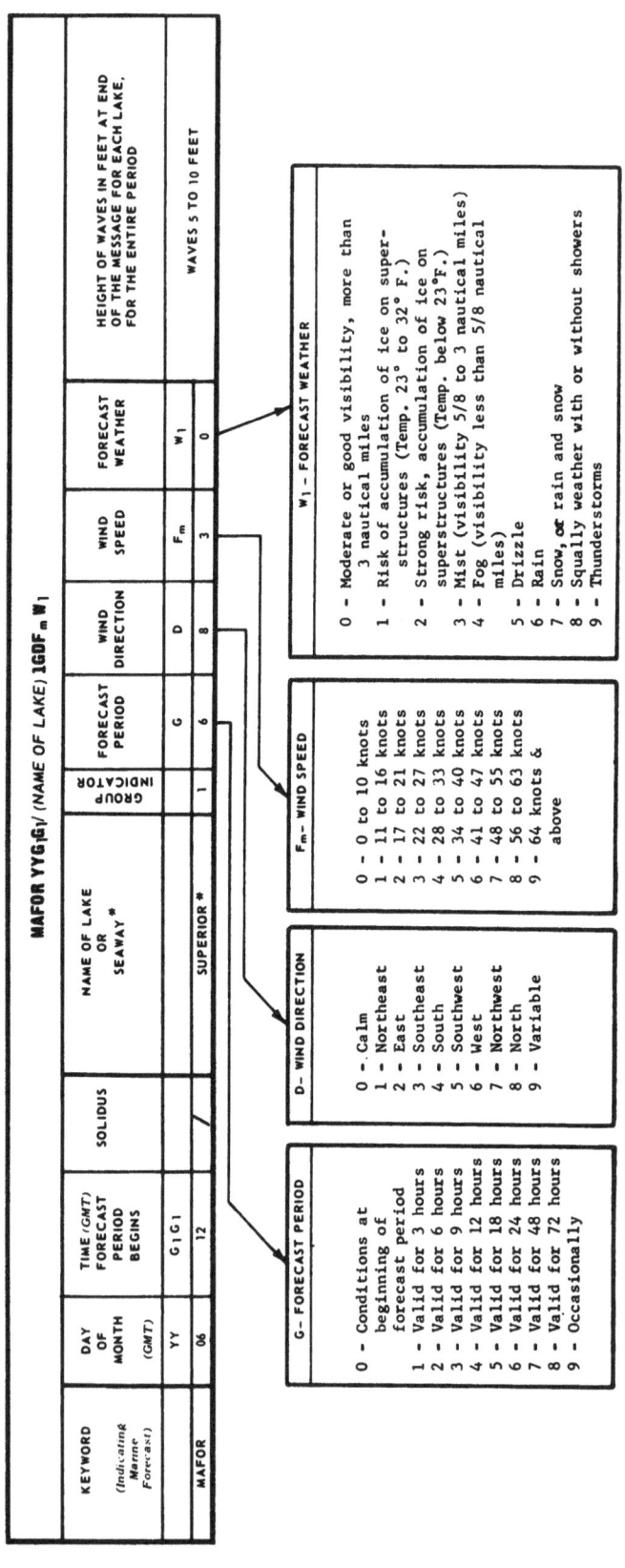

Recreational boating forecasts are given every six hours at 6:45 and 12:45 a.m. and p.m., EST, on 162.55 $_mH_2$.

WEATHER INFORMATION CAN BE OBTAINED FROM THESE OFFICES IN ONTARIO

OFFICE	Telephone
Hamilton (Mt. Hope)	416-524-2035
Kingston	613-389-8349
London	519-451-3172
Muskoka	705-687 103
Sarnia	519-542-6051
Sault Ste. Marie	705-779-3144
North Bay	705-472-9110
Peterborough	705-743-5852
Simcoe	519-426-0941
St. Catharines	416-688-1847
Thunder Bay	807-577-3921
Toronto International Airport	416-676-3066
Toronto Island Airport	416-369-4281
Wiarton	519-534-2760
Windsor	519-969-7585

MAFOR

The first figure is an identifying figure required by international practice. For the Great Lakes forecasts the number will always be one.

The second figure indicates the period of time the forecast conditions will persist. (table one)

Third, fourth and fifth figures represent conditions.
    The third figure, the forecast wind direction. (table two)
    The fourth figure, the forecast speed of the wind. (table three)
    The fifth figure, the forecast of the weather. (table four)

TABLE I
G—Period of time covered by forecast
0—conditions at beginning of forecast period
1—forecast valid for 3 hours
2—forecast valid for 6 hours
3—forecast valid for 9 hours
4—forecast valid for 12 hours
5—forecast valid for 18 hours
6—forecast valid for 24 hours
7—forecast valid for 48 hours
8—forecast valid for 72 hours
9—occasionally

TABLE II
D—Forecast direction of wind
0—calm
1—northeast
2—east
3—southeast
4—south
5—southwest
6—west
7—northwest
8—north
9—variable

TABLE III
Fm-Forecast speed of wind
0—Beaufort number 0-3 (0-10 knots)
1—Beaufort number 4 (11-16 knots)
2—Beaufort number 5 (17-21 knots)
3—Beaufort number 6 (22-27 knots)
4—Beaufort number 7 (28-33 knots)
5—Beaufort number 8 (34-40 knots)
6—Beaufort number 9 (41-47 knots)
7—Beaufort number 10 (48-55 knots)
8—Beaufort number 11 (56-63 knots)
9—Beaufort number 12 (64-71 knots)

TABLE IV
W—Forecast Weather
0—moderate or good visibility (greater than 3 nautical miles)
1—risk of accumulation of ice on superstructures
2—strong risk of accumulation of ice on superstructures
3—mist (visibility less than 5/8 to 3 nautical miles)
4—fog (visibility less than 5/8 mile)
5—drizzle
6—rain
7—snow or rain and snow
8—squally weather with or without showers
9—thunderstorms

Example: MAFOR ... HURON 12646 translation: the first six hours of the forecast period ... wind west 28-33 knots, with rain.

Chapter 7

FAIRS, FESTIVALS, RACES & REGATTAS, SUMMER EVENTS CALENDAR

"They talk about the good times they had,
and the good times to come. . ."
Waylon Jennings/Willie Nelson

The following summer events calendar has been created to expose the many special celebrations surrounding the Lake St. Clair region. In compiling this original Pirate's Guide Summer Calendar the editing process included annual water related fairs, festivals, shows and beach parties. The theory behind this unique calendar is that the recreational yachtsman could arrive at his or her boat on Friday night of the weekend or holiday weekend and review the many unpublished special events that don't receive the gale of international PR, that many of these small towns can't afford and until the Pirate's Guide, never had a platform to expose. The Chambers of Commerce surrounding Lake St. Clair and some throughout Michigan and Canada were contacted for a listing of annual special events, boating related, or that would interest the boating community. The editing process excluded the tap dancing contests and concentrated on the unique. At the top of the list are celebrations like the Curious George's 5th annual Kite Festival (on the beach), the Sandcastle competition, with $2,700 in prizes, Hot Air Balloon Fiestas, Fishing Derbies, Bikini Contests, boat shows and beach parties. The important things. These many local delights offer family and friends a slice of international liquid treats until this time, unknown except to the local folks. The majority are free. Like in the world of romance, dates change, call ahead to the Chamber of Commerce or Ministry of Tourism for the affirmative. As stated in the famous Shedd quote "A ship in a harbor is safe, but that's not what ships are built for." The international relationship between Canada and the United States is the envy of the world, where else could you sail through international waters for a hot air balloon ride?   Bon Voyage.

GOING TO CANADIAN WATERS

If you plan to cruise over to the Canadian side from the U.S. there's a few things you should know. First obtain an I-68 form from any U.S. Immigration Service, such as the one located at the Detroit-Windsor Tunnel or Ambassador Bridge. Bring your proof of citizenship, such as birth certificate, baptismal certificate, voter registration card or valid passport.

Every person on your boat should have an I-68 form.

Canadian Customs Marine Officers require U.S. boat visitors to call customs when they hit Canadian soil. The number for the Detroit area is 800-265-5633. For the Wallaceburg-Sarnia area the number is 800-265-1440.

Pirate's Guide Summer Calendar

MAY

MAY 1:	Joseph Schneider Haus (Shearing, Dyeing, Weaving)	KITCHENER.
MAY 13 – JUNE 15:	Idelwyld. An Era of Elegance Designers Showcase Victorian Mansion	LONDON, ONT.
MAY 24 – JUNE 1:	Budweiser Fishing Derby	PARRY SOUND.
MAY 26 – JUNE 1:	Jaycee Fair	CHATHAM
MAY 30 – JUNE 1:	Games for the Disabled	OWEN SOUND
MAY 30 – AUGUST 31:	Art Display / Juried	CHATHAM.
MAY 31 – JUNE 8:	Doon Renaissance Festival, 15th Century Chivalry & Romance	KITCHENER

Pirate's Guide Summer Calendar

EARLY MAY:	Tent Chautauqua	GREENFIELD VILLAGE, MI.
EARLY MAY:	Greek Festival	WYANDOTTE, MI.
EARLY MAY:	Easter Flower Show	BELLE ISLE, MI.
EARLY MAY:	Art Fair	MT. CLEMENS.
EARLY MAY:	Captive Nations Festival	DETROIT.
EARLY MAY:	Downtown Hoedown	DETROIT.
EARLY MAY:	Art Fair	MT. CLEMENS.
MID-MAY:	Fiddler's Jamboree	PORT HURON.
MID-MAY:	Village Antiques Show	GREENFIELD VILLAGE, MI.

MID-MAY:	Blue Water Salmon Classic	PORT HURON
MID-MAY:	Ukrainian & Slovak Festival	DETROIT.
MID-MAY:	Waterford Spring Craft	WATERFORD
LATE MAY:	Mexican Festival	WYANDOTTE.
LATE MAY:	German Festival	WYANDOTTE.
LATE MAY:	Greek Festival	DETROIT.
LATE MAY:	Around the World Festival	DETROIT.
LATE MAY:	Feast of the St. Clair	PORT HURON.
MAY 13 – JUNE 15:	Idelwyld. An Era of Elegance Designers Showcase Victorian Mansion	LONDON, ONT.

JUNE

JUNE 1:	Baldoon Annual Golf Tournament (Open to Everyone)	WALLACEBURG
JUNE 1 – SEPTEMBER 21:	Windsor Art Gallery Display	WINDSOR
JUNE 2 – AUGUST 24:	Celebration '86 London Embroiderer's Guild	LONDON.
JUNE 6 – 8:	Blue Grass Camp-out Concert (Largest in North America)	CARLISLE

JUNE 6 – 8:	Shrine Circus	LONDON.
JUNE 6 – 8:	Games for the Disabled	PARRY SOUND
JUNE 6 – 8:	12th Annual Couchi-Cat Regatta (Hobie Cat)	ORILLIA
JUNE 7:	Spring Tea/Antique Cast Iron Toys	SOMBRA, ONT.
JUNE 7–8:	12th Annual International Air Show (Largest in Canada)	LONDON, ONT.

Pirate's Guide Summer Calendar

JUNE 7 – 8:	Dockside Show/Entertainment	MEAFORD.
JUNE 7 – 15:	Newport Maxiboat Series.	
JUNE 8:	Bermuda 1-2 Race.	
JUNE 11 – 21:	Indian Village/Iroquois Legend, Seneca Legend of Moon Goddess	LONDON
JUNE 12 – 15:	Junefest Windsurfing Regatta	WASAGA BEACH.
JUNE 14 – 15:	Grand Riverfest Water Ski Party	CAMBRIDGE.
JUNE 14 – 15:	18 & Under Boardsailing Championships (Ont. Sailing Assoc.)	ROSSEAU
JUNE 15:	Ausable River Marathon Canoe Races	GRAND BEND.
JUNE 15:	Annapolis to Newport Race.	
JUNE 19 – 22:	Burgerfest - On The Beach	GRAND BEND.
JUNE 20 – 22:	Fifty Point Boat Show	WINONA.
JUNE 20 – 22:	Sounds of Summer (Rock, Jazz, Country and Folk Concerts)	WATERLOO
JUNE 20 – JULY 1:	Riverfest (Bikini Contest, Rock 'n Roll Revivial, Fish Fry and Beach Party)	BROCKVILLE

JUNE 20 – JULY 5:	International Freedom Festival/Tugboat Race	DETROIT RIVER, WINDSOR/DETROIT.
JUNE 20 – 22:	Michitario Games International Friendship Games	SARNIA.
JUNE 21:	Marion-Bermuda Cruising Yacht Race.	
JUNE 21 – 22:	19 & Under Lightning World & Triple Handed Championships	TORONTO
JUNE 22:	Pioneer Day/19th Century Crafts	COLCHESTER
JUNE 22:	Town & Country Meet (Antique Cars/Children's Magic)	KITCHENER
JUNE 22:	4th Annual Triathlon	ST. MARYS.
JUNE 22:	Mixed Two Ball Invitational (Open to Everyone)	WALLACEBURG
JUNE 22 – 29:	Kiel Week.	
JUNE 23 – 28:	Block Island Race Week.	
JUNE 24 – JULY 4:	Yachting's Regatta Time in Abaco.	

Pirate's Guide Summer Calendar

JUNE 25 – 29:	Sound of Music Festival (5 Out-door Stages all Music)	BURLINGTON
JUNE 25 – JULY 1:	Canada Week Celebrations (Fishing Derby, Parade and Picnic)	WALLACEBURG
JUNE 26 – JULY 1:	Rainbow Festival/Carnival	MISSISSAUGA.
JUNE 26 – JULY 1:	Canada Week Celebrations (Music Festival)	GODERICH
JUNE 27 – 30:	Funtastic Days/Barbeque/Parade ("Whisky Jack" Music Co.)	ARKONA
JUNE 27 – JULY 1:	Gala Gananoque (Model Boats, Antique Boat Show)	GANANOQUE
JUNE 27 – JULY 1:	Canada Week Celebration (Entertainment Beach Park)	OWEN SOUND
JUNE 27 – JULY 1:	Canada Week Celebration (Blue Water Park)	WIARTON
JUNE 28:	Canada Day Celebration (Parade to Waterfront)	PARRY SOUND
JUNE 28 – 29:	Beach Party/Dance/Sail Past	SOUTHHAMPTON.
JUNE 28 – JULY 1:	CHIN International Picnic (Boat Races/Bikini Pageant)	TORONTO
JUNE 28 – JULY 6:	Heritage Quilt Show & Sale	GRAND BEND.
JUNE 28 – JULY 19:	Summer Salmon Search & Great Walleye Hunt (Over $25,000)	PORT STANLEY
JUNE 29:	Curious George's 5th Annual Kite Festival at the Beach	CHATHAM
JUNE 29:	Buffalo Barbeque	PORT STANLEY.
JUNE 29:	Canada Day (Parade, Entertainment)	SARNIA.
JUNE 29 – JULY 1:	Liberty Cup.	
JUNE 29 – JULY 6:	Multicultural Festival	CHATHAM.
MID-JUNE:	Grand Prix	DETROIT

EARLY JUNE:	Oak Apple Art Festival	ROYAL OAK.
EARLY JUNE:	Governor's Cup Hydroplane Races	YPSILANTI.
EARLY JUNE:	Irish Festival	DETROIT.
MID-JUNE:	Muzzle Loaders Festival	GREENFIELD VILLAGE, MI.
MID-JUNE:	Le Rendez-vous De Salt & Fiddler's Jamboree	SAULT STE. MARIE
MID-JUNE:	Hungarian Festival	WYANDOTTE.
MID-JUNE:	Country Festival	CANTON.
MID-JUNE:	German Festival	DETROIT.

Pirate's Guide Summer Calendar

MID-JUNE:	Set Sail for Summer	PORT HURON.
MID-JUNE:	Bay Rama Fish Fly Festival	NEW BALTIMORE.
LATE JUNE – EARLY JULY:	International Freedom Festival	DETROIT/WINDSOR.
LATE JUNE:	Grand Prix	DETROIT.
LATE JUNE:	Arts & Craft Show	MONROE.
LATE JUNE:	Michigan Storytellers Festival	FLINT.
LATE JUNE:	International Freedom Festival	DETROIT/WINDSOR.
LATE JUNE:	Unlimited Hydroplane Race	DETROIT.
LATE JUNE:	Freedom Festival	DETROIT.
LATE JUNE:	St. Clair Art Fair	ST. CLAIR, MI.
LAST WEEK IN JUNE:	Blue Grass Festival	LEAMINGTON ARENA.

★   ★ ★   ★ ★   ★

JULY

JULY:	Old Time Fiddler Contest	BELLE RIVER.
JULY 1:	Canada Day / Riverside Park	CAMBRIDGE
JULY 1:	Canada Day/Parade-Music	CHATHAM.
JULY 1:	Canada Day/Fireworks-on the Beach	GRAND BEND
JULY 1:	Canada Day Celebration (Museum of Indian Archaeology)	LONDON
JULY 1:	Canada Day Celebration (Night-time Sail Past)	TORONTO.
JULY 4:	Transpac '85	
JULY 4 – 6:	Flower Show in Church (Local Flowers Antiques and Treasures)	KINCARDINE
JULY 4 – 6:	10th Annual Bass Derby	FORT ERIE.
JULY 6:	19th Annual Fly-In (Barbeque & Air Show)	WOODSTOCK, ONT.
JULY 7:	Marblehead-to-Halifax Ocean Race.	
JULY 7 – 28:	Women's Keelboat Series	TORONTO.
JULY 9 – 22:	One Ton Cup.	
JULY 10 – 12:	Grande Olde Days (Antiques & Classic Boat Show)	WALLACEBURG
JULY 10 – 12:	Festival Days (Caribbean Theme, Street Dances)	PORT PERRY.
JULY 10 – 13:	Escape XII (Exciting Scenic Powerboat Excursion)	KENORA.
JULY 11 – 13:	Antique Car Show	OWEN SOUND.
JULY 11 – 13:	Women's Canadian Championships	KINGSTON.
JULY 12:	Annual Picnic & Parade Fishing Derby	WILKESPORT.
JULY 12:	Star Great Salmon Hunt (Over $300,000 Cash & Prizes)	TORONTO

Pirate's Guide Summer Calendar

JULY 12 – 13:	Under 16 Singlehanded Championships	CORNWALL.
JULY 12 – 13:	Gold Cup Races (Powerboats)	PICTON.
JULY 12 – SEPTEMBER 2:	A Salute to the Artisan (Woodcarving/ Photo/ Cricket Games)	KITCHENER
JULY 13:	Chicago-Mackinac Island.	
JULY 14 – 19:	Yachting's Whidbey Island Race Week.	
JULY 18 – 19:	Antique Show/Sale	PORT ELGIN.
JULY 18 – 20:	Waterfront Festival & Folklorama (Triathlon/Fishing/Sail Past)	BELLEVILLE

JULY 18 – 20:	Home Country Folk Festival	LONDON.
JULY 18 – 20:	Country Music Festival	OWEN SOUND.
JULY 19:	Antique Boat Show (Up to 100, 1900-1940)	PORT CARLING
JULY 19:	Hillside Festival (Riverside Band Shell)	GUELPH
JULY 19:	Pork Barbeque & Jamboree	KINCARDINE
JULY 19 – 20:	Summer Antique & Classic Boat Show	TORONTO.
JULY 19 – 20:	Walpole Island Powwow	WALLACEBURG/ WALPOLE ISLAND
JULY 19 – 20:	Boardsailing Championships	ORILLIA.
JULY 20:	Port Huron-Mackinac Island Race.	
JULY 25 – 29:	Great International Steamboat Flotilla (40 Steamboats, Cruise)	KINGSTON
JULY 26:	Barn Raising & Bee Frolic (See How It's Done)	KITCHENER
JULY 26:	Fiddlers Contest (On the Lawn)	SOMBRA.
JULY 26:	Tecumseh Trophy Race (Keel and Centreboard Race)	PENETANQUISHENE
JULY 26 – 27:	Women's Singlehanded & Double	WHITBY.
JULY 27:	Sailing Regatta Around Lake in Woods	KENORA.
JULY 28 – AUGUST 2:	MORC International Regatta.	
JULY 29:	Caribana (Colorful Festival of Caribbean Music)	TORONTO.
JULY 29:	'Round the Island Race.	
JULY 29 – AUGUST 16	Admiral's Cup.	
EARLY JULY:	Pickerel Tournament	ALGONAC.
EARLY JULY:	Champagne Cruise	CHARLEVOIX.
EARLY JULY:	Down Home Days	UTICA.
EARLY JULY:	Mill River Days	MILFORD.
EARLY JULY:	Italian Festival	DETROIT.

Pirate's Guide Summer Calendar

EARLY JULY:	Far Eastern Festival	DETROIT.
EARLY JULY:	Pickerel Tournament	ALGONAC.
EARLY TO MID-JULY:	Blue Water Festival	PORT HURON.
EARLY TO LATE JULY:	Pickerel Tournament	ALGONAC.
MID-JULY:	Port Huron-Mackinac Island Yacht Race	PORT HURON.
MID-JULY:	Colonial Music & Military Muster	GREENFIELD VILLAGE, MI.
MID-JULY:	Blue Water Festival	PORT HURON.
MID-JULY:	Floral City Festival	MONROE.
MID-JULY:	Czechoslavak Festival	WYANDOTTE
MID-JULY:	Street Art Fair	WYANDOTTE.
MID-JULY:	Founder's Festival	FARMINGTON.
MID-JULY:	Polish Festival	WYANDOTTE.
MID-JULY:	Afro-American Festival	DETROIT.
3rd WEEK IN JULY:	Tomato Tour	WINDSOR.
LATE JULY:	Ann Arbor Arts Fair	ANN ARBOR.
LATE JULY:	Fire Engine Muster	GREENFIELD VILLAGE, MI.
LATE JULY:	Brown Trout Festival	ALPENA.
LATE JULY:	Venetian Festival	CHARLEVOIX.
LATE JULY:	Little Traverse Bay Regatta	HARBOR SPRINGS.
LATE JULY:	International Canoe Race	AU SABLE RIVER.
LATE JULY:	Coast Guard Festival	GRAND HAVEN.
LATE JULY:	Arab World Festival	DETROIT.

AUGUST

AUGUST:	Salmon Bonanza Tournament	HARBOR BEACH.
AUGUST:	Comber Fair	COMBER, ONT.
AUGUST:	Hot Air Balloon Fiesta	LONDON, ONT.
AUGUST 1 – 4:	Hot Air Balloon Fiesta	LONDON, ONT.
AUGUST 1 – 4:	Calipso Weekend/ Boat Parade	PORT STANLEY.
AUGUST 2:	Lake EXPO, Water Resource & Protection	CHEBOYGAN.
AUGUST 2 – 3:	Great Plains Anglers Tournament	ST. CLAIR, CANADA.

Pirate's Guide Summer Calendar

AUGUST 2 – 3:	Canal Days (Ship Models, Knot Tying and Music)	PORT COLBORNE.
AUGUST 2 – 3:	Laser II Championship	ORILLIA.
AUGUST 2 – 4:	Holiday Homecoming (Yacht Race for Tiger Cup)	LION'S HEAD.
AUGUST 2 – 4:	Summerama (Powerboat Races)	PENETANQUISHENE.
AUGUST 2 – 11:	Prince of Wales Festival (Triple Crown Horse Race)	FORT ERIE
AUGUST 6 – 10:	Royal Canadian Henley Regatta (World's Largest 5-day Regatta)	ST. CATHARINE
AUGUST 7 – 11:	Yachting's One-of-a-Kind Regatta.	
AUGUST 8 – 9:	Antique Show/Sale	GODERICH
AUGUST 8 – 15:	Wayfarer World Championships	ORILLIA.
AUGUST 8 – 23:	Chinook Classic Fishing Derby (Over $100,000 Cash & Prizes)	SOUTHHAMPTON
AUGUST 9:	11th Annual International Antique & Classic Boat Show	MANOTICK

AUGUST 9:	Sandcastle Competition ($2,700 in Prizes)	GRAND BEND.
AUGUST 9 – 10:	Singlehanded Laser	PORT CREDIT.
AUGUST 9 – 15:	Lightning North American Championship	KINGSTON.
AUGUST 15 – 17:	Summerfolk-Folk Festival	OWEN SOUND.
AUGUST 16 – 22:	Canadian Olympic Regatta – North American & Canadian	KINGSTON
AUGUST 23:	Bluegrass Music Festival	LION'S HEAD
AUGUST 23 – 24:	Summer Festival (Lake Erie Perch Dinners)	PORT DOVER.
AUGUST 24:	Outdoor Concert	SOMBRA.
AUGUST 30:	Bruce Peninsula Fishing Derby (Over $10,000 Cash & Prizes)	LION'S HEAD
AUGUST 31:	Classic Yacht Regatta.	
EARLY AUGUST:	Brown Trout Festival	ALPENA.
EARLY AUGUST:	Brown Trout Festival	ALPENA.
EARLY AUGUST:	Motor Muster	GREENFIELD VILLAGE, MI
EARLY AUGUST:	Nautical City Festival	ROGERS CITY.
EARLY AUGUST:	Bluegrass & Traditional Arts Festival	FLINT.
EARLY AUGUST:	Wayler Sailboard Nationals	LAKE CHARLEVOIX.
EARLY AUGUST:	Fish Sandwich Day	BAY PORT.

Pirate's Guide Summer Calendar

EARLY AUGUST:	Concours d'Elegance	ROCHESTER.
EARLY AUGUST:	Scandinavian Festival – Festival of India	DETROIT.
EARLY AUGUST:	Polish Festival	DETROIT.
EARLY AUGUST:	Nautical City Festival	ROGERS CITY.
EARLY AUGUST:	Water Festival	ST. CLAIR.
MID-AUGUST:	Waterfront Art Fair	CHARLEVOIX.
MID-AUGUST:	Great American Folk Art Festival	BRIGHTON.
MID-AUGUST:	Scandinavian Festival	WYANDOTTE
MID-AUGUST:	Waterfront Art Fair	CHARLEVOIX
MID-AUGUST:	Antique Boat Show/Festival	HESSELL.
MID-AUGUST:	Art on the River	FLINT.
MID-AUGUST:	Russian Festival	WYANDOTTE.
MID-AUGUST:	Venetian Night Boat Parade	GRAND HAVEN.
MID-AUGUST:	Balloon Classic	FLINT.
MID-AUGUST:	Art at Meadow Brook	ROCHESTER.
MID-AUGUST:	Mexican Festival	DETROIT.
MID-AUGUST:	Maritime Days	MARINE CITY.
LATE AUGUST:	Michigan Renaissance Festival	CLARKSTON.
LATE AUGUST:	State Fair	DETROIT.
LATE AUGUST:	Gas & Steam Engine Meet	GREENFIELD VILLAGE, MI.
LATE AUGUST:	Stroh Salmon Derby	SAULT STE. MARIE.
LATE AUGUST:	Regional Soaring Championships	IONIA.

LATE AUGUST:	Farm City Festival	MT. CLEMENS.
LATE AUGUST:	Maritime Festival	WHITEHALL.
LATE AUGUST:	Renaissance Festival	CLARKSTON
LATE AUGUST:	Montreux Jazz Festival	DETROIT.
LATE AUGUST:	Olympic Triangle Sail Race	LAKE CHARLEVOIX.
LATE AUGUST:	Coho Festival	HONOR.
LATE AUGUST:	Tagged Salmon Derby	MUSKEGON.
LATE AUGUST:	State Championshiop Snowmobile Water Race	BITELEY.
LATE AUGUST:	Red Fox Regatta	LAKE CHARLEVOIX.
LATE AUGUST:	Art Fair	ALGONAC.
LATE AUGUST:	African World Festival	DETROIT.
LATE AUGUST:	Farm City Days	MT. CLEMENS.
LATE AUGUST:	Montreux Jazz Festival	DETROIT

Pirate's Guide Summer Calendar

SEPTEMBER

LABOR DAY WEEKEND:	Hamtramck Festival	HAMTRAMCK.
SEPTEMBER 14 – 22:	North American One Ton Championship.	
SEPTEMBER 15 – 22:	Big Boat Series.	
SEPTEMBER 28:	4th Whitbread Round the World Race.	
EARLY SEPTEMBER:	Montreux Jazz Festival	DETROIT.
EARLY SEPTEMBER:	Old Car Festival	GREENFIELD VILLAGE, MI.
EARLY SEPTEMBER:	Coho Festival.	
EARLY SEPTEMBER:	Straits of Mackinac Fishing Festival	ST. IGNACE.
EARLY SEPTEMBER:	Boat & Fishing Show	PORT HURON.
EARLY SEPTEMBER:	Fall Festival	W. BLOOMFIELD.
EARLY SEPTEMBER:	Yugoslav Festival	DETROIT.
MID-SEPTEMBER:	Latin-American Festival	DETROIT.
MID-SEPTEMBER:	Antique Classic Boat Show	PORT HURON.
LATE SEPTEMBER:	Yesterday's Tomorrows	GREENFIELD VILLAGE, MI.

REGATTA SCHEDULE

SATURDAY	MAY 17	GREAT LAKES YACHT CLUB
SATURDAY	MAY 24	DETROIT YACHT CLUB
SATURDAY	MAY 31	BAYVIEW YACHT CLUB
FRIDAY	JUNE 6	TOLEDO YACHT CLUB/ STORM TRYSAIL CLUB
SATURDAY	JUNE 14	DETROIT BOAT CLUB
FRIDAY	JUNE 20	WINDSOR YACHT CLUB
SATURDAY	JUNE 21	SOUTH PORT SAIL CLUB
SATURDAY	JUNE 28	GROSSE POINTE CLUB
SATURDAY	JULY 5	GROSSE POINTE YACHT CLUB
SATURDAY	JULY 12	GROSSE POINTE SAIL CLUB
SATURDAY	JULY 19	BAYVIEW YACHT CLUB MACKINAC

SATURDAY	JULY 26	CHICAGO YACHT CLUB MACKINAC
SATURDAY	AUGUST 2	GROSSE ISLE YACHT CLUB
SATURDAY	AUGUST 9	FORD YACHT CLUB
SATURDAY	AUGUST 16	EDISON BOAT CLUB
FRIDAY	AUGUST 22	PORT HURON YACHT CLUB
SATURDAY	AUGUST 23	CRESCENT SAIL YACHT CLUB
SATURDAY	AUGUST 30	ALBATROSS YACHT CLUB/ ST. CLAIR YACHT CLUB/ THAMES RIVER YACHT CLUB
SUNDAY	AUGUST 31	PORT HURON YACHT CLUB/ SARNIA YACHT CLUB
SATURDAY	SEPTEMBER 6	DETROIT YACHT CLUB
SATURDAY	SEPTEMBER 13	BAYVIEW YACHT CLUB
SATURDAY	SEPTEMBER 20	GROSSE POINTE YACHT CLUB
SATURDAY	SEPTEMBER 27	BAYVIEW YACHT CLUB
SATURDAY	OCTOBER 11	LAKE SHORE SAIL CLUB

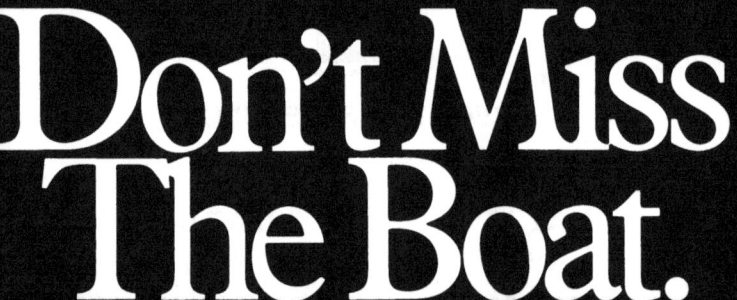

Don't Miss The Boat.

Some loan applications take so long to process, your ship could sail without you.

Your biggest problem should be deciding which new model to choose. Let First of America take care of the rest.

We've got quick and easy marine loan financing. If you qualify, we'll usually get your loan through the very same day.

And our Detroit office has over 30 years experience in helping people get the boats they want. We'll even explain all about rates and terms.

So call our First of America marine loan financing office at 965-LOAN.

Our staff will help you get the money you need so you'll be sailing away in no time at all.

FIRST of AMERICA
WORKING TOGETHER TO BE FIRST.

Members FDIC.

Gulf Stream Northern

—B.B.

The west Palm Beach Marina has all the characteristics of the perfect harbor. The rich and reckless are on one side of Lake Worth, the water people on the municipal docks. Teaching sailing from the municipal docks became another rewarding experience of blowing into port, sea stories in one hand and a hand shake in the other. Frank and Ginny ran a wing on wing sailing club. Wing on wing is a great sailing position, but I always have the feeling the wind is too unpredictable to allow things to stay in this expanded position for too long. Both people are an absolute joy. Our meeting occurred during a liquid withdrawal experienced only by the truly addicted. The tremors had developed a search for an ocean going vessel, Frank and Ginny had just that — four ocean going vessels to be exact. Now for the juice.

"If you join our club you can use the boats for a small rental fee." Following a bit of digging and a few martini's, what the club really needed was a sailing instructor, or at least I convinced them, they needed one that would teach for a few gold dabloon's, periodic swills of rum and access to the fleet. A true Pirate's deal had been struck. The Vassar college girls, those from the rich and reckless side and the many barmaids and waitresses from the municipal side, enhanced the booty.

About once a month the members of the club, mostly amateur, would sail to West End, Grand Bahama, departing Thursday night and returning Sunday night. The crossing takes about eight hours depending on Oden's mood at the time. It's sixty miles by sea. Four boats were scheduled for departure ranging from 26-30 feet, one or two a bit too tender for the Gulf Stream.

In my miles of dock walking, especially prior to a voyage, I'm always silently searching for that wind burned, quiet, man or woman of the sea, who isn't sitting around with that martini in one hand and a list of who's who in the other. They are usually tucked away scrubbing down the Sea Princess or Moon Dancer. Beer in one hand, scrub brush in the other, the respect they have for the Mother Ocean is the respect you best have for them and the Sea Princess. It's a mutual arora.

Garth McNabe was one of those men. Garth had been watching me and the activities of the marina for months. As I danced the islander through the harbor, sometimes under straight sail, my credibility became good enough to eventually rate a seasoned nod of approval from this man of the sea.

The Thursday evening a few hours prior to the sail to West End and feeling a bit apprehensive of the crossing, I walked down the dock, subconsciously looking for Garth. Garth was adjusting his lines, tucking the Princess in for another night of safety. The Princess settled in after Garth had moved, tightened, loosened and adjusted a final perfect network of line, vessel, wind and anticipated weather. It is a job that developes maritime fiber stronger than manila line. Garth gave me a brief acknowledged nod.

Maybe the distant sounds of the pre-voyage rigging and provisioning signaled him or my rare evening appearance to Garth and his Princess. "Going out tonight?" I think so, suppose to take a light crew over to the Bahamas, try to hit West End at day break, four boats going."

Stay together, what do you think."

"Don't go, not tonight, and not for a few days, it's a Gulf Stream Northern."

My anticipation, respect for this man, the sea and the safety of the dock under me unfurried the obvious Great Lakes question. What's a Gulf Stream Northern? My every sense activated to the movements and sounds of the only man I respected during months of discreet observation. "Tell the others, too. It happens about once a year for about three days. The wind clocks around, runs into the stream and all Hell breaks loose. You leave the harbor, maybe one foot seas, maybe like glass. You get to the stream, hit a wall of water, 30-40 foot seas, grab your boat, beat ya for days, maybe take ya." Don't go. The words struck throughout my system similar to my vision of 30 foot seas grabbing out tender armada. The Princess was safe, Garth was safe. The sounds of the sea lapped peacefully against all things built by man, reminding me who was in charge, and who was allowed temporary access to this liquid culture. "Have a nice night, thank you, Garth."

My apprehension built up as the sounds of "more beer" and "don't forget your bikini" got closer. I felt the approaching confrontation would be briefly disappointing, acknowledged, then moved to a local saloon for future planning, with a minimum of out-bursts or individual mutiny. To my dismay, the news wasn't accepted amidst crys of how this weekend had been planned for weeks and the switches that had taken place with employers and fellow employees. The weekend warriors were off to West End, come Hell or high water. They were unresponsive to the news of just what they were going to get. This is no time to test the force and rath of Oden and Mother Nature, this is a time to respect the sea and the wind. Anyone who gets in the way will be spit out and maybe swallowed. Sorry, we're going.

GULF STREAM NORTHERN

The boats jerked out of their slips like bulls from a bull pen. Eager to fight the Conquistadore's of the sea. The may-day calls came in approximately eight hours later. The Palm Beach Coast Guard refused to respond. Their small search and rescue crafts couldn't handle the now reported 40-50 foot seas. The 186 foot cutters in Miami had to assist. The cutters left Miami battened down and ready for war. The tender crews and tender 26 footers were experiencing the rage of Mother Nature's rule "Hell has no fury like a woman scorned." Two and a half days later the boats sporatically returned, the crews either green with sea sickness or opaque white with fear. The reports ranged from to sea sickness to making radio contact with the Devils' Triangle.

They were not the victory hails of the conquering, but the moans of the conquered. A Gulf Stream Northern had been inflicted on eighteen more souls. Oden and Mother Nature were returning to another mood, and the hailrards on the Sea Princess gently chimed another song to her masters.

First Time Out
-B.B.

"John just called and he asked if we would like to go sailing for the day?" Sailing?, I didn't know John had a boat. He doesn't, his friend Pat does."

This conversation will be repeated thousands of times in every dialect around the world, from now until man doesn't float anymore. Excitement usually follows by numerous calls to anyone that has ever worn foul weather gear at a local saloon or blazers and white slacks to a cocktail party. S.O.S. calls for an immediate history on yachting etiquette follows.

Etiquette is defined by Webster as: A prescribed or accepted code of usage in matters of ceremony, and "Yachting" is a ceremony. Many a marriage has failed or a business deal been dumped due to spills on the teak or guacamole on the deck. There are exceptions to all rules of order, and the following accents sailing. A Sunday outing with Uncle Charlie on his 24 foot boat can make the feuds on Dallas look like prototypes of your next ten years with Uncle Charlie, because you burned a cigarette hole in his Captain's chair. (Bar chairs on luxury yachts can cost $5,000 per chair, that's Five thousand dollars per chair.)

Never fear, say "Yes" and I will navigate you from the click of the receiver to become an informed, safe and enjoyable crew. The intriquing part about boating, especially sailing, is your direct relationship with Mother Nature. No other sport demands the respect for the vehicle or the elements more than boating. Flying (no way) is like a car with wings. The engine stops, down you go and who cares what you wear. The only thing you hope is that you're wearing a parachute. And boating is more intriquing because you can tie up on the islands, you can't tie up on the clouds. The other advantage to boating is that you are in most cases, in charge of your vessel. In other sports there is usually an engine or animal involved, one that can stop. For those of you who have never been skippering a 72 footer at 14 knots, the thrill is unbelievable, don't let the speed deceive you. The only parallel for rush is flying 120 m.p.h. two feet above the South China sea in a four man open helicopter. And I don't recommend either one First Time Out.

Open your closet and start with the most important thing in the eyes of your host. The shoes. Topsiders are accepted footwear, but you don't have to rush out and spend $70 or frantically search for a Marine store or mall that's open Sunday afternoon. Tennis shoes, jogging shoes, anything that has a rubber sole will work. The shoes are very important, not just from the stand point of preventing a nick or scratch on what most hosts consider a Grand piano, but also from a safety perspective. You will be moving around the boat, at some times very rapidly, water on the top sides, which are either, teak, wood, or highly polished fiberglass. Walked across a Corvette lately? When it's all wet, you need the traction. Any shoes with a soft rubber sole are mandatory equipment. Socks, at your discretion, placed in a duffle bag, which will be covered later, have saved many a preppy from frozen ankles after the sun goes down. Slacks or blue jeans, will pass on almost all occasions, corduroys and khaki will also work, depending on the weather. On the upper half anything goes. Sun glasses and hats for Great Lakes day sails are not mandatory; long distance and ocean going, they are mandatory. Foul weather gear is the nautical term for rain gear. Local sporting goods stores sell it and prices range from $10 to $200. Again if you have an attractive waist length casual rain coat, you can carry it. Most well prepared skippers have a few extra on board, but it's nice to be prepared. Sweaters show the same weather insight, the point is, after the sun goes down it can get mighty chilly. The Irish coffees taste much better with the cool breezes just going around your face and hands and not through your rib cage.

Now for the duffle bag.

With the insurgence of work outs/ marathons/ tennis doubles and sportmania, many canvas or soft material bags are usually around or easily purchased no matter what the time of day. Look at the duffle bag and contents to place in it, as a small soft suitcase, with some common sense allergies. No glass containers; boats bounce, glass breaks, people sit or grab, people get cut. No paper openers or pointed sharp containers. Spray cans contain gases, most flammable gases. Canvas

FIRST TIME OUT

packed away in very compact areas could possibly cause a problem. Included are butane lighters and lighter fluid. The purpose of the duffle is extra clothing, hygiene, bandannas and Pirate's Guides.

Take that extra sweater, socks, rain gear, soap, shampoo (plastic bottle), tooth brush, tooth paste, razor, towel and Bob Seger tapes, stick to the basics. Floyd Hinsby, seasoned yatchsman, travels only with duffle. Want to sail to Australia? Floyd's ready. If, after your first encounter with boating, you plan to continue, pick up a duffle. As stated earlier the negative result of ignorance is no excuse for the law. Being prepared can expose positive individual characteristics to that Vice President or future Commordoress, regarding what you take. Now you are dressed and ready to go.

Off to Jefferson Beach Marina or the Great Lakes Yacht Club. You passed the party store, so your offer to bring refreshments, snacks and sandwiches wasn't accepted? Right. You also asked directions, once in the harbor to the boat and well number. Good. Most marinas and yacht clubs have some type of security gate or entrance. Guards sometimes require guests' names or clearance from the owner to allow entry. Some private parks and clubs are so strict, you'd think they were ex-border guards from East Berlin. Once in the harbor drive slowly to the well, road dust and boats don't mix, they incite riots. Dust, stones and fast vehicles don't go in the Cisteen Chapel, and many a dock boy, deck hand or captain consider their boats eligible for placement in the Cisteen Chapel. Boats are washed, painted and expertly varnished and an impatient motorist can cause hours of damage and heartache. Boat yards are, along with places to have fun, working communities. Cars are parked, not in the way of any launch sites, Travel-lifts or other boats on land that could be on a list to drop in the water that day. Great. It's down the dock and welcome aboard.

Now the fun starts.

Power boats, row boats and sail boats all have one mutual characteristic: you can get hurt and you can die. Proceed with cautious anticipation. The majority of skippers respect and safely navigate the waterways, but like bad apples, there's always a few. Your decision to go for a pleasurable afternoon of sun and fun should be just that, pleasurable and fun. A pie eyed captain or inexperienced captain can turn that afternoon into tragedy. Don't let the excitement of the opportunity overcome common sense. It is not my intent to frighten or instill paranoia with this bit of direction, just to lay out some ground rules, to make that afternoon pleasurable and fun. Once on board you are the captain's crew, and the captain's word is Law. If he says move, move. Until he is no longer capable of piloting his vessel, give him his or her due respect. With the many lines, cleats, pieces of steel, wood and aluminum, this is not the place to unknowingly assist prior to a captain's or crew's request for such assistance. Once on board you will start to realize you are moving into another dimension. Let the pilots of that dimension pilot. Once the cruise is off ask questions about what is going on, that's part of the beauty of the sport, you never stop learning. High side, low side, port, starboard, red right returning. Now that the harbor is being left behind, you have one thing in common with every other person on board, they have never experienced that sail, cruise or ride under the same conditions, and neither have you. They have been in similar conditions or similar routes but never identical ones. The Coast Guard laws on licensing are very realistic from the stand point that you don't get your license or certificate until you have completed a prescribed amount of Running Time, time that was documented on the water, from Point A to B. Thus part of the tradition developed in the Log, the Captain's record of what took place that day, week or hour. Recreational vessels don't require documented logs, but the IRS does, if you want to write off part of the boat's expense as business expenses. Experience is the certified teacher in boating. Some of that experience can be gained through class room or home study, but putting those lessons to use takes place during running time. Settle back, open your mind and start to learn, especially on sail boats, how to use Mother Nature to go from point A to point B.

Captain John Walker had commandered power boats for years and turns an afternoon on his yacht into one of the most enjoyable experiences available, for the very simple reason he knows what he's doing and will explain what he's doing just for the asking. The true and time tested qualities of a captain. Not how fast he can go, but how did you get there? A nervous wreak, or sipping on a perfect Bloody Mary and watching a school of Dolphins play, swim, jump and summersault, glistening on a background of three dimensional, full color, climate control, fresh air wonder of the World, the Sea. The same experience is repeated on the Great Lakes, exchanging some of the players with new scenes. Good captains, good boat rides. Good crew, good boat rides. For the First Time Out can be the start of a life long affair with something you can never totally control, the Forces of Mother Nature, Oden and the wind Maria. The key is to work with it, not against it. In the words of Captain John Walker, "Everybody wants to go for a boat ride!"

Golden Doubloon Awards

Pirate's regarded gold and silver coins as the greatest booty of all. The coins held the highest value due to the ability to equally and easily divide the treasure. In 1716 pirate Henry Jennings Plundered a Spanish Galleon off the coast of Florida containing 350,000 pieces of eight. The Atocha that Mel Fisher found after years of heartache and frustration awarded the treasure hunting crew with millions of gold and silver coins. It is in the spirit of the Atocha, the Whiddo, Jean Lafitte, Long John Silver and the many legends that risk life and limb for the prized Golden Doubloon that we grant the following Awards. The people and places graced with this unique honor may not be the fastest or the biggest, but the best. 1st mate, "May I have the treasure chest please"

Best Bartenders	Jim Machris, Tim Shannon, out of country Floater
Best Marina	Kean's Detroit Harbour
Best New Yachtman	Pat Wheeler
Best All Around Waterman	Al Wagner
Best Maritime Teachers	Simon / Pat Hinsby / George Uznis
Best Drink	Sindbad's
Best Canadian Saloon	Bell Bouy
Best Company	Ludington News
Best Event	Guitar Army Concert
Best Book Buyer	Charlie Przygocki, Diane Ewing
Best 7:00 a.m. Saloon	Honest John's Marine Bar & Bosnan's
Best Party Yacht	Helene
Best D.J.'s	Karen Savelly, Arthur Penhallow
Best Talk Show	Peter Werbe - Night Call
Best Morning Show	J.J. and the Morning Crew
Best Marine Photographer	Robert "Spike" Neesley
Best American Humor	Johnny Carson
Best Detroit River Pirate	Bob Armond
Best Treasurer Hunter's	Mel Fisher, Barry Clifford
Best Party Band	Keel Haulers, Harbor Springs, Michigan
Best Party Store	Dick's Party Mart, N. River Road

Chapter 8

CHARTERS, RIDES & INSTRUCTION

"Mother, Mother Ocean, I have heard you call,
wanted to sail upon your waters
since I was three feet tall,
you've seen it all..."
— Jimmy Buffett
A Pirate looks at forty
Recorded LIVE, Atlanta, Ga.

This chapter will explain the many ways of enjoying the water without either a major investment, or a taste of the sea prior to selling the house and finding out that ping pong is easier on your metabolism. Settle back and find out how, where and when to go yachting, fishing or diving at a portion of the cost.

The chartering of a boat can range from a 14-foot sunfish at Metropolitan Beach to a 75-footer that will scream through the Bermuda Triangle. No matter what your pleasure a little knowledge goes a long way. I have taught sailing and worked on all types of power boats, and I learned one main thing, you can never learn too much and even the most experienced always can use someone around who knows what to do when smoke starts to come from the engine room.

The first place to start is the United States Power Squadron. They wil also be listed in the chapter under associations. These people are great. They are sincere, they love the water and nothing makes them happier than to inform, instruct and assist people of all ages in the maritime arts. They can be contacted at 9149 E. Jefferson, Detroit or call 821-4900. Almost any boat yard, yacht club or ships store can give the address and phone number of the Power Squadron facility in your area.

There are many private schools of instruction that range from 2-hour classes to two weeks on the high seas. The Power Squadron is usually free, except for course materials. Private classes are not free. I taught for a private organization and felt the people definitely got what they paid for and most do give competent instruction, but like all parts of business, not everyone is fair and honest. Topics offered by the Power Squadron cover how to read a compass, read charts, handle a boat under normal and adverse conditions, government's regulations concerning equipment and good seamanship. Persons who successfully complete the course are awarded a boating safety certificate. If you plan to do any chartering in different states or countries, this certificate will at least show you've had some formal instruction. The classes are usually at night or on the weekends and well worth the time, and fun.

Young boaters 12-16 years of age can participate in several free boating safety training programs to receive their Michigan Boating Safety Certificate. This certificate is required by law if they operate a motorboat powered by six or more horsepower while not accompanied by an adult. The basic course consists of six, one-hour sessions with the sixth class being used for review, examination and award of certificates and patches to successful students. It is offered through participating Sheriff's Departments, YMCA's, YWCA's, Red Cross, as well as the U.S. Power Squadron.

Several sailing classes are held on Lake St. Clair. The Anchor Bay Sailing School offers courses in basic and advanced sailing for adults. Teens 15-17 may enroll if accompanied by a parent. Courses are limited to four students and consist of three four-hour classes. Classes meet at the Jefferson Beach Marina and are conducted aboard new, completely rigged 25-foot keel sailboats. The Olympic Sailing School of Mt. Clemens features an 18-hour racing class with three people per boat in addition to its regular programs of basic and advanced sailing. For teens it has a special Junior Sailing Program that meets for three weeks starting in August. Wayne County Community College takes to the lake after a six-week classroom study in sailing. Instructor Bill Smith, Deputy Director of Detroit's Department of Community and Economic Development, has taught a wide range of students the fine art of sailing.

A relatively new innovation in sailing instruction is the "learn to sail vacation" and the sailing club. Offshore Sailing School Ltd. has resorts on Martha's Vineyard, City Island, N.Y., Hilton Head, S.C., Captiva Island, Fla., Sarasota, Fla. and Tottola British Virgin Islands. In a one-week vacation, amidst deluxe resort accommodations, guests are taught to a 27' Olympic class solely by experienced instructors. Gulf Stream International offers free sailing instruction to members through its local sailing clubs.

I taught sailing for the Gulf Stream Club in Palm Beach, Fla. for about eight months. The club was run by Frank and Gini Bostwick, two great people who took me in after becoming aware there was one thing I came to Fla. for, to sail the ocean. went out twice a day on anything from a 18-footer to one of the greatest boats ever sailed, an Islander 29'. A dream for the ocean and islands. In seas close to 30 feet and the boat handled them like an absolute dolphin. My time with those people and their club was something I will never forget. mastered the sea and all my students were pleased with what they received for their payment, except maybe for one that went into a minor catatonic state when we got into some large seas in the gulf stream. First time on a boat, and between my sea stories, the sea turtles, dolphin and flying fish, it was a bit much. I quickly got her and her husband back to a martini in a nice dry bar. The rougher the sea, the more I liked it. Many of my students didn't quite agree. But It's a great deal if you want to find out what sailing is all about.

caught between the clet and the line. The next thing , blood was pouring all over his boat and he calmly stated he had severed his finger. We retrieved the finger and maydayed a passing power boat, then contacted the hospital in Palm Beach and informed them of the accident. The power boat sped the man to shore to a waiting ambulance and into the emergency room for the operation. They sewed the finger back on and the man survived. Line changes and moving parts on a boat can be deadly. In a split second you can lose a limb, have your teeth knocked out or be knocked out and drowned. Be careful, respect the forces around you. They can be the most beautiful in the universe or violent killers.

Most people I found really had too much of a Hollywood image of the sport. Being out on the water can be a very dangerous experience, it kills, its inhabitants kill and sometimes it's not while you're sleeping. Knock on wood, only had one accident while teaching and it wasn't my fault. A man had run aground and requested my assistance to pull him off the sand bar. I agreed and he threw me a line. Just a note here. When people are in distress have them throw you the line and then you are not liable. Some have been known to sue after you save them. Anyway, he threw me a line but didn't clet it. made my pass, cletted my line and as the slack was spinning out of the line he tried to clet his end. His hand got

Courses in these clubs range from celestial navigation to dead reckoning. I may add I have delivered boats from Florida to the East Coast and no matter what electronic equipment that is on board someone should have a working knowledge of celestial navigation prior to any long distance yachting, not so much for the Great Lakes because if you stay in one direction you will hit shore but in the ocean you may not. Celestial is the navigation by the stars, sun and moon. It's a real art, I truly respect anyone who has mastered it, they are true blue water seamen. Celestial navigation to the yachtsman is like open heart surgery to the surgeon. The seconds, formulas and decisions make the difference between success and failure. In addition, the typical sailing club offers charter boats to its members at discount rates and organizes sailing parties, diving activities, weekend trips and extended trips to international ports of call.

For the heartier of the Great Lakes Sailors is the Trade Winds Charter Yachts of Milwaukee, Wisconsin and Sailboats, Inc., Charters of Excelsior, Minnesota. Sailboats Inc. specializes in cruising the unspoiled Apostle Islands of Lake Superior. Bareboat charters are on 24-35 foot boats including many C&C's or you can be accompanied by a combination guide/sailing instructor. For those short on time, Trade Winds specializes in trip planning with travel arrangements and one-way charters in the Green Bay and Northern Lake Michigan area.

The following information has been assembled for a guide to Lake St. Clair and Lake Huron Boat Charters. For additional information concerning the total Great Lakes area contact Pirates Guide to Lake St. Clair.

The Great Lakes are the home of many famous cruising grounds. Michigan charter services in the Charlevoix-Traverse area feature bareboat and crewed charters on Lake Michigan to Beaver Island, Little Traverse Bay, Grand Traverse Bay, Manitou Islands, Fox Islands, Mackinac Island and the North Channel. The Urban Yacht Service has its headquarters in Rochester, Michigan, but maintains a charter service and navigation school in Boyne City on Lake Charlevoix. Northern Charter Properties has a full service yacht yard in Mt. Clemens and in Harbor Springs, where it has the new Tartan 37 and many other fine boats. Summer charters off Charlevoix has sailboats from 26 to 42 feet — sloops, ketches, gas and diesel — for bareboat charter cruising. The Sail Shack of Traverse City offers hourly sailboat rental rates for such boats as its Prindle 16 in addition to its sailing school and charter service.

Caribbean yacht charters are for many the ultimate in a cruising adventure. Northwind Charters of East Lansing, Lansing, Michigan, has Morgan Out Islands that sail from Biscayne Bay, Fla. From the point of departure the course can range from the casinos of Grand Bahamas and Freeport, Paradise Island, to the best deep sea fishing in the world. For the purist, just pick an island and go. There are approximately 700 islands in the chain and many are uninhabited. This is my pleasure, no phones, TV, or people, except for that special lady that looks better with her bikini off than on, and prefers it that way.

Watch out for 20th century pirates. They're around. Be cautious of strangers wishing to purchase your boat. Quite a few boats have been hijacked in the islands mostly by dope dealers. They come on board kill the captain and crew, take the boat, make a dope run and sink the boat. 60 Minutes did a special report on the situation, so really take it easy and remember not all boaters are as mellow as the Hollywood image makes them out to be.

Caribbean Yacht Charters, Virgin Island Charters and Stevens Yachts of Annapolis sail the Caribbean Windward, Leeward and Greadine Islands. Oceanus, New Jersey, specializes in the "Other Caribbean" with charters stopping at ancient seaports such as Haiti, Honduras and Cuba. Sail the Silver Banks where you see and hear 5,000 singing whales or explore a sunken pirate ship. Each Caribbean Island has its own unique flavor and this area is considered the best cruising in the world. If you can ever do it, fly right by Ft. Lauderdale and Palm Beach and hit the out islands by yacht. You will understand why Hemingway moved there and commuted to the Big Apple. Definitely the best of both worlds. Itineraries are limited only by your imagination and pocketbook. The basic cost is about $230/wk based on six persons bareboat rate. Provisions range from basic to the most lavish foods and liquors. This market has become very competitive so shop around.

The windjammer cruises are another avenue to check out, but check it out carefully. I have read a few articles that the management of these cruises is questionable. But the yachts are beautiful. They range from the Fantom, built for the Duke of Westminster as a private floating palace, to the Yankee Clipper, Flying Cloud, Polynesia and Yankee Trader, who have equally colorful histories. The boats are huge, approximately 282 feet, but check them out before you get into a definite commitment. The Maverick managed by Westindiaman Cruises and Tiki managed by Seven Seas Yachts also sail the Caribbean. If you'd enjoy visiting Maine's outer island on one of these classics shops, try the three masted windjammer Victory Chimes run by Maine Coast Cruises. The Victory Chimes is the largest passenger sailing vessel under the American flag. Other ships cruising the New England Coast are the Mary Day, Coastal Cruises, Stephen Taber, Yankee Packet, Timerwind, Schooner Isaac H. Evans, Richard Robbins, Shenandoah, Coastwise Packet Co., Mystic Whaler.

If houseboats are more of your liking, Egan Marine has a fleet of Pigeon Lake in the Trent-Severn Canadian Waterway. This waterway is located in one of the continent's most beautiful and picturesque inladn routes with 240 miles of protected cruising through 20 lakes, rivers and canals. From Pigeon Lake in the heart of the Kawarthas you can travel in either direction on the Trent-Severn Waterway. To the east, through Buckhorn, Lovesick and Stoney Lakes there are bays, uninhabited islands and towering pine trees. Continuing, the waterway wanders to Peterborough, with a spectacular 65' hydraulic lift lock that is worth the trip for home movies. To the west of Pigeon Lake are some of Ontario's crystal lakes and summer villages — Sturgeon, Camerson and Balsam Lakes; the towns of Bobcaygeon, Fenelon Falls and Rosedale, all lie on the borders of this waterway on the route to Lake Somcoe. September is an especially good time to reduce the cost of this vacation. Off season fares are about half of the peak summer rates, but either would be enjoyable. The houseboats are equipped with furnaces for those cool autumn nights.

FREIGHTER TRAVEL

For those of you who would love to just float down the lazy river, freighter travel is for you. If you think the air lines have low fares and bargain fares check out your local or international freighter captain and find out what you've been missing. In lay man terms, its cheap, good food, if not superb, friendly, if not brotherly and you will come away with more sea stories to tell your grandchildren from men who have sailed the high seas all their lives. Reg and Rose Clark have founded the Freighter Travel Club of America and just for some of the information about the vessels a tramp steamer they're not. Sauna's, swimming pools, cinema, library, gymnasium, hospital and air conditioning.

The passenger-carrying freighter generally takes about 12 passengers in addition to crew and cargo. The cargoliner is often referred to as a freighter but carries around 60 passengers and up to 300 in some instances. Todays deluxe freighters are almost exclusively Scandinavian, German, British, or Netherlands flag ships which generally charge less than equivalent American freighters. You dine with the officers and are served the same well-cooked meals along with several exotic dishes and foreign specialties. On ships with East Indian stewards you will be waited on almost hand and foot, in a manner that

EGAN MARINE
8201 Keele Street
Concord, Ontario

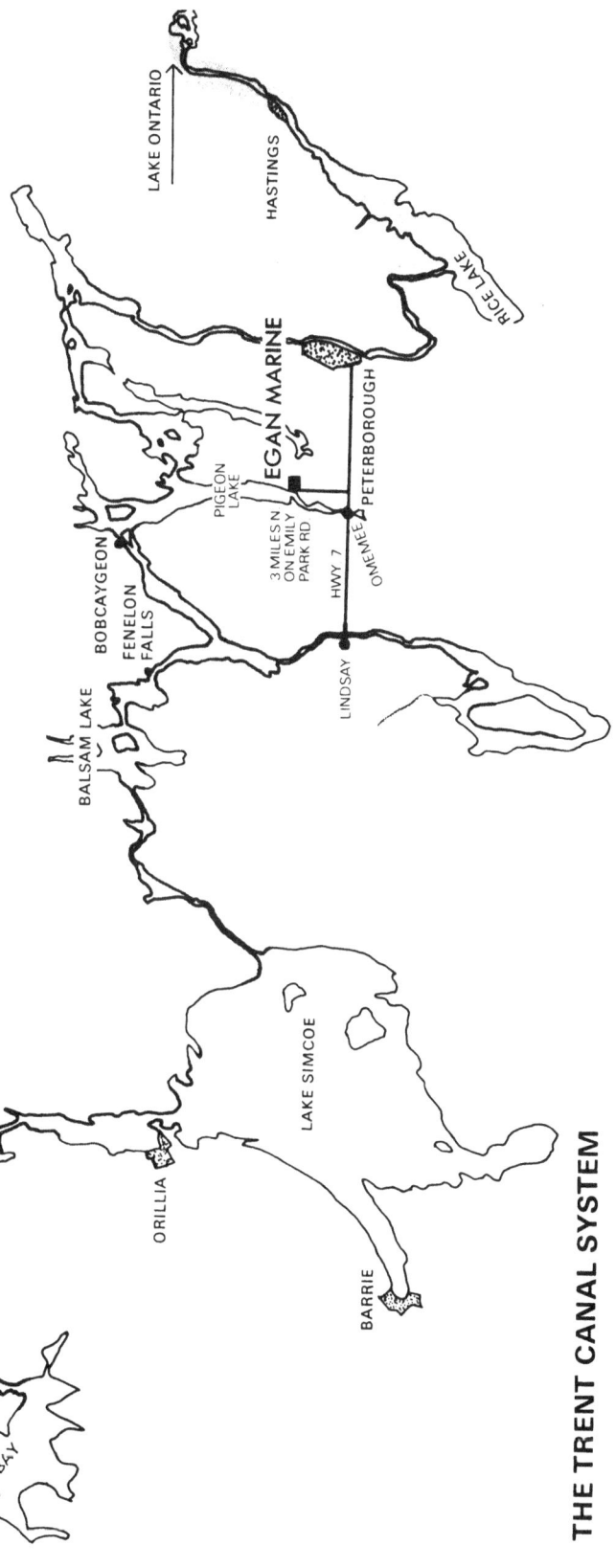

THE TRENT CANAL SYSTEM

is completely unknown to Americans and most Europeans.

Intrigue and foreign adventure go hand in hand on this wonderful, unique cruise. The Norwegian Barber S.S. Lines carries 12 passengers on a 100 day Far East adventure from New York to Newport News, Charleston, Panama, Los Angeles, San Francisco, Manila, Hong Kong, Bangkok and Singapore; returning to Port Kelang, Belawan, Keelung, Kobe and Yokohoma. The American Export Line has Mediterranean routes from New York to Barcelona, Naples, Istanbul, Genoa and Mareille. Freighter Club of America organizes a yearly schedule of cruises.

Pearl's Freighter Tips, Inc.
Suite 306
175 Great Neck Road
Great Neck, N.Y. 11021
Phone:

This unique organization offers information on true maritime travel. The length of the trips range from a few days to often four, five and more weeks. Don't expect an Astrology cruise, but the Captain and crew can tell you stories of the stars. The accommodations vary, from ship to ship, the Edmund Fitzgerald was decorated by the J.L. Hudson Company. Once on board you are part of the crew, in most cases. Such welcomes include dinner with the Captain, at the Captain's table. Generally about 12 passengers are carried. For Great Lake passage the best place to start is the Port Authority and import export brokers. The Brokers work with the Freighter's on a daily basis, many know Captains and freighter that take passengers. If the QE 2 isn't your bag, maybe an Exxon Super tanker is.

1846. MONEY AND TIME SAVED!! 1846.
FARE REDUCED,
AND SPEED INCREASED!!!

THE WELL KNOWN STEAMER

BROTHERS,
CAPT. WALTER EBERTS,

Commenced making regular trips for the season Monday, April 6, from Chatham to Windsor, Detroit and Amherstburg, and vice versa, as follows:

Leaves Windsor and Detroit for Chatham every Tuesday, Thursday and Saturday mornings, at 10 o'clock, A. M. Leaves Chatham for Windsor and Detroit every Monday, Wednesday and Friday mornings, at 8 o'clock, A. M., in connection with a Daily Line of Post Coaches; through by daylight to London; thence to Brantford, Hamilton and Queenston.

The road between Chatham and London is in complete repair. From London to Brantford the road is McAdamized, and throughout the entire line is one of the best roads in Canada. This route offers every facility to travelers with private carriages, or by the public conveyances, which are not to be equalled in any other part of America.

ABOUT: To take an opposite tack.
AFT: Rear or stern end of boat.
AMIDSHIPS: Midpoint of boat between bow and stern.
ASTERN: Toward the rear or stern of boat.
BECALMED: A boat that's not moving because the wind has died.
BELOW: Under the main deck, or the next level down.
BEND: A joining Knot.
BERTH: A "parking" spot; place where boat is docked.
BOW: Front or forward end of boat.
BULKHEAD: A wall or partition used to divide space.
CAPSIZE: That which gets larger after you win a race!
CAULKING: Material used to fill cracks and separations on a wooden boat.
CHAFING GEAR: Fenders or other objects used as buffers against scraping.
DRAFT: The minimum depth a boat requires to avoid scraping bottom.
EBB: Outgoing tide.
FATHOM: Nautical measure, equal to six feet.
FLOOD: Incoming tide.
FLOTSAM: Floating objects, driftwood, garbage.
GALE: Strong wind, bewtween 28 and 55 knots.
HALYARD: Small lines used for raising sails, flags, etc.
HEAD: Toilet.
J & B: Joyful Boating!
JIB: A forward sail.
KNOT: Measurement of distance; one nautical mile.
LEE: Sheltered side of the boat — away from the wind.
LUFF: What makes the world go round!
OVERBOARD: When something or someone goes over the side.
PAINTER: A line attached to a dory or other small boat.
PART: Separate or break.
PORT: Left.
SECURE: Battening down all loose objects.
SHIPSHAPE: Keeping things neat and orderly.
SMALL STUFF: Thin rope, as opposed to the heavier line.
STARBOARD: Right.
STERN: Rear or back end of boat.
STOW: To arrange or store.
TOPSIDE: Levels above the deck.
WAKE: Trail of white water that marks a boat's path.

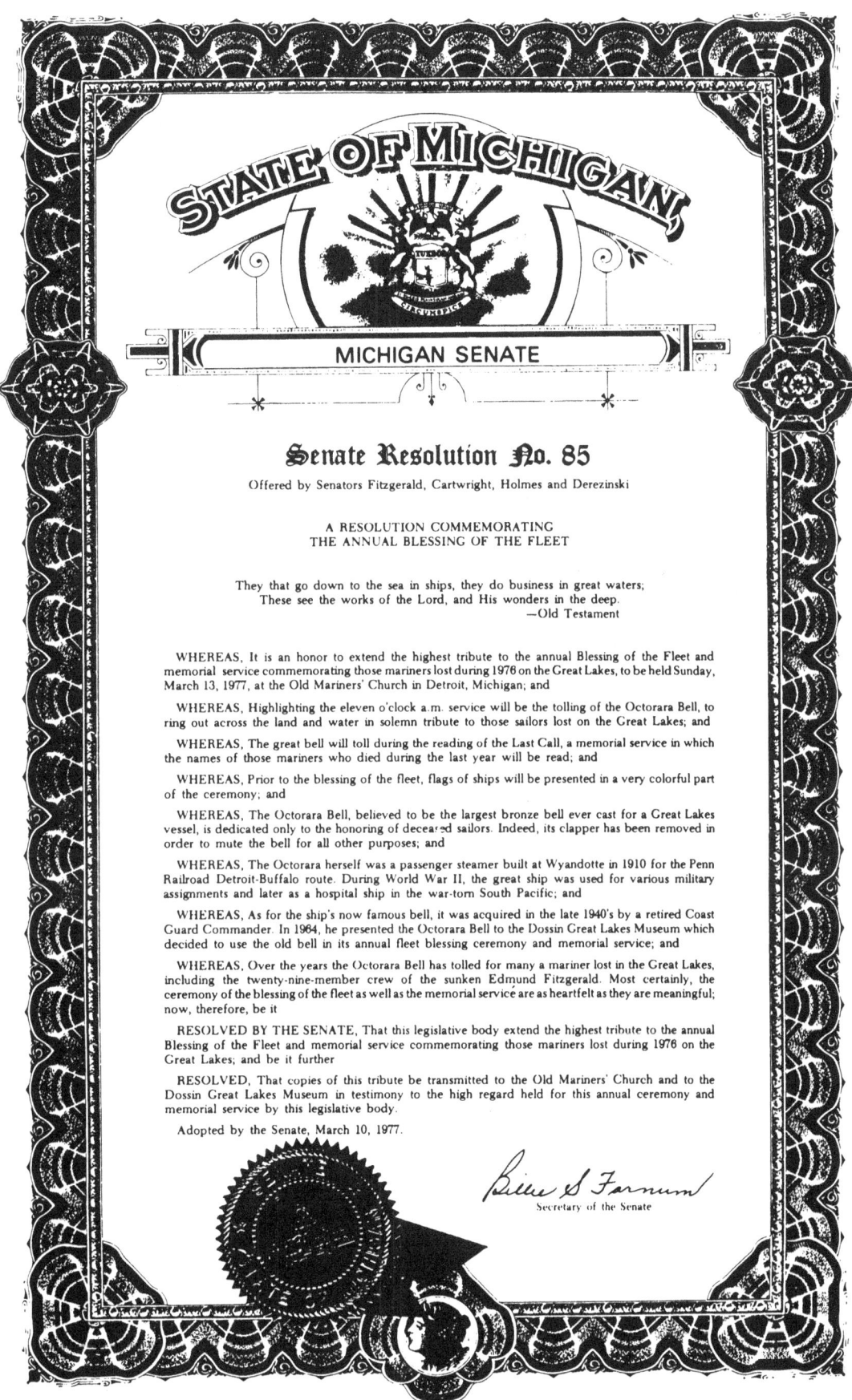

𝔖enate 𝔑esolution 𝔑o. 85

Offered by Senators Fitzgerald, Cartwright, Holmes and Derezinski

A RESOLUTION COMMEMORATING
THE ANNUAL BLESSING OF THE FLEET

They that go down to the sea in ships, they do business in great waters;
These see the works of the Lord, and His wonders in the deep.
—Old Testament

WHEREAS, It is an honor to extend the highest tribute to the annual Blessing of the Fleet and memorial service commemorating those mariners lost during 1976 on the Great Lakes, to be held Sunday, March 13, 1977, at the Old Mariners' Church in Detroit, Michigan; and

WHEREAS, Highlighting the eleven o'clock a.m. service will be the tolling of the Octorara Bell, to ring out across the land and water in solemn tribute to those sailors lost on the Great Lakes; and

WHEREAS, The great bell will toll during the reading of the Last Call, a memorial service in which the names of those mariners who died during the last year will be read; and

WHEREAS, Prior to the blessing of the fleet, flags of ships will be presented in a very colorful part of the ceremony; and

WHEREAS, The Octorara Bell, believed to be the largest bronze bell ever cast for a Great Lakes vessel, is dedicated only to the honoring of deceased sailors. Indeed, its clapper has been removed in order to mute the bell for all other purposes; and

WHEREAS, The Octorara herself was a passenger steamer built at Wyandotte in 1910 for the Penn Railroad Detroit-Buffalo route. During World War II, the great ship was used for various military assignments and later as a hospital ship in the war-torn South Pacific; and

WHEREAS, As for the ship's now famous bell, it was acquired in the late 1940's by a retired Coast Guard Commander. In 1964, he presented the Octorara Bell to the Dossin Great Lakes Museum which decided to use the old bell in its annual fleet blessing ceremony and memorial service; and

WHEREAS, Over the years the Octorara Bell has tolled for many a mariner lost in the Great Lakes, including the twenty-nine-member crew of the sunken Edmund Fitzgerald. Most certainly, the ceremony of the blessing of the fleet as well as the memorial service are as heartfelt as they are meaningful; now, therefore, be it

RESOLVED BY THE SENATE, That this legislative body extend the highest tribute to the annual Blessing of the Fleet and memorial service commemorating those mariners lost during 1976 on the Great Lakes; and be it further

RESOLVED, That copies of this tribute be transmitted to the Old Mariners' Church and to the Dossin Great Lakes Museum in testimony to the high regard held for this annual ceremony and memorial service by this legislative body.

Adopted by the Senate, March 10, 1977.

Billie S. Farnum
Secretary of the Senate

SAILING WITH AMERICAN YOUTH HOSTELS
Michigan Council American Youth Hostels
3024 Coolidge Hwy.
Berkley, Michigan 48072

The Michigan Council of American Youth Hostels (AYH) has developed a unique sailing program designed to meet the needs of the novice as well as the experienced sailor. The sail program consists of a series of instructional levels, designed to teach basic sailing skills on 18' centerboard sloops (Skipper Program) and more advanced sailing on 26' and 30' keelboats (Captains Program, Ensigns and Voyager Programs).

Successful completion of each level of instruction earns the student a rating (Skipper, Captain, Ensign and Voyager) and the opportunity to sail the club boats which correspond to that rating.

And for those who seek a more competitive sailing experience, AYH offers an Interlake Yacht Racing program which takes place on Kent Lake at Kensington Metro Park, during the sailing season.

No other sail instruction program in the midwest allows you to learn so much and sail so often, for so little!

Skippers Program
Basic class instruction for novices is offered in the Spring of each year. It consists of two evening shore school sessions and two full days of hands on sailing experience, plus a maintenance class. Students learn basic sailing skills and nautical terms, including regulations and the "rules of the road" with emphasis on safe boating and handling.

To qualify for the "Skippers" rating the student must pass both a written and an on-the-water test. Testing may be taken immediately after completion of the course or at any time during the season when the student feels ready. In preparation for testing, students can schedule an unlimited number of practice sails at Kent Lake. Practice sails are held every evening of the week with a rated AYH sailor in charge of each boat to assist the new student.

Since the sail program operates on a cooperative volunteer basis, each participant and rated sailor is required to contribute a minimum of fourteen (14) work hours per year, to the program.

For prospective "Skippers" who miss the Spring session, AYH offers a Fall Class Weekend. It begins with a Friday night shore school and continues with on-the-water instruction all day Saturday and Sunday. Students stay at the Foote Hostel in Milford, Michigan during this seassion.

Skipper Class Schedule

CLASS #	SHORE SCHOOL	ON-THE-WATER CLASS
1	5/15 & 5/29	5/17 & 5/31
2	5/15 & 5/29	5/18 & 6/1
3	6/5 & 6/12	6/7 & 6/14
4	6/5 & 6/12	6/8 & 6/15
5	6/19 & 6/26	6/21 & 6/28
6	6/19 & 6/26	6/22 & 6/29

Shore School
Shore School will be held at Sixma School, 28500 Alden in Madison Heights. Class time is from 7 p.m. until 10 p.m.

On-The-Water Classes
On-the-water classes are held at Kensington Metro Park and Stony Creek Metro Park from 9 a.m. until 4 p.m.

American Youth Hostels
American Youth Hostels is a non-profit organization which promotes a wide variety of educational and outdoor recreational activities for people of all ages and backgrounds. The Michigan AYH offers day, weekend and extended trips and activities involving sailing, skiing, hiking/backpacking, canoeing and bicycling.

ATTENTION:  STOP!

Planning To Build Something or Do Some Work in a River, Stream, Lake or Wetland?

Before You Start, Contact The U.S. Army Corps of Engineers

Federal laws require that a permit be obtained from the U.S. Army Corps of Engineers for most construction activities and dredging/filling operations in navigable waters of the United States. The U.S. Army Corps of Engineers wants your assistance in protecting the nation's water quality.

For further information and/or a review of your construction plans, contact:

Regulatory Functions Branch
Detroit District,
Corps of Engineers,
P.O. Box 1027,
Detroit, MI 48231
or telephone: (313) 226-6827 for additional information.

AMERICAN YOUTH HOSTELS INC.

Social events include theatre parties, barbecues and square dances as well as a number of fund raising events for AYH members and their guests.

The AYH council offers instruction in a myriad of educational sessions such as nature seminars, bicycle repair, first aid classes and leadership training.

Membership in AYH opens the door to more than 6,000 hostels world wide, 275 across the U.S. and over 20 in Michigan. Hostels provide inexpensive accommodations for individuals, families and groups of likeminded people. Membership may be individual or family.

The first step to the AYH sail program is to become a member of American Youth Hostels. Each participant in the sailing program must become an AYH member to participate.

Sailing Opportunities For Occasional Sailors

AYH members (and guests) not in the sail program may still enjoy sailing as a passenger. You may hitch rides at Kent Lake anytime on weekends and holidays for just $2.00. Just sign-in with the Dockmaster when you arrive.

The program consists of a series of instructional levels designed to meet the needs of the novice as well as experienced sailor. Basic sailing skills with an emphasis on safe boating and handling are taught on 18' centerboard sloops with qualified instructors. The program includes shore school and on water classes with unlimited practice sails.

Advanced sail instruction is available on our 26' and 30' keelboats on Lake St. Clair; members can charter boats and participate in evening pleasure sails throughout the season. And for those seeking a competitive sailing experience, the AYH now offers an Interlake yacht racing program.

You may also make reservations through the AYH office for evening sails on Lake St. Clair. Evening sails depart at 6:30 p.m. from the Jefferson Beach Marina.

```
26' Commanders – all season
Sailpass Holders          $3.00
Non-Sailpass Holders      $5.00

     30' Cruising Boats
Sailpass Holders          $4.00
Non-Sailpass Holders      $6.00
```

The folllowing sailing fees must be paid:
    Sailpass $ 55.00
    Instruction $100.00
    Total $155.00

Note: If more than one member of your family is taking the classes, you may purchase a Family Sail Pass (husband/wife and/or children under 18). The minimum age for sail students is 16 years old.

Cancellation and Refund Policy

A cancellation fee of $15.00 will be assessed for any cancellation of sail classes which is not made 30 days prior to the beginning of the class.

Refunds on evening sails will be made only if the office is notified by the Captain that the sail was cancelled.

AYH MEMBERSHIP

Name:
Address:
City:
Home Phone: Zip:
Work Phone:
New: Renewal:
How did you learn about our sail Program?

MEMBERSHIP FEES

Senior (18-59 yrs.)	$ 22.50
Junior (under 18)	12.50
3 yr. Senior	52.50
Family	32.50
Life Membership	202.50
Senior Citizen	12.50
Total	

The above prices include a subscription to the Michigan AYH Beacon.

Sail Fees

Single Sailpass	$ 55.00
Family Sailpass	70.00
Skipper Class Fee	100.00
Captain Class Fee	70.00
Ensign Class Fee	70.00
Total	

All sailors must buy a sail pass. Please send a separate check for the membership and one for the sail fees. Make all checks payable to AYH.

Sail Pass

The AYH sail pass is the basis for active participation in the sailing program (not required for evening sails). A sail pass is required to validate ratings ("Skipper," "Captain," "Ensign," "Voyager") and to participate in an entire season of regular day and evening sailing activities at Kent Lake, and (at a reduced fee) on Lake St. Clair.

To Enroll in Beginning Sail Classes

You must be an AYH member and subscribe to the Beacon.

Walker Boat Building

WHY NOT GIVE YOUR OLD BOAT NEW LIFE?

Walker Boat Building can make your old boat sparkle like new. Skilled in modern and traditional methods, we will repair, refinish or custom build a vessel for you.

Give us a call today
(613) 542-0841

P.O. Box 272 Kingston, Ontario, Canada K7L 4V8

What is Walker Boat Building?

Walker Boat Building specializes in the custom building, repair and restoration of wooden boats. We have the skills and facilities to employ all types of wooden construction, simple or complex, using either traditional or modern methods. Our experience includes the building of small conventional and up-to-date vessels in solid lumber, plywood and cold molding, and the construction of larger multihulls in plywood and epoxy. We are also the only shop in North America now producing wooden Tornado catamarans using cold molding and vacuum bag techniques. Because the demand for traditional wooden vessels is quite limited in today's market, Walker Boat Building is very versatile in our modes of construction. We are therefore willing to supply quotes for and bid on any type of wooden design that you may receive inquiries about from your clients.

Why Walker Boat Building?

Apart from the high quality of our workmanship, being in Kingston, Canada puts Walker Boat Building in an especially advantageous position for American customers. We have access to good suplies of very economical materials (local lumber includes white oak, cedar and marine plywoods); the difference in the dollar which favours U.S. currency by 25 percent; and low import duties into the States from Canada. Kingston itself is located at the eastern end of Lake Ontario on a super-highway halfway between two major supply centres, Toronto and Montreal. The St. Lawrence Seaway and Erie Barge Canal are close by for easy access to the Atlantic and eastern seaboard. The economic structure of the area allows us to keep our hourly shop rate extremely low by current standards, at only $20. Our shop consists of 4400 square feet of heated space, 10,000 square feet of yard, and has lake access and a railway spur 200 feet away. Transportation is therefore no problem, and our space gives us the capacity to build boats up to 45 feet in length and the capability to expand for larger projects. Furthermore we are equipped with air tools to provide efficient use of the time available for each job.

The Owner

The owner, Willie Walker, grew up in Devon, England and has acquired a great deal of ocean sailing experience throughout his thirty-four years. He has worked in the repair and construction of glass and wood boats in England, Canada and the U.S.A., has a marina management diploma from Sheridan College and 3 years study at Guelph University.
He thus became very well versed in all aspects of boating at a very young age. A one year course in wooden boat building at The Landing Boatshop school in Maine, further supplemented his knowledge before he embarked on setting up his own one-man shop in Kingston in the fall of 1980. He presently employs six people, and has developed and expanded a high-quality leisure business in a period of economic restraint.

SCHOONER ISSAC H. EVANS
 & SCHOONER RICHARD ROBBINS, SR.
Box 482
Rockland, ME 04841

CAPT. ROBERT S. DOUGLASS
Coastwise Packet Co., Inc.
Vinegard Haven, Mass. 02568

MARINE COAST CRUISES
Capt. Frederick B. Guild
Rockalnd, ME 04841

CAPTAIN MIKE ANDERSON
Yankee Packet Co.
Box 736
Camden, ME 04843

MYSTIC WHALER
7 Homes Street
Mystic, Connecticut 06355

WESTINDIAMAN CRUISES
1539 Washington Lane
West Chester, Pennsylvania 19380

SEVEN SEAS YACHTS
Box 36
City Island, New York 10464

DISCOVER BELIZE
Hanns Ebensten Travel
55 W. 42nd Street
New York, New York 10036

ALSO TRAVEL CLUBS LIKE THE
 MATTERHORN SPORTS CLUB
3 West 57th Street
New York City, New York 10019
feature short Charters and "Weekend Learn to
 Sails" for their members.

CARIBBEAN YACHT CHARTERS
P.O. Box 583
Marblehead, Mass. 01945

VIRGIN ISLAND YACHT CHARTERS
239–F Delancey Street
Philadelphia, Pennsylvania 19106

STEVENS YACHTS OF ANNAPOLIS
100 Severn Avenue
Annapolis, Maryland 21403

OCEANUS
Box 431Y11
Ho-Ho-Kus, New Jersey 07423

FREIGHTER TRAVEL CLUB OF
 AMERICA WORLD TRAVEL
Box 4229
Anaheim, California 92803

WINDJAMMER BAREFOOT CRUISES
P.O. Box 120
Miami Beach, Florida 33139

MICHIGAN SEA GRANT PROGRAM
Something in it for you

Michigan residents are drawn to lakes — especially to the Great Lakes. Year-round recreation opportunities are the chief attractions: boating, fishing, SCUBA diving and just looking at the scenery. The Michigan Sea Grant Program sponsors research, education and advisory services to help solve problems and plan for balanced use of Great Lakes resources. We are constantly looking for ways to preserve and improve recreational opportunities along the State's shorelines.

The Michigan Sea Grant Program is a cooperative effort of the University of Michigan and Michigan State University. We welcome your ideas and offer you some useful publications listed below. Order them from:

The Michigan Sea Grant Publications Office
University of Michigan
2200 Bonisteel Blvd.
Ann Arbor, Michigan 48109

SOLVING SHORELINE PROBLEMS: If you own, or are planning to purchase shoreline property, you will be concerned with erosion problems. Try these informational booklets. All are free for single copies:

1. Shore Erosion: What to Do. MICHU-SG-100
2. Shoreline Protection Guide for Property Owners. Insight 2
3. Buying Shoreline Property. MICHU-SG-75-101
4. Shoreline Erosion: Special Problems for Realtors. MICHU-SG-76-302

SOMETHING FOR FISHERMEN: Here are some booklets which have resulted from our fisheries research.

1. Great Lakes Fish Cookery. 16 pages. Free for single copies.
2. Fishes of the Grand Traverse Bay Region. Illustrated. 54 pages. $1.00.
3. Salmon Eggs: Bait and Food. PB257242/ AS/ MICHU-SG-76-100

ATTENTION SCUBA DIVERS: We have an extensive Underwater Technology program at Michigan Sea Grant. Training, safety and medical research, and the hyperbaric rescue chamber are important services. The following publications are free for single copies.

Ocean Research and Education Society, Inc.

ORES is an independent nonprofit corporation with home offices in Boston. The Society was formed for the purpose of promoting research, knowledge and conservation of the ocean environment. Students of the Society serve as research assistants and working crew aboard the "Regina Maris." The Society is funded by interested foundations and individuals. Operating income is derived from expeditions, research grants and tuitions.

The ship: "Regina Maris" is a three-masted barquentine built in 1908 by Ring Anduson of Denmark for service between Hamburg and Canada. Because the North Atlantic winter is one of the roughest in the world, she was very strongly built of heavy oak planks on oak frames with special strengthening for work in ice. The hull has been well looked after throughout her life and remains in class with Lloyds Register. Her last hull survey was in August 1975 when she passed with only two small repairs to a stanchion on deck.

The vessel traded from 1908 to 1957 and was laid up until 1965 when she was bought by a Norwegian shipowner who re-engined her, re-rigged her with new spars and stainless steel rigging and re-fitted her out under Lloyds Survey.

Her new equipment included a 220v electrical system with two 15 Kw and one 5 Kw alternators, electrical ventilating system to the accommodation, hot water heating and domestic water boiler system, and a modern bilge and fire pumping system.

Navigation equipment includes MK 22 Decca navigator system, Kelvin Hughes MK 17 radar, Simrad 200 fathom echo sounder, standard compass and binnacle, steering compass, azimuth mirror and ship chronometer. In 1975, two new radio sets were fitted, a Sailor V.H.F. 18 channel and a Sailor M.F. radio telephone.

Since 1966 the ship has been round the world via Cape Horn. She visited Panama, Mexico, Chile, Australia, New Zealand, Tahiti, Honolulu and South Africa. The "Regina Maris" was recently used in the making of a film by the Polish government.

She has accommodation for 36 persons and a British D.T.I. Solas certificate for fire and life safety equipment.

She is a traditional sailing ship with very beautiful lines, capable of withstanding the worst weathers in safety and comfort and able to make long ocean passages at any time and in any weather.
Length Overall: 144' (43.60 m)
Water Line: 103' (31.50 m)
Beam: 26' (8 m)
Draft: 11' (3.30 m)
Engine: G.M. 230 h.p. V 8.

Since the students work the ship, expedition participation requires a minimum age of 18 and good health as well as an interest in pursuing a career in ocean sciences and marine biology. For application and information write: ORES, Inc., 51 Commercial Wharf 6, Boston, Massachusetts 02110, (617) 523-3455.

Sailing Singles

P.O. Box 717
Royal Oak, MI 48068

If you'd rather furl a jib than fumble with the weekend TV lineup — if you'd prefer cruising the lakes to cruising the singles' bars — COME SAIL WITH THE SAILING SINGLES.

Over five years old, SAILING SINGLES originated with a group of single friends trying to combine their two favorite things — good sailing and good company. The club now has grown to over 200 members from all over the metro Detroit area. Many of the members own sizeable cruising boats or smaller trailerable sloops or catamarans. The rest of the members act as crew, putting their sailing skills to practice or learning to sail for the first time.

Members come from Northville, Livonia, Union Lake, Royal Oak, Troy, Grosse Pointe, Detroit, St. Clair Shores, Warren, Mt. Clemens and everywhere in between. It's a diverse group with a variety of levels of sailing experience.

To satisfy their yearning for the sea, SAILING SINGLES' activities include, day, evening, and overnight cruises on the Great Lakes, as well as picnic-sail parties and windsurfing on some of the smaller, inland lakes. Many of the events are free to members or involve a small fee or food and drink contribution.

The season officially starts with the semi-formal Commodore's Ball, but many an anxious skipper can be found chasing the last of the ice flows down to the Detroit River. On the second Thursday of the month, May to September, SAILING SINGLES meet at Bonnie Brook Country Club, Eight Mile and Telegraph, for an informal meeting and dance. The charge for non-members is $6.00. Educational programs on sailing technique, safety skills, or even dockside gourmet cooking open the evenings at 7:30 p.m. By 9:00 p.m., everyone's on the dance floor and the party continues until 1:00 a.m. Non-members are encouraged to attend these socials to learn more about the club and meet its members. Throughout the spring and summer, special activities are held across the tri-county map, occasionally at some of the better-known boat and yacht clubs along the waterfront. Other activities include a white water rafting trip, Tiger baseball games, Bob-Lo moonlight cruises, to name a few.

Summer is, of course, the busiest time for SAILING SINGLES. But, don't think this group hibernates all winter! During the non-sailing months, the socials move to Friday night at Bonnie Brook and an impressive list of ski parties, happy hour get-togethers, and winter sport spectaculars is put into plan.

As with any club or organization, the key to enjoying SAILING SINGLES is to get involved. It is a very active and well-organized group and the secret to its success is the time and energy volunteered by its members.

Whether you're a skipper with your own boat, an enthusiastic deck hand, or would like to learn to sail while making new friends, SAILING SINGLES is waiting to welcome you aboard.

Chapter 9

SURROUNDING WATERS

For their interflowing aggregate,
those grand freshwater seas of ours,
Erie, and Ontario, and Huron,
and Superior and Michigan, . . .
possess an ocean-like expansiveness,
with many of the ocean's traits;
with many of its rimmed varieties of races
   and climes.

HERMAN MELVILLE
Moby Dick

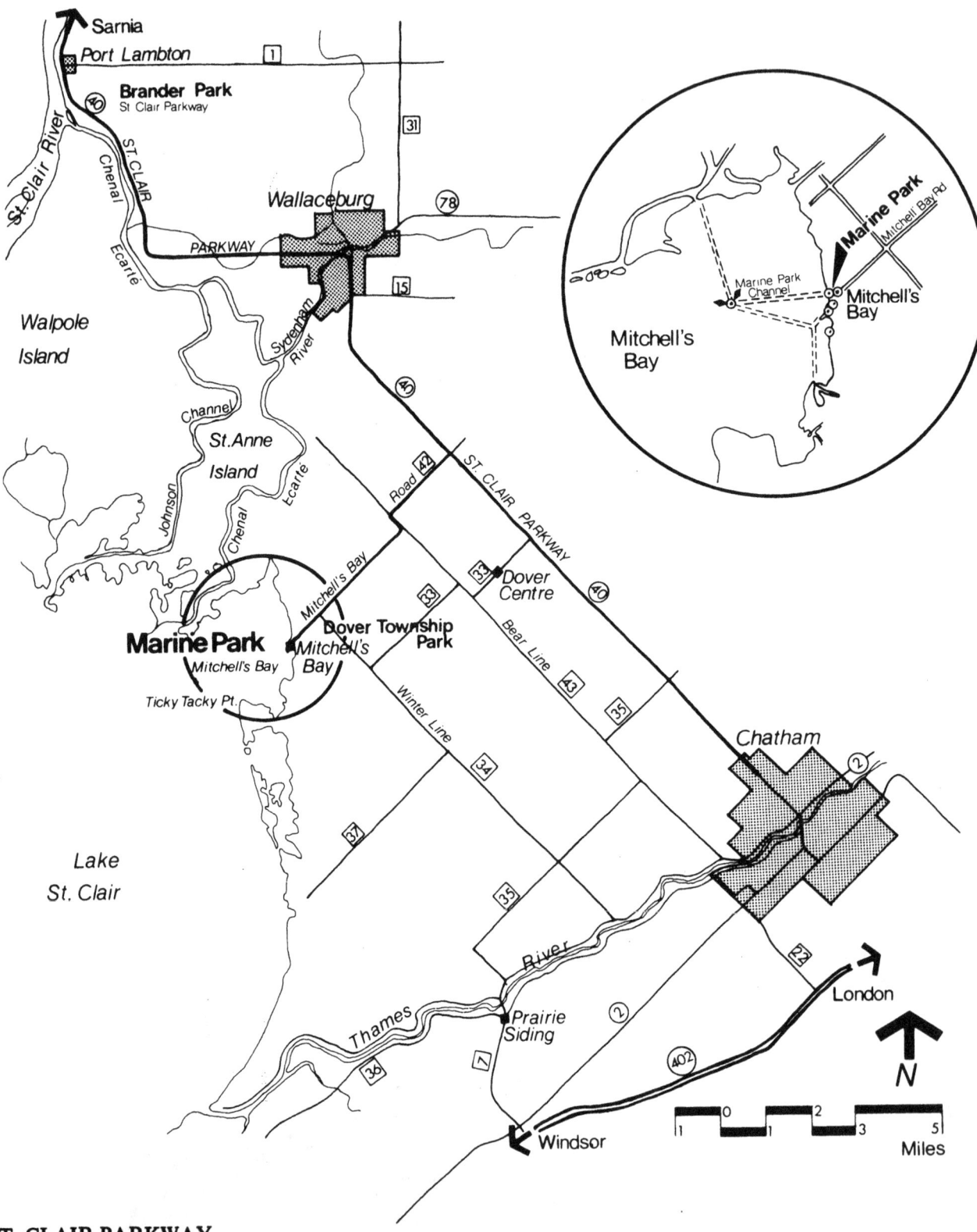

ST. CLAIR PARKWAY

Watching the Boats Go By . . .

Visitors to the Parkway note that their favorite pastime is Seaway observation. There is always a wide variety of river traffic; lake freighters, commercial vessels, an assortment of pleasure craft, and "salties" from all over the world.

The St. Clair River-Lake St. Clair-Detroit River area is the busiest section of the Great Lakes shipping system, with a ship entering the St. Clair River every seven minutes. Over 100 million tons of cargo is transported through this river every year, which is more than the Panama, Keil and Suez Canals combined.

SHIPWRECKS

General Information

Fathom Five Provincial Park offers an unlimited variety of diving opportunities suitable for all levels of sport diving experience, from the novice snorkeler to the highly skilled and advanced diving enthusiast. Visitors are reminded that while the sport can be enjoyable and a safe pastime, there is no substitute for adequate training and the following of safe practices. Divers are encouraged to adhere to all safety guidelines taught by the training organizations and further outlined in this pamphlet.

The Diving Rules

The Ministry of Natural Resources, in co-operation with the Ontario Underwater Council, the Association of Canadian Underwater Councils and the National Association of Underwater Instructors, Canada, supports and encourages all divers to adhere to the following safe diving practices.
1. NEVER DIVE ALONE: The buddy system is your protection in the event of unexpected problems.
2. CERTIFICATION: All divers should be trained and certified by a recognized organization. Trainees must be under the supervision of a certified diving instructor.
3. USE THE DIVE FLAG: Always display a fully visible and recognized dive flag when in the water. Restrict all diving to within 100 feet (30 metres) of the flag and do not confuse boaters by flying the flag when no activity is underway. In turn, boat operators must use extreme caution when operating near a displayed dive flag.
4. UNATTENDED BOATS: Never leave a boat unattended especially when it is used for diving. At least one person must be left on board when the boat is anchored or moored.
5. COLD WATER: Low water temperatures in this area can create special hazards. Only experienced divers should exceed 60 feet (18 metres) in depth. Regulator freeze-up can occur, so divers should take appropriate precautions.
6. RESTRICTED AREAS: Avoid diving in restricted areas such as vessel channels and docking areas. Details regarding these restricted areas are available at the park Visitor Centre.
7. NIGHT DIVING: Only experienced divers should engage in night diving. Each diver should be equipped with an adequate underwater light and should never exceed 30 feet (10 metres) in depth.
8. DRUGS AND ALCOHOL: The use of alcohol or drugs when diving can have disastrous effects.

Regulations

Visitors are reminded that certain Regulations under the Provincial Parks Act may affect their behaviour and conduct. Some are produced here for your guidance and information. You should be aware that these as well as other applicable laws are enforced within the park. Additional information may be obtained from the park Visitor Centre.
Ont. Regulation 822 (General) Revised Regulations of Ont.
2 (1) No person shall,
  a) remove, damage, or deface any property of the Crown; or
  b) damage or deface any relic, artifact, or natural object or any site of archaeological or historical interest,
  within a provincial park.
(2) Except with the written permission of the Minister, no person shall,
  a) cut or remove any plant or tree;
  b) remove any relic, artifact or natural object;
  c) disturb any site of archaeological or historical interest;
  d) make an excavation for any purpose; or
  e) conduct research,
  within a provincial park. (Ont. Reg. 399/79 s.2)
29a (1) In this section "dive" means to engage in the sport of underwater swimming while using any self-contained underwater breathing apparatus or any other type of apparatus, except a snorkel, designed to supply the user with an air supply while submerged.

(2) No person shall dive within Fathom Five Provincial Park without first registering at the park office.
(3) A person found diving within Fathom Five Provincial Park shall, on demand of an officer produce proof of registration.
(4) Every registration expires March 31 next following the date of registration.

The park Visitor Centre contains displays and information concerning park resources and the local area. Staff are available to assist in providing information regarding local conditions, site selection and general enquiries. Special group service programmes, intended to enhance the diving experience at the park, may be arranged during your visit to the Centre.

All divers are required by regulation to register and obtain an annual diver registration at the park Visitor Centre. By so doing, important safety and management messages will be provided, thus increasing the quality of your diving experience while at Fathom Five.

Harbour Area Sites

Except for those areas that are designated on the map, the Tobermory harbours are restricted to diving. Extreme care should be taken at all times, since considerable vessel traffic may be encountered at all locations.
The use of a towed float with a dive flag is recommended. Vessel operators are requested to use extreme caution when piloting a boat in the area of all diving activities.

1. SWEEPSTAKES - schooner
   built: Burlington, Ontario, 1867
   length: 119 feet
   depth: 20 feet (7 metres) maximum
   This vessel was abandoned and later sank, June, 1896. It is an excellent site for all levels of diving experience.
2. CITY OF GRAND RAPIDS - steamer
   built: Grand Haven, Michigan, 1879
   length: 122.5 feet
   depth: 15 feet (5 metres) maximum
   This vessel was burned and sank in October, 1907. Its rudder and propeller are displayed at the Tobermory and St. Edmunds Township Museum, Tobermory.
   This is an excellent site for all levels of diving experience.

3. BIG TUB LIGHTHOUSE
   This is an area of interesting geological features.
   depth: to 75 feet (23 metres)
   Limited parking is available at this access point. It is a good location for check-out dives in the shallower depths. For your safety, please contain your diving activities to the area inside the restricted boating buoys.
4. THE ANCHOR
   This large wooden stocked iron anchor from an unknown vessel provides an interesting viewing opportunity.
   depth: 70 feet (21 metres)
   Access can be gained by approaching the site by boat or by swimming from the "gap" access area.
   It is recommended that you stay close to shore and please respect the rights of the adjacent private property owners.
5. THE TUGS
   Wreckage of four small steam tugs, (The JOHN AND ALEX, ROBERT K., BOB FOOTE and ALICE G.) are

located in this area.
depth: 40 feet (13 metres) maximum
Please contain diving activities to the area inside the restricted boating buoys.
This is a good site for all levels of diving experience.

6. CASCADEN - schooner
   built: Southampton, Ontario, 1866
   length: unknown (138 tons)
   depth: 20 feet (6 metres) maximum
   This vessel was wrecked in October, 1871. The wreckage is badly broken up and spread over a large area.
   Larger groups do not find this a popular site.

7. CHINA - schooner
   built: Port Robinson, Ontario, 1863
   length: 137 feet
   depth: 10 feet (3 metres) maximum
   It was wrecked on the China Reef in November, 1883. Today the wreckage is badly broken up with the main portion being close to shore.
   This is not a popular location for group dives.

8. JOHN WALTERS - schooner
   built: Kingston, Ontario, 1852
   length: 108 feet
   depth: 15 feet (5 metres) maximum
   The JOHN WALTERS was wrecked circa 1899.
   It is an excellent site for snorkelers and novice divers as it provides a lot to see and touch.

9. W. L. WETMORE - steamer
   built: Cleveland, Ohio, 1871
   length: 213.7 feet
   depth: 30 feet (10 metres) maximum
   This vessel was wrecked in a storm in November, 1901. In addition to the large amount of timber wreckage, some of the impressive machinery including the boiler is still in place. Surrounding the site are interesting glacial scours in the bedrock.

10. JAMES C. KING - schooner/barge
    built: East Saginaw, Michigan, 1867
    length: 175 feet, 3 inches
    depth: 25 to 95 feet (7 to 30 metres)
    The KING was wrecked while under tow to the WETMORE in November, 1901. The second barge on tow, the BRUNETTE, was later salvaged.
    This site is good for advanced levels of experience. It is not recommended for novices or trainees.

11. NEWAYGO - steamer
    built: Marine City, Michigan, 1890
    length: 196 feet
    depth: 25 feet (8 metres) maximum
    This vessel was wrecked during a storm in November, 1903. Although the wreckage is scattered, the main portion lies flat on the bottom.
    This is an excellent site for all levels of diving experience.

12. PHILO SCOVILLE - schooner
    built: Cleveland, Ohio, 1863
    length: 139 feet, 6 inches
    depth: 25 to 95 feet (7 to 30 metres)
    It was wrecked in a storm in October, 1889. The bow portion can be found at the deeper depths and the anchors are located about 100 feet (30 metres) east of the main wreckage.
    Persons with advanced levels of diving experience find this a popular site. It is not recommended for novices.

13. CHARLES P. MINCH - schooner
    built: Vermillion, Ohio, 1867
    length: 154.7 feet
    depth: 20 to 50 feet (6 to 16 metres)
    The MINCH was driven onto the rocks in October, 1898. The wreckage is broken up and spread over the bay with the main portions being found close to the shore near the head of the cove.
    This is an excellent site for all levels of experience.

14. ARABIA - barque
    built: Kingston, Ontario, 1853
    length: 131.6 feet
    depth: 120 feet (37 metres)
    The ARABIA foundered in October, 1884.
    This site is recommended only for advanced diving groups under the direction of a dive master.

15. MARION L. BRECK - schooner
    built: Kingston, Ontario, 1863
    length: 127 feet
    depth: the major portion is in 90 feet (28 metres)
    This vessel struck the rocks and broke up in October, 1900, leaving some scattered wreckage in the shallows.
    This is not a popular site and is recommended for experienced divers only.

16. FOREST CITY - steamer
    built: Cleveland, Ohio, 1870
    length: 216.7 feet
    depth: 60 to 150 feet (18 to 46 metres)
    It struck the island in the fog, slid off and sank in June, 1904.
    This site is suitable for highly advanced divers only. Not recommended for sport divers.

17. THE CAVES
    Located along the cliffs of Cyprus Lake Provincial Park, 12 miles (19 km) east of Fathom Five Provincial Park.
    depth: submerged grotto entrance in 20 feet (6 metres), rock face drops off to much deeper depths.
    These caves are most accessible by boat from Tobermory.
    Use of a dive light is recommended.
    A most pleasant and interesting geological dive, it is suitable for most levels of experience.

18. DAVES BAY - (Little Cove)
    Interesting geological formations such as pitting, glacial erratics and layered dolomite can be found along the south shore of the Bay.
    depth: to 40 feet (13 metres)
    Limited parking is available at this access point. Please respect the rights of the private property owners to the north of this access point.
    This area is suitable for diver check-outs.

19. DUNKS POINT
    Interesting geological formations, including good examples of "pitting", can be found in this location.
    depth: up to 40 feet (13 metres)
    Vessel access only.
    Divers with all levels of experience will find this an interesting location.

In addition, many other geological and fish observation sites may be found throughout the park. Information concerning these sites may be obtained by visiting the park Visitor Centre.

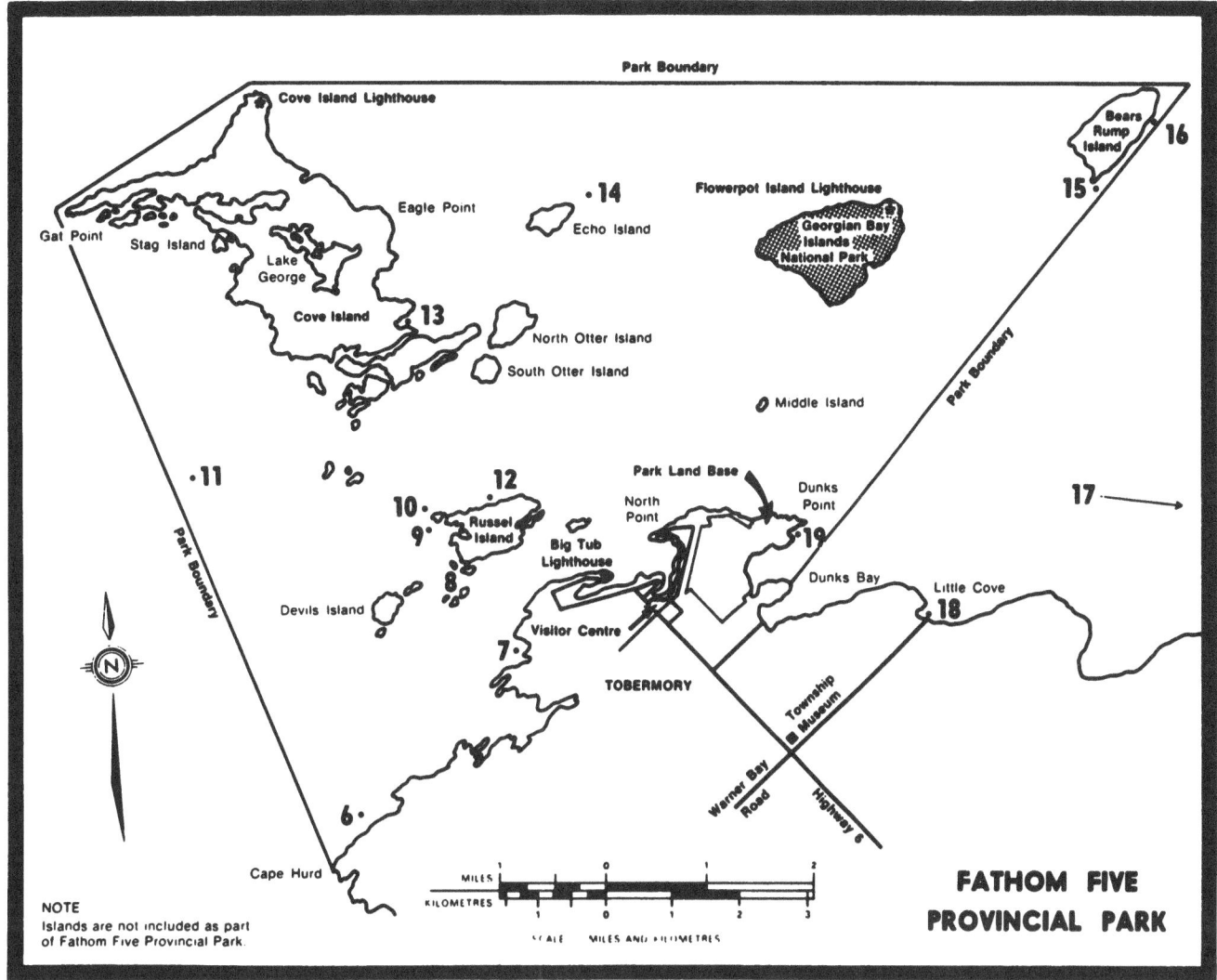

DIVER REGISTRATION PROGRAMME

Each year, thousands of sport diving enthusiasts are attracted to Fathom Five Provincial Park by the water quality and abundance of protected submerged historical and geological sites. To ensure a safe and enjoyable visit, it is imperative that basic safe diving practices are followed.

Diving safety is a primary concern of the park programme. It is important that each diver is aware of the relevant data concerning local conditions, safety measures and management messages. In order for this exchange of information to occur, each diver is required by law to register, prior to diving, at the Park Office/Visitor Centre.

Diving registration is available, free of charge, at the Visitor Centre and is valid for the entire season for which it has been issued. The Visitor Centre is open daily (early May to mid October) from 8 a.m. to 5 p.m. and on Friday and Saturday evenings as required. On subsequent visits, registered divers are encouraged to drop into the Centre and advise staff of their visit.

At the time of registration, the diver is provided with maps and information designed to aid in planning a safe and enjoyable dive. Informative displays and knowledgeable staff are available to provide additional information and assistance.

PROVINCIAL PARKS ACT, ONTARIO REGULATION 822/81 (GENERAL) REVISED REGULATIONS OF ONTARIO.

28 (1) In this section "dive" means to engage in the sport of underwater swimming while using any self contained underwater breathing apparatus or any other type of apparatus, except a snorkel, designed to supply the user with an air supply while submerged.

(2) No person shall dive within Fathom Five Provincial Park without first registering at the Park Office.

(3) A person found diving within Fathom Five Provincial Park shall, on demand of an officer, produce proof of registration.

(4) Every registration expires March 31 next following the date of registration.

22 (1) Every person who contravenes any of the provisions of this Act or of the regulations is guilty of an offence and on summary conviction is liable to a fine of not more than $500.

The ONTARIO UNDERWATER COUNCIL, the sport governing body for skin and scuba diving within Ontario, has represented and served its members on a variety of levels for almost 25 years.

1. The Deep Diving Syndrome.
2. Bends and the Sport Diver.
3. "It won't Happen to Me" Syndrome: Preparation for an Emergency and Recreational Surface-Supplied Diving. 21 pages. MICHU-SG-76-309 and MICHU-SG-76-310.
4. The Hyperbaric Chamber. MICHU-SG-73-102

NEWS ON THE GREAT LAKES: If you'd like to keep up to date on policy and issues on the Great Lakes, we have a bi-monthly newsletter called Upwellings. Ask to be put on the mailing list. And if you want to know more about our program, ask for our Annual Report.

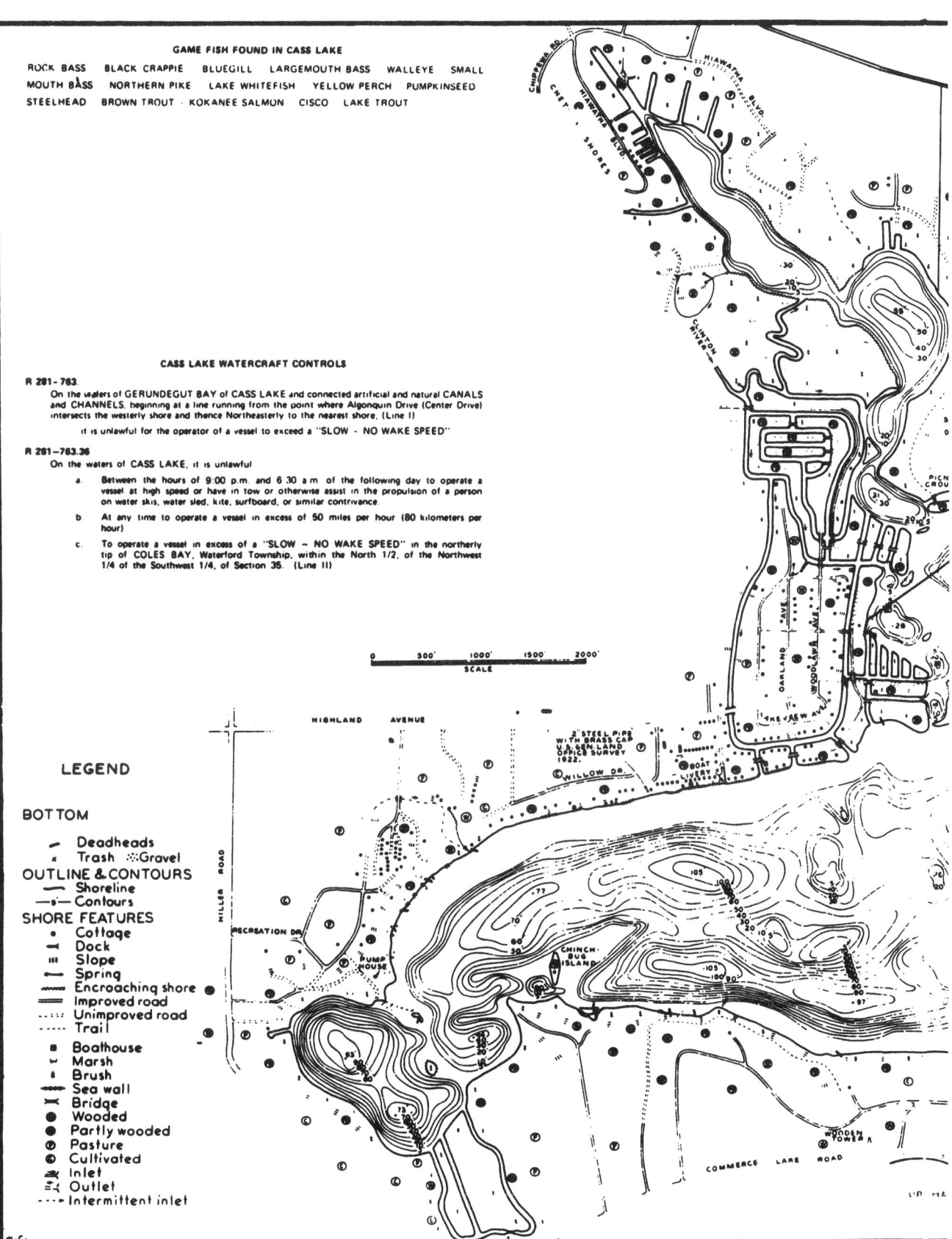

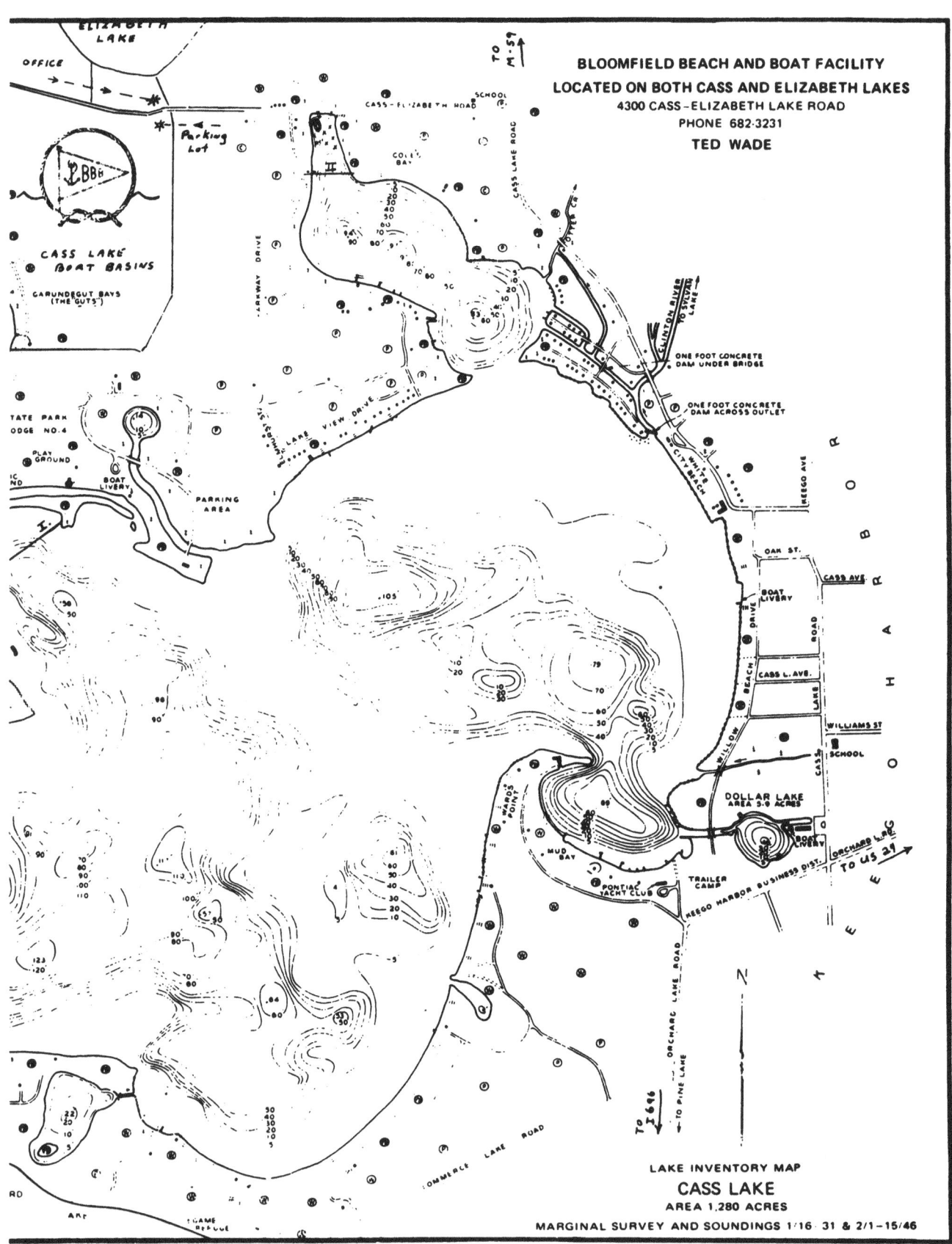

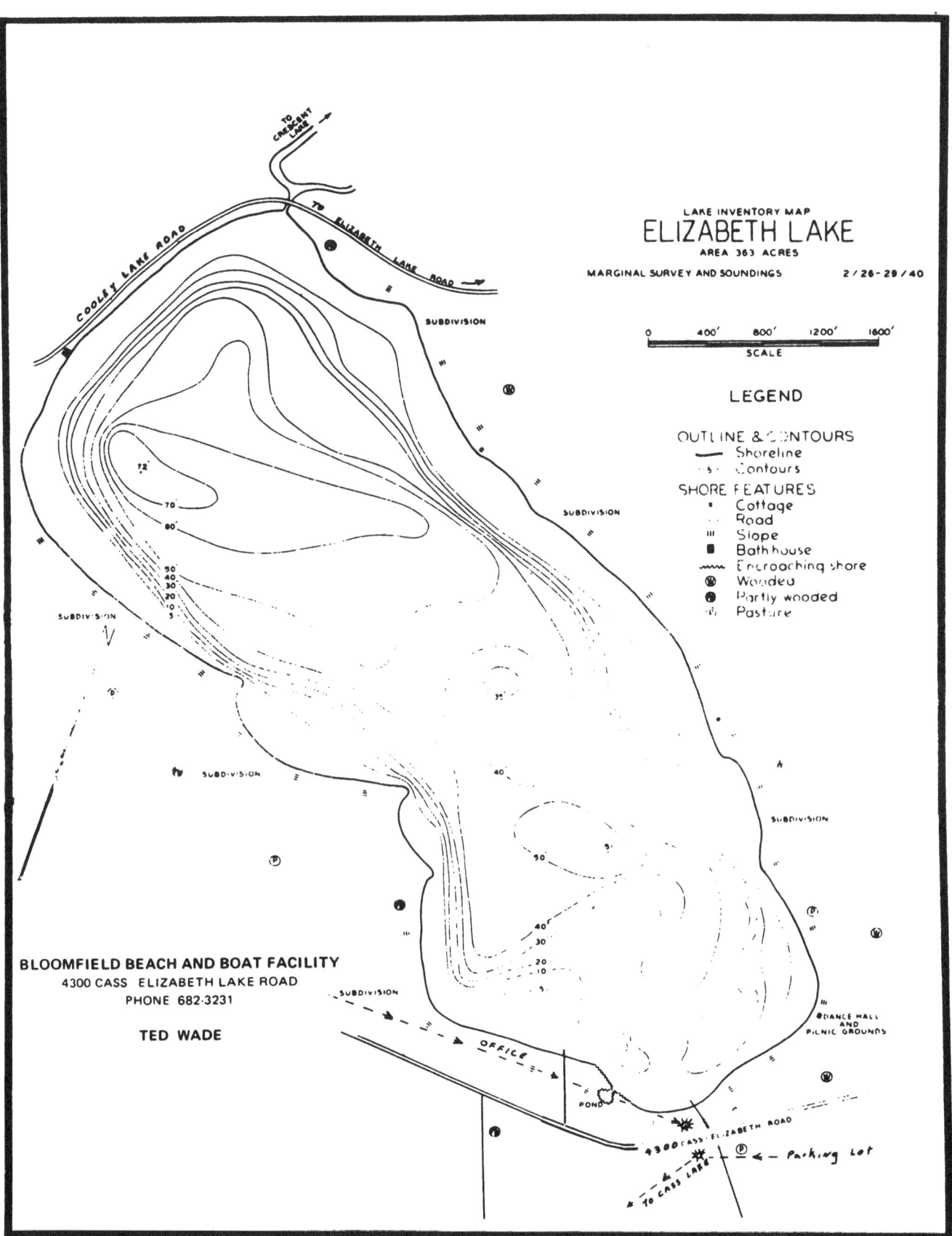

Dockage

Bloomfield Beach & Boat
4300 Cass Elizabeth Rd.
Pontiac, Michigan 48054
Phone (313) 682-3231

Boating Is "Our" Business

TWO MARINAS
CASS LAKE *ELIZABETH LAKE*

SAIL BOATS
HOBIE CATS
SAIL BOARDS
SERVICE
PARTS
RENTALS
ACCESSORIES

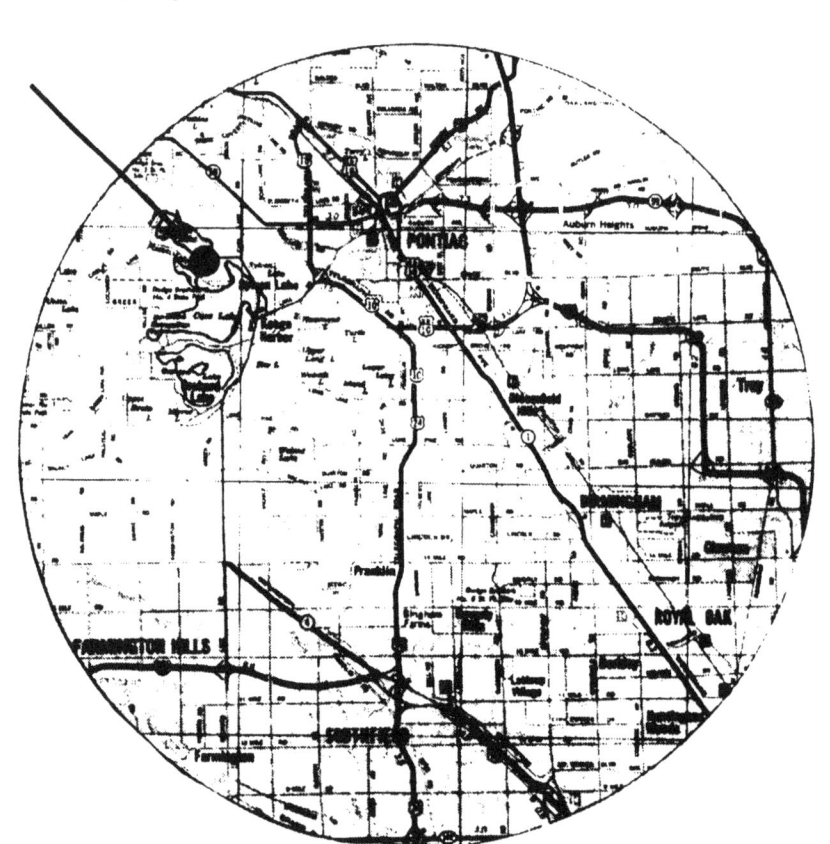

Family Owned for 37 Years!

GLORIA GOEDDEKE

RAFTED   24 x 30   OIL   M.I. MARINA   24 x 30   OIL

HAVE YOUR YACHT RENDERED IN PEN AND INK OR OIL.

GLORIA GOEDDEKE'S WORK IS INCLUDED IN BOTH PUBLIC AND PRIVATE COLLECTIONS. A PARTIAL LIST INCLUDES YACHTSMEN D. SCHMIDT, "SASSY" MT. CLEMENS, MI.; J. MILLER, "HARRAH," BLOOMFIELD HILLS, MI.; D. WHARTON, "TORTUGA," CHICAGO, ILL.

PUBLIC COLLECTIONS INCLUDE THE HYATT REGENCY, DEARBORN, MI.; BUTTERWORTH HOSPITAL, GRAND RAPIDS, MI.; GINO'S SURF SUPPER CLUB, MT. CLEMENS, MI. AND SAND POINT INN, TITUSVILLE, FLA.

GOEDDEKE'S STUDIO III   37680 Mapplehill, Mount Clemens, MI 48085

Chapter 10

NAUTICAL PUBLICATIONS

"Knowledge is of two kinds.
We know a subject
ourselves, or we know
where we can find
information upon it."
Boswell, Life of Johnson (1775)

The following chapter includes the many publications directed from Windsurfer to 12 Meter's. The publisher's of the world design, research, illustrate and educate readers on subjects as clear and complex, as the lakes, rivers and sea. The directory and reviews have been included so you, the reader, may expand your interest, knowledge and resources, regarding region, philosophy and appetite. The length of the review is no reflection on the quality or quantity of the publication. This section has been compiled to navigate you to your specific information harbor.

I would like to thank the many editors, secretaries and publishers that have responded to my requests for information to make this NAUTICAL PUBLICATIONS chapter possible.

Anchor's Away!

Sailing

Devoted to "the beauty of sailing" for the devoter of sail". Sailing magazine published monthly by Port Publications, Inc. at 125 E. Main St., Port Washington, WI. 53074. Directed to Sailboat connoisseur, this publication is totally unique. My second reason for the Logo, it's size — It's physically much larger than the other magazines, approximately 15" by 11", with excellent full color photos, also suitable for framing. The publication covers everything from racing, to hidden islands in the Carribean, good news coverage on products and opinions. For someone interested in, addicted to or fascinated by Sailing and Sailboats, this is the magazine for you.

Published monthly
524 Thames Street
Newport, R.I. 02840
$18.00 per year U.S.
$22.00 in Canada

A beautiful publication with consent sections of Canvas classes, shoreline, Passage Notes Fitting Out, and editorial opinions. Directed to the cruising sailor, for the cruising sailor. How to, Where to and When to. The infamous Tristan Jones did articles on "A Rendezvous with a Gale" to give you an idea of what an Atlantic crossing is like in a raging storm. Anyone who classifies a gale "playful" can really give you some tips. The quote was "It was a precocious gale, a playful gale, and, because gales have no respect for late sleepers, it was an early morning gale." I have been close to gale force winds, if not in so, and I didn't need a wake up call. When this man speaks, read on. The magazine covers it all. Great photos, with a true coarse for the person who wants to master cruising on the Great Lakes, or the oceans, Cruising World is exactly what the name delivers. A market place is included for sailboats for sale, and cruising products like Bimini Tents. A complete bookshelf which is really a library of all maritime subjects, adventures, maintenance, even a full color video "Celestial Navigation Simplified," by William F. Buckley, Jr. just for a jib run.

The Cruising World reader, is a Cruising World leader.

Yachting

P.O. Box 1200
5 River Rd.
Cos Cob, Conn. 06807
$19.98 per year, U.S.
Monthly

The symbol of the Yachting image. Yachting magazine is directed to the connoisseur of liquid assets. If you are in the market for a 40 to 100 footer, the majority of Yachting's display advertising exhibits these vessels. Power boats and Sail boats receive equal editorial copy. The publication is for the serious yachtsman or yachtswoman. Serious, in the category of tax bracket. Yacht design, book reviews, storm tactics, weather forecasting to mention some of the sections. A complete international brokerage and charter department, puts the world a phone call away. For the cruising Yachtsman, international ports of call are traveled with award winning photographs and charts to support editorial copy. The publication also forges issues like Federal fuel legislation. Yachting symbolizes the true traditions the name projects.

TELESCOPE
Dossin Great Lakes Museum
Belle Isle
Detroit, Michigan 48207
Published six times a year.
Membership $10.00 per year
Sustaining memberships $15.00 with the extra funds to Museum Development Fund.

The history of the Great Lakes continued thru the present encompasses this organization and publication. The Great Lakes Maritime Institute sponsors exhibits and displays. Meetings are held with guest speakers and maritime films. It never ceases to amaze me that organizations such as this great one, can include you in the fascination that surrounds the Freighter history, Sea stories and events for such a reasonable price. The Coast Guard officer that conducted the investigation into the sinking of the Edmund Fitzgerald was one of their dinner speakers with slides and professional insights to the tragedy and investigation. The museum has a pilot house from a freighter, the wood carvings that equal a maritime scale of the cistine chapel. Miniature models of Lake Freighters, coming and going thru locks.

The Curator John Polacsek has produced CAPTAIN OF THE FLEET, a game designed to teach players the economy and geography of the Great Lakes. A map of the lakes is printed on a vinyl surface with ports and shipyards. The object is to complete the required number of trips while overcoming obstacles such as weather delays, mechanical breakdowns and collisions. The game is available at the museum for $14.50, plus $2.50 postage. Sea sick pills and foul weather gear not included. A delightful organization and intriguing museum. For a family outing, where you can learn something interesting and important. Highly recommended. The publication will target a shipyard and list what ships were built when (photos included). Great Lakes and Seaway News documents current activities of vessels that sail the Great Lakes. Thank you Dossin, the State of Michigan and members.

"Canada's National Sailing Magazine"
95 Berkeley St.
Toronto, Ontario M5A 2W8

Published 10 times annually, one year subscription $26.95. ($6.95 for "Sourcebook"). Crew Notes lists regattas, events, projects and waterline information. "From the Helm" directs a series of articles on specific subject or specific author. Tides are covered in the navigation section and maintenance for repair and prevention. The publication is not limited to Canadian subjects, sailing events thru-out the globe are covered. Racing techniques are accompanied with photos and illustrations. The issue reviewed had a complete and in-depth series on a Mediterranean Odyssey right down to the time the Russian tea was served on board. Cruising information is covered on specific Canadian harbors and bays. Books are reviewed, first aid and general product introductions. A very professional, visually attractive magazine.

Cruising Guide to the Florida Keys
By Capt. Frank Papy
Edited by Barbara Methven
$12.95 plus $1.00 postage and handling/Annual
Frank M. Papy
208 Hendricks Isle
Fort Lauderdale, Florida 33301

A complete cruising guide to the Florida Keys, with Florida West Coast Supplement. Capt. Papy is also a charter Captain with licenses to 1000 tons. The Guide includes magnificent illustrations by Award winning Florida artist Millard Wells. From "Bonefisherman on the Flats, Bayside" to "Loggerhead Light, Dry Tortugas" the illustrations expose the reader to the colors, wind and wildlife of the Keys. Charts are complete with aerial satellite photos to enhance the formal maritime harbor and coast line charts. Weather information, underwater activities, marinas, with detail on each key. Special information sections range from suggested cruises, what to wear, equipment check list, fishing (with illustrations of fish), to galley guide. Approximately 20 special interest sections. The author has researched and sailed the keys from all angles. A must for a Key Cruise, a mental vacation for the armchair sailor. The information provided about each Key navigates you thru all routes with recommended weather and season routes. A technical guide with the direction and hands-on knowledge of its author and Captain.

SAIL AND POWER PORTRAITS BY

216-752-9882
2888 LUDLOW ROAD
CLEVELAND, OHIO 44120

Savor the Wild
Edited by Kay L. Richey
Sportsman's Outdoor Enterprises, Inc.
P.O. Box 192, Grawn, MI 49637
$ 13.00 postpaid

Yachtmen, sailor's and buccaneer's recieve fame and fortune usually by knowing a shrewd bargain and seizing it. Savor the Wild should be added to this list of Galley Gold. Kay Richey has recruited 57 famous outdoor writer's from the U.S. and Canada in this unique and useful cookbook. 133 pages in length, 280 mouthwatering recipes educate the reader from preparation to pan. The chapter titles include; 1. How to Cook Freshwater Gamefish 2. How to Cook North America's Big Game & Small Game 3. How to Cook North America's Gamebirds 4. Marinades, Sauces and

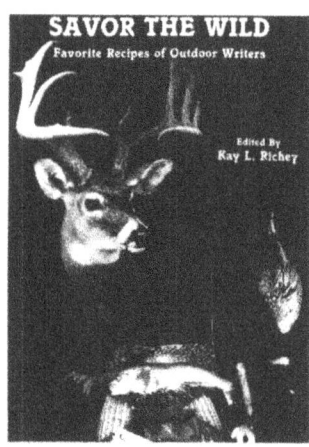

Bastters 5. Meet the Outdoor Writers (all members of the Outdoor Writer's Association) Delights like Sunshine Bass, Truite Au Bleu (Blue Trout) and Quebec Style Stuffed Northern Pike grace the Freshwater gamefish section. How about a Bear Roast? page 43. right after the Bear burger Pie, and prior to the Mountain Goat Stew. Also available are mini-cookbooks for $2.50 each titled My 10 Favorite Venison, Salmon-Trout, Walleye, Gamebird and Small Game recipes. Fisherman may wish to contact Kay for a list of five other books, titled, Great Lakes Steelhead Flies, Michigan's AuSable River, Today & Tomorrow, Making & Using the Dry Fly, Fly Fishing and Manistee and the Fly Hatches. Savor the Wild is a delightful publication for Yachtman or Landlover!

Ontario Out of Doors
Magnus Publishing Ltd.
3 Church St.
Toronto, Ont.
M5E 1M2.
10 times a year
19.95 per year
$6.00 add outside Canada

In depth, tightly designed magazine directed toward fishing, camping and hunting. Sections include Fishing, Wildlife, News of the Out of Doors, on Target, Boating. Special features cover detailed features regarding fishing rights, weather, Events Calendar with excellent Classified section on where to go, Fishing, Hunting and Camping. From Fly-In Services to Bear and Moose Lodges. Photographs are superior.

Should you ask me whence
   these stories?
I should answer, I should tell
   you
From the forests on the
   prairies,
From the great lakes of the
   Northland.

Henry Wadsworth Longfellow
Song of Hiawatha

Yachtman's Guide to the Great Lakes

Seaway Publishing Co.
16 South Elm St.
Zeeland, MI 49464
Annual

The 8½ x 11, approximately 290 page publications covers the complete Great Lakes area. Aerial photographs and many charts help the Yachtman cover this vast area. Points of interest are periodically included. Yacht clubs are listed to assist the boater in over night dockage. Many of the Chamber of Commerces also accompany the charts and maps of ports of call. Divided into approximately eight sections 1. General information, 2. Lake Michigan, 3. Lake Superior, 4 Lake Huron, 5. St. Clair River, Lake St. Clair and Detroit River, Section 6. Lake Erie, Section 7. Lake Ontario, and Special Interest sections on Emergency Procedures, First Aid etc. Marinas listing includes for most chart or photo, with address and phone number. With the maritime charts just directing you to the harbor, it's nice to have additional information and details for entry to the harbor, the Yachtman's Guide to the Great Lakes provides this data.

MICHIGAN HOSTLE NEWS

Published by the Metropolitan Detroit Council American Youth Hostels, 3024 Coolidge Road, Berkley, Michigan 48072.

A monthly tabloid newspaper with some really good information about camping, sailing, hiking and bike riding. That may sound fairly general and a little off beat for publications directed to the boating community, but the thing that I think is valuable about this little newspaper is the information about instruction and the many trips day sailing and involvement these people have right here at your fingertips. The organization, owns and maintains their own fleet of boats, which for many is a great way to get involved in the water without the large expense it takes for most. Just to give you an example of cost. Five days of sailing thru out Lake Huron and Les Cheneaux Islands cost $179.00. Price includes food, instruction, maintenance and licensed Captain on board. Many three day trips on Lake St. Clair also available.

Cruising Guide to the Great Lakes
by Marjorie Cahn Brazer
496 Pages
75 B&W photographs, numerous charts
Hardcover $29.95

The author has written "Well Favoured Passage" a guide to the North Channel and "Sweet Water Sea", a guide to Georgian Bay. Her stated objective is "to help cruising sailors to plan cruises, to tell them where to go and why. Special interest information on the harbors is included. A cruising guide and not a pilot only about ten percent of the book is spent explaining how to get into the harbor. Where to get supplies, fuel, pump-out and even whether a jacket is required at the Yacht Club. How to make VHF phone call, weather and proper customs procedures. Ms. Brazer covered this vast area mostly by boat, some by car, she has 20 years cruising experience on the Lakes. I hope she has the Pirate's Guide, to find out where you don't have to wear a sportcoat.

THE BOATING INDUSTRY

Publisher, Whitney Communications Corporation, 205 East 42nd Street, New York, N.Y. 10017.

The business magazine of boating. Distributed to the marine dealers, distributors, boatbuilders marinas, manufacturer's respresentatives and manufacturers.

Address all subscription mail to Circulation Department, Boating Industry, 639 Marine Blvd., Marion, Ohio 43302. Include name, title, and marine industry association. A magazine for the business men in the wholesale, retail etc. position of the boat business. Good articles on economic conditions, and a variety of services to those involved. Marketing services offer. Boating Product News, The Marine Buyers Guide, Information Cards, OEM Specifier's Fact Book, Direct Mail Services, Merchandising, Showtime Showcase, Trade Show Dailies.

SAIL

Published monthly by United Marine Publishing, Inc., 38 Commercial Wharf, Boston, Massachusetts 02110.

Attractive magazine for the sailor of the world. A pure sail publication in both advertising and editorial. Promoted as the largest circulation of sailors than any other publication in the world. Editorial on racing and cruising. Great photos and large classified section on brokerage and equipment, services.

MOTOR BOATING AND SAILING

Published monthly by the Hearst Corporation, 224 West 57th St., New York, N.Y. 10019.

LAKELAND BOATING
729 Brookside, Ann Arbor, Michigan 48105

Published monthly.

The freshwater Yachting Magazine that covers cruising, racing and product development. In depth coverage on region races and manufacturers.

SHIPPING DIGEST

Published every Monday by Shipping Digest, Inc., 25 Broadway, New York, N.Y. 10004.

Editorial directed to the Export and Transportation Executives. Established January 17, 1923. A weekly information source on shipping schedules and shipping brokers. International in depth complete time table of international shipping schedules. A very unique publication from the stand point that it's weekly and a great deal of detailed shipping information.

WISCONSIN SPORTSMAN
Box 1307
Oshkosh, WI 54901

BRANDON'S SHIPPER AND FORWARDER

Published Weekly at One World Trade Center, Suite 3169, N.Y., N.Y. 10048.

A publication with the Official Steamship Schedules. Definity for the commercial international shipping personnel.

AMERICAN SEAPORT

The Official magazine for the American Association of Port Authorities. Published independently as World Ports / American Seaport by Amundsen Publications, Inc. General Offices, P.O. Box 39092, Washington, D.C.

Issued eight times per year. Trade publication directed to the management of cargo ports, fairly technical.

AMERICAN BOATING ILLUSTRATED
Recreation Publications, Inc.
2019 Clement Ave.
Alameda, CA 94501

A how-to-do and technical monthly tabloid aimed for boat owners who like to tinker with their own work aboard. Articles cover all manner of onboard engine repair and installation, electronics, hull and deck repairs, as well as features on cruising, sailing and fishing. Boating Illustrated is the genuine bolts and nuts offering step - by - step solutions to your building, fixing, installing, cruising and fishing problems. Also carries an Update Section on latest marine gear, unusual products and gives the general news concerning navigation and safety legislation. Plenty of photos and illustrations. Audience: Above average income and education, ages 21–65.

For nearly half a century, the American Merchant Marine Library Association has fulfilled the seaman's need for books—for inspiration, information, relaxation. At eight port offices it provides books to vessels of the American Merchant Marine, U.S. Coast Guard and other U.S. Government waterborne operations.

AFLOAT: in 1968 AMMLA distributed 338,520 books and 483,640 magazines to 1079 ships in 4836 library units.

ASHORE: thousands of individuals used AMMLA library facilities in eight port cities.

AMMLA now needs funds to carry on—to collect books, sort them, assemble them into library units, deliver them to ships, and to maintain shoreside library facilities.

Your contribution to the American Merchant Marine Library Association is tax deductible. It will benefit the morale, the knowledge and the skill of the American seamen on whom our maritime trade depends.

Give a gift that's one for the books.
Give to AMMLA.

AMERICAN MERCHANT MARINE LIBRARY ASSOCIATION
Public Library of the High Seas

Headquarters: U.S. Customs House,
1 Bowling Green, New York, N.Y. 10004

Port Offices: Boston, Mass.; Norfolk, Va.; New Orleans, La.; San Pedro, San Francisco, Cal.; Seattle, Wash.; Sault Ste. Marie, Mich.

THE WORK BOAT
Peace Publications
P.O. Box 2400
Covington, LA. 70434
$20.00 per year
Monthly

Tug Boats, Barges, Oil Rigs and Marine Cranes. Harry L. Peace, editor, could probably tell you what was wrong with Noah's Ark. Diesel engines and steel ships, working ships. A trade publication for the maritime community that builds locks and supplies the oil rigs. New designs and concepts are covered with such items as 26 meter cat boats (85½ feet long x 31½ feet wide) cruising at 30 knots with 300 passengers. Repair Shipyards are also included, but don't expect Buffy's Boat Livery, try 3000 ton docks, 250 x 68 inside with two 500 ton Marine railways. The Offshore industry, Waterways, Equipment, Navigation and Communication and Boat Building are covered with the 20th century Mike Finn in mind.

THE FISH BOAT
Peace Publications
P.O. Box 2400
Covington, LA 70434
$20.00 per year
Monthly

The second of Harry Peace's commercial publications. The Fish Boat is for the commercial fisherman, suppliers and operators. Fishermen that use steel cables for their nets and 155 factory trawlers, for a night of casting. International fishing regulations, quotas etc. inform, educate and supply the farmers of the sea to issues that concern all of us and will continue to be a pointed issue as we feed more and more of the human race. New fishing boats are reviewed with such details as freezers that are capable of freezing 50,000 pounds of filets in 24 hours, high tech fishing, no worms allowed. A Product and Service Guide has a directory of Fish, Oyster, Shrimp, Crabmeat, Frog Legs etc. that could come in handy for the restauranteur, Fish store owner, or large party giver. The distributors are advertised with some selling 1–2 lb. packages. Order right from the source.

MICHIGAN FISHERMAN
P.O. Box 977
E. Lansing, MI 48823
$8.00 per year
Bi-Monthly

For the editorial direction and focus of Michigan Fisherman, the editor, Ken Darwin, states "to help you catch more fish. So, you can expect to read about my personal experiences and locations where the action is worthwhile. My goal is to pinpoint fishing action based on established patterns, and also give you information on methods or tactics that work. Every article is limited to materials regarding angling in your home state. You'll notice that we like to talk about the water near your home. Each issue is written specifically for you." The publication includes waterline information regarding indian fishing and treaty agreements, record holders, and cash tournaments. For the serious fisherman or the novice, Michigan Fisherman also has the Sportsmans Kitchen with delightful recipes on preparation. Kay Richey, field editor has edited a 133 page spiral bound book, with approximately 280 recipes, titled SAVOR THE WILD. The book is divided into chapter on cooking freshwater gamefish, North America's big and small game, gamebirds, how to prepare tasty marinades, sauces etc. Top magazine and newspaper outdoor writers prepare bass, trout, salmon, venison, rabbits, woodcock, quail, wild turkey,

caribou, elk, turtle, etc. Copies are available from Kay L. Richey, Dept. P–G, Box 192, Grawn, MI 49637 for $13 each, postpaid. All books autographed by the editor.

Great Lakes Trolling Annual
Published by Michigan Fisherman
$3.00

Special annual is packed with all information regarding trolling for the Great Lakes angler. Where-to, how-to, and reveal the techniques, tackle, and equipment. Would you believe that 1.54 million fishing licenses are sold annually in Michigan, join the action.

SEA HISTORY

Published by Sea History, 2 Fulton St., Brooklyn, N.Y. 11201. Quarterly publication, explores maritime heritage.

POWERBOAT MAGAZINE
15917 Strathern St.
Van Nuys, CA 91406

For "performance-conscious" boaters. Extensive "How-To" pieces, with a monthly rundown on the latest development in boating, and listings of national and major event competitions.

BOATING NEWS
26 Coal Harbour Wharf
566 Cardero St.
Vancouver, British Columbia, Canada V6G 2W7

The monthly bible and marine log to navigating the Western' Canadian waterways. Emphasis on sail and power boating, useful boating tips, plus news on local commercial fishing.

MARINA MANAGEMENT/MARKETING
Box 373
Wilmette, IL 60091

A monthly magazine — directed to operators of boatyards, clubs and marinas — complete with profiles and interviews of marina owners and other personnel. The publication's material includes "in house" information on dockage, repair services, maintenance and related how-to articles of successful merchandising techniques. There's even info related to adjoining recreational facilities and motel management, as well as rental concessions. Circulation: 15,000 plus.

SOUNDINGS

Published monthly at Essex, Connecticut 06426, A very large tabloid newspaper. This newspaper covers from Florida to Ontario and all the east Coast. They publish a Great Lakes edition which includes, Western New York, Pennsylvania, Ohio, Indiana, Michigan, Illinois, Wisconsin, Minnesota and Ontario. Editorial emphasis is on news, maintaining the newspaper format to supply up to date news faster and more current than magazines that have much more production time included in printing schedule. Good newspaper, established 1963.

WATERWAY GUIDE

Published by Waterway Guide, P.O. Box 1486, Annapolis, Md. 21404. Northern Edition — New York to Cape Code, Maine, the Canals, Canada and Lake Ontario.

Mid-Atlantic Edition — New York Harbor to the Georgia / Florida line. Chesapeake Bay and the Intercoastal Waterway.

Southern Edition — Georgia/Florida line to the Keys, the Bahamas, the Gulf Coast to Texas and Lake Pontchatrain.

This publication is not only one of my favorites, but one of the most useful if you decide to do any cruising or deliveries in these areas mentioned above. I have delivered boats from Florida to different parts of the east coast and wouldn't leave port without a copy of this publication for the trip. Not only does the publication include charts and sounding but also information on the communities, restaurants, hardwares etc. Billed as the "Yachtsman's Bible for the cruising Sailor". Published since 1947 continually advising the cruising sailor ... taking up where the charts leave off. I have noticed that they have added another service which is a book of charts for Delaware and Chesapeake Bays, so I think they may change there image to taking, up, over and control of where the government leaves off. Great publication.

NATIONAL FISHERMAN
National Fisherman, Camden, Maine 04843

A large tabloid newspaper published by Journal Publications, Inc. Camden, Maine 04843 classified as "Down - To - Sea Coverage of Fishing, Boats and Boatbuilding. Established in 1919 and published monthly, this newspaper is to boating and fishing, like the Wall Street Journal is to Business and finance.

Orientation toward daysailing and cruising – and in traditional boats, at that. This newspaper covers everything from diving to cooking, fishing, to grants available, in reviewing it all I can say is you'd have to see it, to believe it. I wonder if United Parcel Service is their newsboy.

OUTDOORS
Outdoors Bldg.
Columbia, MO 65201

A monthly magazine geared toward the boating families and outdoor fishing enthusiasts. Boat campers will be interested in the seasonal hints and tips and area profiles. Fishing enthusiasts should key into the monthly fishing local rundown, telling where the big (and little) ones are biting.

INTERNATIONAL YACHTSMAN
Hixson Industries, Inc.
4519 Admiraly Way
#206 Marina del Rey, CA 90291

A quarterly magazine of worldwide circulation. Sea spirits should be captivated by exceptional photographic and literary excellence of this 72-page design. Yachtsman articles and photos cover every aspect of the "exceptional experience afloat." Among regular departments are sections for the historian, the artisans, galley gourmets and model builders. Fashions Afloat, Classic Cruises, celebs on the high seas, and sketches of the various resorts and harbors and profiles on the glamourous vessels and global skippers – make this publication a must for international yachtsmen.

BOATING

Editorial offices at One Park Avenue, New York, N.Y. 10016. Send all subscription correspondence to Boating, P.O. Box 2773, Boulder, Colorado 80323. Ziff-Davis Publishing Company. Each issue features a Boat Test, a frank evaluation of performance and design of a current powerboat. January issue includes a broad directory of boats and equipment for the upcoming year. Publisher states more boatmen read Boating than any other boating magazine in the world. Good human interest stories, I really enjoyed their coverage of Newport, R.I. for the Americas Cup.

SAILBOAT AND EQUIPMENT DIRECTORY
Published in October by the United Marine Publishing, Inc., 38 Commercial Wharf, Boston, Massachusetts 02110. A comprehensive reference / buying guide for people interested in sails, engines, boats, sailing gear and equipment. This is an annual publication.

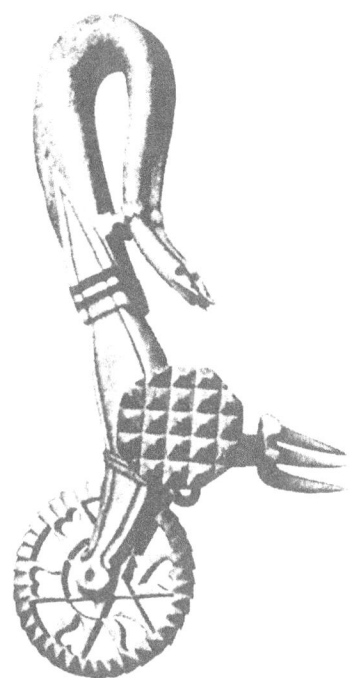

*This is the crimper
that whalemen carved
to give to wives
to close the crusts
of pies that baked
in open hearths
of homes that stand
today
at Mystic Seaport.*

A century's passed, but much is here to capture the excitement of seafaring days. It needs your membership to keep alive the ships, homes, workshops, and artifacts of this unique maritime museum. Join Mystic Seaport today.

MYSTIC SEAPORT

Mystic, Connecticut
Where the ships are!

For information about dues and member benefits, complete this coupon and mail to Flora C. Fairchild, Mystic Seaport, Mystic, CT 06355.

Name _____
Street _____
City _____
State _____ Zip _____

A handy illustrated guide for warm-weather vacationing along Michigan's 3000-mile shoreline

The Long Blue Edge of Summer

A Vacation Guide to the Shorelines of Michigan

By Doris Scharfenberg

Packed with a wealth of useful information, this colorfully written guide by a native Michiganian and experienced travel writer will take you on a tour of Michigan's magnificent shorelines.

Section by section, you'll learn all about the cities, beaches, lighthouses, fishing piers, museums, festivals, wildlife sanctuaries, sand-dunes, ghost towns, ferry boatrides...and much more. And special in-depth articles provide information on freighters of the Great Lakes, local history and customs, parks, harbors, camping, birds, fish, and shipwrecks.

No other guide has such an abundance of nitty-gritty facts and useful information for the Michigan vacationer. It's an invaluable resource for the family with children, a picnic hamper in the back seat and fishing gear on the roof, as well as for the solitary back-packer or retirees with a trailer...or for anyone who loves the sight of that long blue horizon.

Paper, $8.95

WM. B. EERDMANS PUBLISHING CO.
255 JEFFERSON AVE. S.E. / GRAND RAPIDS, MICHIGAN 49503

To order by mail:

Please send me _____ copies of *The Long Blue Edge of Summer* (7044-9) @ $8.95 each. I enclosed 50¢ postage/handling for each copy ordered.
Check one (Sorry, no billing):
____ Enclosed is my check/money order for $ _____
____ Please charge $ _____ to: ☐ VISA ☐ Mastercard ☐ American Express
Acct. No. _____ Expiration _____
Name _____
Address _____
City _____ State _____ Zip _____
Complete and mail to: Wm. B. Eerdmans Publishing Co., 255 Jefferson Ave., S.E., Grand Rapids, MI 49503   To Order By Phone, Call: 616-459-4591

SEAWAY REVIEW

A quarterly magazine published by Seaway Review, Harbor Island, Maple City Postal Station, Michigan 49664. This publication is directed precisely to Great Lakes commercial shipping. Publisher stating the only maritime magazine devoted exclusively to the Great Lakes. It has been cited as the best written, best designed and most authoritative magazine in its field. For anyone involved in or interested in Great Lakes—St. Lawrence Seaway region this is the journal covering the maritime industry. A very specialized publication. Included with the information I requested was some promotional literature from the Superior Publishing Company, Seattle, Washington about two books written by Jacques Les Strang. One SEAWAY covering the birth, construction and the current exciting activity of the St. Lawrence Seaway. The second LAKE CARRIERS written about the fresh water merchant marine of the United States and Canada. Stories of heroic sailings during winter months with accounts of the crews and the company's that operate the ships.

MARITIME PRESERVATION NEWS

Published by Maritime Preservation office of the President, National Trust, 740 Jackson Place, N.W., Washington, D.C. 20006. A tabloid newspaper covering the preservation and restoration of existing historic properties, including large vessels, small craft and shore side facilities. The organization also is responsible for many maritime programs and efforts, one of the most recent and spectacular Operation Sail.

NAUTICAL QUARTERLY

Published by Nautical Quarterly, Inc. 141 Lexington Ave., New York, N.Y. 10016. Four times a year at $35.00, a saving of $13.00 over the four issue bookstore price of $48.00. Or a sample issue is yours for approximately $10.00. This publication covers the best of boating and the boating experience. Stories range from America's Cup history, offshore powerboats to the adventurous days of rum-running. A very slick, professional magazine with photos suitable for framing.

SPYGLASS

Published by Spyglass, 2415 Mariner Sq. Drive, Alameda, CA 94501.

Positioned as the most informative sailing guide on the market. Concentration on sailing equipment and explanation of the most advantageous way to use it. I would have to assume this is an annual publication. Approximately 425 pages.

Yachtsman's Guide to the Bahamas
Originally compiled by Harry Etheridge
(1910-1957) Harry Kline, Editor Emeritus
Meredith Helleberg Fields, Editor
Tropic Isle Publishers, Inc.
P.O. Box 610935
North Miami, Florida 33161-0935
Phone: (305) 893-4277
$13.95, U.S. post paid. Annual

A '30 year tradition for the cruising Yachtsman. Another "Don't leave the Dock without it" Guide. Anchoring, Air Sea Rescue, Communications, Security, etc. The publication displays the years of research, charts, drawings and editorial knowledge from bow to stern. Pen and ink drawings navigate the channels, coves and harbors. Depths, directions, and tides include information to support the maritime charts for safe and pleasurable passage. Tide charts and complete Light List accompany medical and emergency information.

CANOE MAGAZINE
The Webb Co.
1999 Shepard Rd.
St. Paul, MN 55116

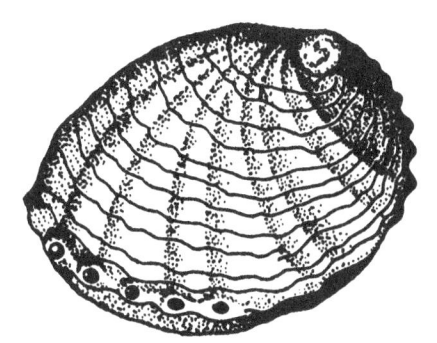

Editor John Viehan says: "We publish a variety of canoeing and kayaking articles, trips and competitive events — for an audience ranging from the weekender to the olympic - calibre racer. Stories cover all 50 states. We are also interested in use of the American waterways dealing with conservation issues, safety, training and expansion of the sport throughout the country. Published bimonthly with a hefty circulation of over 150,000.

MICHIGAN OUT-OF-DOORS

Published monthly by the Michigan Wildlife Foundation and the Michigan United Conservation Clubs (MUCC), an independent, statewide organization of affiliated clubs incorporated under Michigan laws as a non - profit organization. Subscription is through membership in MUCC. Fifty cents of dues buys a years subscription. The office is located at 2101 Wood St. Lansing, Michigan 48933. All communications regarding advertising, editorial, circulation or MUCC should be sent to P.O. Box 30235, Lansing, Michigan 48909. The publication covers the majority of outdoor activities in Michigan. Fishing, hunting and boating and camping. The organization that publishes also is involved in may conservation activities surrounding wildlife and ecology in Michigan. One of their other services is a book section that covers books ranging from Wilderness Cooking to a Home Guide to Muzzle Loaders. Inquires should be sent to the above address.

BAY & DELTA YACHTSMAN
Recreation Publications
2019 Clement Ave.
Alameda, CA 94501

Primarily for the small boat owners and recreational yachtsmen in Northern California, nevertheless — you may want to someday drop anchor in the San Francisco region and this would be your tab passport. A lot of valuable info for both power and sailboat enthusiasts who just simply cannot get their hands on enough good boating materials.

THE OUTDOOR PRESS
  (Tabloid weekly newspaper)
N. 2012 Ruby St.
Spokane, WA 99207

OUTDOORS TODAY
  (weekly tabloid)
569 Melville
St. Louis, MO 63130

SALT WATER SPORTSMAN
10 High St.
Boston, MA 02110

SOUTHERN ANGLER'S GUIDE
P.O. Box 2188
Hot Springs, AR 71901

MOTORBOAT AND EQUIPMENT DIRECTORY

Published by United Marine Publishing, 38 Commercial Wharf, Boston, Massachusetts 02110, Similar to the Sailboat directory, published annual providing the community, public and trade, with a definitive reference / buying guide to the motorboats and motorboat products available in the U.S. and Canada each year. A source book / buying guide for purchasing new motorboats, equipment and accessories.

MARINE BUSINESS

Published by the United Marine Publishing, Inc. at 38 Commercial Wharf, Boston, Massachusetts 02110, Publisher's editorial statement. Marine Business is edited for the entire marine industry and trade with emphasis on the marine retailer. The editorial content provides practical sales, merchandising and mangement techniques and ideas, which have been tested in real business situations. The magazine also chronicles events and trends within the marine industry and the business community which impact on the marine retailer. Regular features and management techniques, and planning aids.

MOTORBOAT

Published by the United Marine Publishing, Inc. at 38 Commercial Wharf, Boston, Massachusetts 02110. Publisher's editorial statement. Written for the active motorboat owner, MOTORBOAT is edited to keep the reader abreast of the latest developments in the sport, to report on the introduction of new boats, gear and equipment, and to provide technique and technical information that will help the reader become a more skillful and knowledgeable skipper. Regular columns cover piloting, navigation, weather, boat design, engine maintenance, electronics, sportfishing and seamanship techniques. Feature articles are written to share the adventure of experienced powerboat owners using their boats for inland expeditions, waterskiing, racing, sportfishing, coastal cruising and ocean voyaging.

WOODENBOAT
Box 78
Brooklin, ME 04616

Readership is composed mainly of owners, builders, and designers of wooden boats. Issued bimonthly. Packed (120 pages) with a wordly flotila of innovating and informative materials. Besides the historical details (evolution of boat types of famous designers or builders of wooden boats), How-To (repair, restore, building and maintaining, et al.) and new product lines (completely documented) — Woodencraft includes much advice and consent on repairs / restoration and construction.

BOATING BUSINESS
120-14 Barbados Blvd.
Scarborough, Ontario, Canada MIJ 1L2

A quarterly publication marketed for the Canadian retail marine trade Dealers trade success and operational details, plus give how-to's on selling boats, motors, and marine accessories. Boating business is read faithfully by over 5,000 Ontario-based marine operators and managers.

SEA
CBS Publications
1499 Monrovia Ave.
Newport Beach, CA 92663

With its emphasis on recreational boating — SEA is a potpourri of How-To procedures / techniques, travel pieces, and interviews with boat owners who offer interesting and profitable (they hope) info to other boat owners. Published monthly, with additional holiday and seasonal materials a regular mainstay

AMERICAN SHIPPER
Published by Howard Publications, Inc., 1314 Seaboard Coast Line Building, Post Office Box 4728, Jacksonville, Florida 32201.
David A. Howard, Publisher. A monthly magazine, last subscription price one year 12 issues. Editorial direction, a communication medium from the martime industry to those shippers who provide the major part of $10 billion in cargo revenues which sustain the maritime industry. Directed to the related management personnel who own, operate, represent, serve, design, build and finance ships serving America. Excellent coverage of legislation surrounding and engaged in the Commercial shipping industry.

SPORTS AFIELD
250 West 55th St.
New York, N.Y. 10019

WESTERN OUTDOORS
3939 Birch St.
Newport Beach, CA 92660

JOURNALS AMERICAN BOATING
Box A.
Reno, NV 89506

MUTLI-HULL INTERNATIONAL
Reference Catamaran Racing Associations

THE FLYFISHER
Seattle, WA

BOATMASTER
PO Box 3543
Montgomery, Alabama 36109
Editor, Dave Ellison

THE JOURNAL OF FRESHWATER
Freshwater Biological Research Foundation
2500 Shadywaood Road, Box 90
Navarre, Minnesota 55392
Editor, Richard Hughes

INLAND SEAS
Quarterly Journal of the Great Lakes
  Historical Society
Business Office 480 Main Street
Vermilion, Ohio 44089

— OR —
320 Republic Building
Cleveland, Ohio 44115

The following is a listing of broad-based outdoor and fishing magazines RECOMMENDED BY THE PIRATE'S GUIDE TO LAKE ST. CLAIR:

THE ANGLER/HUNTER IN ONTARIO
Ontario Outdoors Publishing, LTD.
Box 1541
Peterborough, Ontario, Canada K9J 7H7

DAIWA FISHING ANNUAL
Aqua-Field Publications, Inc.
728 Beaver Dam Rd.
Point Pleasant, NJ 08742

FERBER'S FRESHWATER FISHERMAN
(Same address as above)

FISHING WORLD
51 Atlantic Ave.
Floral Park, NY 11001

FUR–FISH–GAME
2878 E. Main
Columbus, OH 43209

ILLINOIS WILDLIFE
P.O. Box 116–13005
S. Western Ave.
Blue Island, IL 60406

ONTARIO OUT OF DOORS
11 King St. W.
Toronto, Ontario, Canada M5H 1A3

OUTDOOR LIFE
380 Madison Ave.
New York, NY 10017

MAGAZINES
Up Great Lakes Sportman
Sportman Publications
26555 Evergreen, Suite 410
Southfield, Michigan

INTERNATIONAL

THE NAUTICAL MAGAZINE–SCOTLAND

ROD & LINE – SCOTLAND

SEA ANGLER–ENGLAND

SEA CRAFT–AUSTRALIA

SHIP AND BOAT INTERNATIONAL

WORK FISHING

SHIP & BOAT INTERNATIONAL
S-15030 Mariefred, Sweden

Everything you wanted to know regarding technical materials in design and construction of commercial crafts. Basically, an international monthly for naval architects, engineers, eequipment manufacturers, consultants and owners.

ADDITIONAL GUIDES AND DIRECTORIES

Country Vacations (Farm, Seashore or Ranch)
Including "Bed and Breakfast"

Canadian Country Vacations Associations
437 Assiniboine Ave.
Winnipeg, Manitoba, Canada
R3C 0Y5

Canadian Hostelling Association
National Office
333 River Road
Vanier City, Ottawa, Ontario, Canada
K1L 8H9

Great Lakes Foundation
2200 North Campus Boulevard
Ann Arbor, MI 48105

News on the Great Lakes
UPWELLINGS — Bi Monthly
Michigan Sea Grant Program

Ontario Marine Operators Association

Michigan Council of the Arts

Michigan Charter Boat Directory

St. Clair Shores Library/Great Lakes Section

Great Lakes Institute, Windsor/Pollution Studies

Detroit River Yachting Association

National Association of Engine and Boat
   Manufacturers, NY, NY

U.S. Power Squadron

Harbor Commission

Ministry of Tourism

Marine Art Clipbook
Edited and Arranged by
Peter H. Spectre and George Putz

Great Lakes Historical Society
 Council of American Maritime Museums
Sons and Daughters of Pioneer Riverman
 Waterways Division — Michigan Natural Resources, 2455 North Williams Lake, Pontiac, MI 48054
Metro-Windsor Waterfront Advisory Committee
Essex Region Conservation Authority
 10 Talbot Street, S.
Essex, Ontario, N0M 1E0

The Pirate Lafite And The Battle of New Orleans
  By Robert Tallant, Landmark Books
  Random House - New York

Jean Lafite - Gentleman Rover
  By Stanley Clisby Arthur
  Harmanson, Publisher, New Orleans, 1952

Lafite the Pirate
  By Lyle Saxon
  The Century Co., N.Y. - London

Pirates Gold
  Lawton B. Evans
  M/B Springfield, Mass.

The seafarers THE PIRATES
by Douglas Botting and the
Editors of Time-Life Books

BOATING

DETROIT RIVER YACHTING ASSOCIATION: 23219 Marter, Suite 214, St. Clair Shores 48080; Organized in 1912. Commodore: Herb Mainwaring. Members include the Alabatross Yacht Club, Anchor Bay Yacht Racing Association, Bayview Yacht Club, Crescent Sail Yacht Club, Detroit Boat Club, Detroit Yacht Club, Edison Boat Club, Ford Yacht Club, Great Lakes Yacht Club, Grosse Ile Yacht Club, Grosse Pointe Club, Grosse Pointe Sail Club, Grosse Pointe Yacht Club, North Cape Yacht Club, North Star Sail Club, Port Huron Yacht Club, St. Clair Yacht Club, Sarnia Yacht Club, Storm Trysail Club, Toledo Yacht Club, Windmill Pointe Yacht Club, Windsor Yacht Club.

MICHIGAN CANOE RACING ASSOCIATION: 58 Union, Mt. Clemens; 469-3694. Organized in 1947. President: Ken Witte. Membership fee: $20 amateur; $5 associate; $2 junior; $20 professional; $10 standard.

NATIONAL WEATHER SERVICE
WARNING STATIONS

Crescent Sail Yacht Club, Municipal Pier, Grosse Pointe Farms Jefferson Beach Marina, Gasow' Boat Livery, Clinton River, Day signals, Selfridge Air Force Base at the Crash Rescue Dock, Salt River Marina, near the mouth of the Salt River, Anchor Bay, Coast Guard Station at the Belle Isle Light, near the upper end of Belle Isle; day signals are displayed on the northerly side of Belle Isle about 700 feet east of the Belle Isle Bridge at the Detroit Boat Club; day signals are displayed at the southwest corner of Detroit Memorial Park Marine Basin about ½ mile upriver from the Belle Isle Bridge.

**Pirate's Guide to Lake St. Clair
and Surrounding Waters**

**Pirate's Guide to Lake St. Clair
and Surrounding Waters**

**Pirate's Guide to Lake St. Clair
and Surrounding Waters**

"Go your own way..."
Fleetwood Mac
Recorded Live

Take it to the limit, one more time...
The Eagles

www.ingramcontent.com/pod-product-compliance
Lightning Source LLC
Chambersburg PA
CBHW081938170426
43202CB00018B/2941